Agreement!

The state, conflict and change
in Northern Ireland

Dedicated to the memory of my dear friend Tom Kay
A great storyteller – among many things – who believed in this story
And who believed in me.

Agreement!

The state, conflict and change in Northern Ireland

Beatrix Campbell

Lawrence & Wishart

LONDON 2008

Lawrence and Wishart Limited
99a Wallis Road
London
E9 5LN

First published 2008

British Library Cataloguing in Publication Data.
A catalogue record for this book is available from the British Library

ISBN 9781905007745

Text setting e-type, Liverpool
Printed and bound by Biddles, Kings Lynn

Contents

Introduction

A THING OF BEAUTY

Emerging out of the brutalising colonial redoubt of Northern Ireland, the Good Friday Agreement was a product of great creativity born of conflict. The state's adversaries improvised a unique template for governance. At the end of the twentieth century, when the legitimacy of representative democracies all over the world was fading, Northern Ireland invented a newly dynamic model of democracy. This was thrilling.

This book is about how the Agreement became a thing of beauty.[1] It is about the tributaries that contributed to the most generous and egalitarian prospectus for government perhaps anywhere in the world – though their journeys into the text confronted a government that had habitually invested in war rather than redress. They prescribed reforms that were reasonable and respectful and yet – if implemented – promised a fundamental challenge to traditional power.

The novelty of the Agreement lay in its description of the duty of the state to engage the people, and particularly the constituencies of the marginalised and the maligned, in the work of making the settlement 'take' – making a new heart to revive the body politic. For the first time Northern Ireland could imagine solidarity as co-operation, as a practice of engagement rather than exclusion.

Even after it was overwhelmingly endorsed and inscribed in legislation, however, the Agreement's constitutional innovations were sabotaged. This book is therefore not just about the ending of the conflict; it is also the story of the struggles to implement the Agreement. The historic resistance to redress, and the obstacles mobilised during the defining years of implementation, continued to be dominated by Britain, through capricious and sinister suspensions of Northern Ireland's elected government at Stormont – manoeuvres that encouraged suspicions that counter-insurgency and collusion were not finished business. The book appears ten years after the deal was done, at a moment when an unexpected historic partnership between former enemies inaugurated a new era in politics – and there is a possibility that Northern Ireland might at last begin to do what it had promised itself a decade earlier.

The Agreement was, in part, a treaty between the British and Irish governments. But it was also a conflicted people's riposte, finally, to the scornful exercise of power – to disrespect that demanded so much and gave so little to people who had been prepared to lay down their lives for it; and to power that gave so much less – and so much worse – to those who dared to challenge the state, the 'narrow ground' of the centre and the political culture that sustained it. It was also, therefore, a rebuke to the paradox of Britain: a liberal democratic welfarist state tangled in an internal armed conflict and killing its citizens

The text was the product of women and men who in April 1998 slept on floors in Belfast's Castle Buildings, under desks, in corridors, hungry, cold, but keen – keener than they'd ever been in their lives to meet a deadline and come to a consensus about change; they were feminists, former warriors, scholars, human rights experts, diplomats from Dublin and London. They didn't do it alone, they were arriving at a destination – an agreement – that could never have been reached without potent friends on 'the out', including the Americans and the Irish on the island and throughout the vast diaspora who had given their vigilance, patience and finally power to the process; and they were supported by civil society's unorthodox coalitions that saw difference as something to be dealt with and not denied. These were movements where gender, class, race, religion, sexual orientation and anti-sectarianism converged. It was their ardent quest for non-violent solutions to injustice and inequality that had exposed a rigid state that appeared to offer no means of remedy – no normal access to courts or elected forums – a state whose extravagant investment in violence had projected the problem as the people themselves.

So this is the story of the people who made the text the novel constitution that it became, and it is also the story of the resistance, of a repressive state apparatus that favoured the defeat of its enemies over consensus and change. (This is not to suggest that the British state was necessarily coherent – it wasn't. But at decisive moments perfidy prevailed.)

The search for non-violent ways to address and redress socio-economic causes harvested an equality movement that gathered momentum at precisely the point when the political wings of armed militias were themselves canvassing a settlement. But Britain all too often blocked progress towards peaceful change: by inertia or sabotage of socio-economic equality, and by the bleak dominion of the repressive security state. Even after the Agreement had been endorsed on both sides of the border as the settled will of the people, they had a way to go. It took almost a decade before intimations of the Agreement's potential became palpable, and this was only after those elements of the establishment that had manoeuvred for defeat rather than a deal had been chastened or controlled; only after the Assembly was enabled to get on with the business of government without interruption or the suspension of its sovereignty by Britain. The Agreement could only appear as fully the settled will when its warrant was embraced even by its enemies, who had contributed nothing to its production and then opposed its implementation; its best chance finally arrived when the purported extremes of Northern Ireland's party politics succeeded where the centre had failed – when the extremes became the centre. Only then could the new constitutionalism test the habits of governance, and only then could it begin to contribute to the creation of consensus where there had been none.

This great story is not widely recognised as the story of the peace process. This book therefore – which is not the story of the entire peace process – is about parallel peace processes and the novelty of the treaty that has been obscured.

There is a tendency to render invisible the political interventions of feminism; but it was women who came up with a template that translated from the specific to a general constitutional duty to address inequalities. There is a tendency to see human rights advocates as oppositional; but in Northern Ireland their concern with the abuse of power connected them with the economy, and with the most powerless – women – and with pro-active institutional solutions. Part I of this book tells the story of the contribution made to the peace process by a wide range of advocates for equality.

There is also a tendency in Britain to represent the period known as the Troubles as a squalid interregnum, a descent into barbarism by religious fundamentalism, republican cruelty and loyalist intransigence, as the bare-knuckle business of tribal paddies. Northern Ireland came to be represented as Britain's burden: Britain was tasked with managing its rowdy and incomprehensible neighbours. The way the deal was represented echoed this view of the conflict. It was seen as the outcome of exhaustion, weary militias needing peace, polarised parties cajoled by benevolent diplomats and wise politicians from both sides of the Atlantic Ocean and the Irish Sea. It was hailed as the triumph of sensible chaps rather than the ingenuity of the society itself. But the Agreement was not just the outcome of politicians guiding the hand of history from on high. It was a moment when popular movements from below converged with statecraft to make history. These included those regarded as the pariah, the paramilitaries from both communities. (Their long journey to the Agreement is discussed in Part II of the book.)

For sure, the Agreement was blessed by ingenious diplomacy. The text and its earlier prototypes, Sunningdale in 1974 and more importantly the 1985 Anglo-Irish Agreement, had produced a new historic compromise between Britain and Ireland, its former colony. The settlement established the terms of the jurisdiction of the governments in London and Dublin in Northern Ireland, and in so doing transcended traditional concepts of borders, nations, states and sovereignty. But the significance of the Agreement was much more than this, and this is what will be explored in this book.

DIFFERENCE, EQUALITY AND THE STATE

A great achievement of the Agreement was its acknowledgement of the legitimacy of both protestant/unionist and catholic/nationalist political aspirations, and of the people who had taken up arms to defend those aspirations. That marked one of the first breaks with earlier peace processes. The civil rights campaigner Michael Farrell argues that the process that produced Agreement was not, as the nationalist politician Seamus Mallon dubbed it, 'Sunningdale for slow learners': the fundamental difference was that the Agreement was 'designed to *bring in* the republican and loyalist paramilitaries, whereas Sunningdale was designed to defeat them'. Histories, aspirations, circumstances that had been so loaded with practices of privilege and humiliation were to be addressed anew. Differences were not denied, they were named. This recognition has often been misrepresented as regressive, but I believe that the Agreement's ingenuity was to affirm difference and diversity by creating structures that aimed to deny any – and indeed all of them – the power of dominion. By naming them it was proposing to deal with difference and diversity as problems of power. Furthermore, the national and religious categories that had defined the arc of the armed conflict were named in the electoral and constitutional arrangements as *political affiliations*;[2] everyone understood these histories as blocs of ideologies. And so identity and ideology were available for fresh interpretations in the shaping of citizenship. Affiliations, interests, orientations, ethnicities and circumstances – advantages and disadvantages, too – were categorised in the electoral arrangements and in the state's constitutional duties in new ways. 'The Agreement makes the question of national identity up for argument in the future', commented Michael Farrell.

And here is the crux: some critics have seen the Agreement's naming of interests and identities as fixing them. I disagree. They could now be conceived not as ways of *being* but ways of *becoming*; they could be imagined as ways of operating within social relationships that would no longer be organised around dominion and humiliation. The Agreement enabled 'identities' to be specified not as being or biology, but as regimes, as relationships. The Agreement prescribed limits on their powers. That, simply, was the point of power-sharing.

Linked to this recognition, citizenship was refreshed within the Agreement as activity in arenas within and beyond the state. At a time when the global political ascendancy of neo-liberalism was promoting the withdrawal of the state, the new Northern Ireland state was expected to be interventionist, re-distributive, and disciplined by a generous dialogue with the civil society. Civil society, which had flourished during, and in response to, the conflict, now expected to be an organic presence in a process of renovation. The state now had a positive duty to engage with, to work with, the new social movements that activated its busy civil society. The Agreement inscribed their right to participate in a new civic space where sectarianism, inequality and injustice 'from whatever source, public or private, can be addressed in a new emancipatory project'.[3]

These possibilities were released, in the first instance, by the Agreement's arrangements for sharing power and entering the Assembly, which obliged elected Members to designate themselves as unionist, nationalist or 'other'; it offered the parties not only their place in the Assembly, but their proportional place in the departments and the executive. So, the significant parties – inevitably both nationalist and unionist – were entitled to share government. The historic blocs – unionist and nationalist – had to manage power co-operatively and consensually. This, too, has been criticised, as muting the normal conflicts of democracy. Again, I disagree. The Agreement was a response to the not-normal. It could not wish away that history; it had to be a product of it. Furthermore, the specification of the historic blocs allowed majorities and minorities. The Agreement allowed them to remain in their blocs, but not only in their blocs – it allowed them to be more than their blocs. Unionists could no longer rule, therefore, without nationalist consent: Unionism could no longer operate unilaterally. Contrary to myth, Members could refuse the dominant alignments, they could be Other, but no one could escape definition in relation to the decisive polarisation that had created in Northern Ireland a failed state and a thirty-year war. And Members who chose to designate themselves as 'Other' always had the option to re-designate within the major blocs, so the Agreement simultaneously specified identities and yet ingeniously allowed the possibilities of multiple and mobile identities. This was dramatised in a moment of grave crisis in the Assembly, when the unionist bloc lost its internal majority, and the Women's Coalition proposed the creative re-designation of its two Members to keep the government alive (see 79–80). Furthermore, these themes of borders and identities and balance of power did not exhaust the Agreement's innovations. The arrangements assumed that everyone was positioned somewhere in the sectarian discourse, but this discourse was now to be mediated through the constitutional duty to practise equality and social justice. The Agreement constitutionalised the duty to promote equality, and then to engage those with an interest in the assessment of it and in policy-making processes. It did so across a span of circumstances and conditions beyond the defining arc of sectarianism. It reached to places where the foundations of modern western democracy – the American Constitution and the French Declaration of the Rights of Man, and the informality and incrementalism of the British tradition – did not reach; though it was, of course, a product of their limits. It inscribed equality, human rights and socio-economic justice as a duty of the state: the state was to promote equality through all policy-making processes. Egalitarianism was, therefore, to change the state. And equality was to be an achievement of the state, an outcome.

So, in an era of laissez faire and shrinking states the Agreement proposed an interventionist state, a state with the duty to make a difference, to do something about the deficits between catholics and protestants, men and women, straights and gays; between White Anglo-Saxon Protestant men – the masters of the universe – and everyone else, between bodies, faiths, faculties, ethnicities and responsibilities. Though class was not named as a specific category (which made it intolerable to some critics), class was present in the redistributive duty to address the matrix between class, sectarianism and sexism that had compromised everything in Northern Ireland. It was also specified in a specific commitment to target poverty in general, and the greater poverty of catholics in particular.

The surprise was that these links had been initiated not by the categories of religion or class, but by gender. Ethno-national conflicts are, of course, always deeply gendered, but peace processes in general conceal that central contradiction. Making it visible involves a 'radical reconception of the nature of the state', and this was the genesis of some of the Agreement's originality.[4] We shall see how the class-religion dimension derived from gender politics and the indispensable creativity of both feminists and human rights advocates, whose concern was not gender but the abuse of power: their shared quest was for ways to make power-holders change the form and content of policy-making.

The duty written into the deal to factor equality proofing into policy-making was accompanied by the duty to engage those with an interest in the process of policy-making. The implementation of policy was to be monitored and measured. Tangible outcomes were the objective. The purpose was to make equality a mission of government, shared with civil society. The implications, therefore, went beyond institutional duty – and moved towards cultural revolution.

Egalitarianism had the potential to infuse 'a new constitutionalism of process, partnership and value'.[5] Equality could be conceived of not as a thing, goods and possessions, but as an ambition vested in social relationships between citizens, and between citizens and states. This approach transcended the limits of classical political philosophy, and envisaged rights not so much as the distribution of goods but as relationships.[6] It was not what catholics and protestants did, or did not, own or earn or receive that was be transformed by the Agreement, but their relationship to each other. Thus, within the new egalitarianism protestants weren't losing anything – except dominion over catholics. Of course, relative privilege had scarcely mitigated working-class protestants' disadvantage within the Unionist universe. That was why the parties representing poor protestants were enthusiastic about the equality duty.

All of this radically re-interpreted the British state's account of itself and its narrative of the conflict. The history of the Agreement's egalitarian discipline had flushed out the state's real interest; and in the promise of partnership civil society gave the state the duty to change itself. It recognised that it had not previously been neutral, as it had claimed; it had not been merely an agent, an arbitrator. It was a subject. It had dominated the place. Inez McCormack summarised the promise of the Agreement as creating the context for transformation. 'None of us have the right to be who we were', she said. Not least the state.

But could the deal do what the society itself had been unable to do? As feminist legal scholar Christine Bell argues, the Agreement encapsulated 'an overtly-value driven constitutionalism'. It did not codify an existing consensus, its aim, rather, was to effect that consensus.[7]

OBSTACLES TO IMPLEMENTATION

The obstacles in the way of implementation, like the provisions of the Agreement itself, were obscured behind the propaganda that Northern Ireland's problem was the paramilitaries. Their reluctance to give up their arms and their practice of rough justice in the most insecure and unprotected communities was mobilised as evidence of their bad faith. Though the paramilitary organisations may have been an obstacle to peace, they were not *the* problem of implementation: this was an international treaty that depended for its implementation not on the paramilitaries but on the polity, whether the devolved state in Belfast or the big British state. If the paramilitaries exasperated the governments who were the Agreement's guardians, it has to be admitted that the British state retained its intransigence and power to thwart, compromise and corrupt the great enterprise.

The legislation to implement the Agreement, like any constitution, was contingent on power and political will. But no sooner was the ink dry than the bureaucracy reasserted its old self, re-interpreted its duties and began the work of betrayal. The equality, human rights and social justice provisions weren't optional, they were the law. But the provisions were located in processes, and in reluctant and unready administrations. This is what Fionnuala Ni Aolain calls the 'under-enforcement' to which all peace treaties are prey.

There was also the major problem of what was not allowed to enter the Agreement: policing, security, justice and public safety. Though the Agreement affirmed 'freedom from sectarian harassment', public space still seemed to be zoned as unregulated – though it is the intensely regulated realm in which we all live; the space of community; the 'space of enunciation', in which speeding and sex and sanitation are regulated, in which pavements and traffic and retail and the quality of air can be controlled – but not, apparently, the performance of sectarianism. Somehow this eluded the public authorities charged with the management of public space. Part III of this book analyses the fatalism of public authority in face of the sectarianisation of space – a phenomenon that was grotesquely rehearsed during the unionist blockade of Holy Cross girls' school, an episode which once more foregrounded the importance of gender in this story, and which is analysed in some detail in this section. Part IV looks at wider aspects of the Agreement's failure to adequately address the issues of policing and security.

An over-arching and corrupting feature of the conflict was the symbiotic partnership between the security state and paramilitarism. Counter-insurgency begets collusion. I describe the dismal effects of collusion, its impact on Northern Ireland's politics in the prelude to the deal, and its implications for the Agreement itself, in Part V. This section focuses on murder, state secrets and the securocrats' struggle to escape scrutiny or censure – during the peace process, the talks and then the reconstruction. It concentrates on the murders of two defence lawyers who were killed by unionist paramilitaries in collaboration with British security services. These murders are analysed as exemplars of Britain's secret assassination strategy. It is the argument of this book that while the combatants were mooting peace towards the end of the 1980s, the state was secretly directing an assassination strategy at its political – in contrast to military – enemy, through the agency of the protestant paramilitaries. The death squads showed the dangerousness of elements within the British state, but also its dependence on confederates that left it vulnerable to disclosure: ultimately these *liaisons dangereuses* exposed a state that was prepared to go *too* far. They therefore became a source of revelation that challenged Britain's burnished reputation as a neutral arbitrator, a peacemaker; they became the raw material – that the British secret state had never expected to see the light of public scrutiny – that showed where the British state had positioned itself in the conflict. These revelations helped to explain the government's implacable resistance to truth as the condition of reconciliation. Yes, the British government set up the vital Saville inquiry into Bloody Sunday, and yes, with the greatest reluctance, Britain bowed to international pressure and conceded inquiries into some emblematic cases of collusion. But it would not subject itself to scrutiny over the pattern, the system, the purpose of collusion as a strategy, and perhaps even as a raison d'etre.

Britain has a tried and tested habit of narrating warmongering as peacemaking. This has endured into the twenty-first century and the era of the new imperialism. Northern Ireland is the classic case; and it counsels a re-consideration of the purpose of Britain's internationalism, and a retreat from the militarism that by the twenty-first century we knew – if we did not know it before – to be a herald of havoc and destruction. Britain's *modus operandi* in Northern Ireland was to defer and thwart the remedies for injustice while stewarding sectarian terrorism. Thus the state poured scorn on the violence of its subjects while simultaneously sponsoring it.

The story of the Agreement is also, therefore, the story of its limits: Northern Ireland needs remedy, truth and reconciliation as the terms of its modernisation – and they are all equally relevant to the renovation of the bigger state across the water.

NOTES

1. Gusty Spence, a former loyalist combatant who loved the Agreement, described it in this way during the referendum campaign.
2. B. O'Leary & J. McGarry, *The Politics of Antagonism*, Blackstaff 2000.
3. John Morison, 'Constitutionalism and Change, Representation, Governance, and Participation in the New Northern Ireland', *Fordham International Law Journal*, April 1999, p1626.

4. Christine Bell, *Peace Agreements and Human Rights*, Oxford University Press 2000, p316.
5. John Morison, op cit.
6. This book's approach is influenced by the pioneering work of the feminist theorist, the late Iris Marion Young, and her germinal texts: *Justice and the Politics of Difference*, Princeton University Press 1990; and *Inclusion and Democracy*, Oxford University Press 2000.
7. Christine Bell, op cit, p307.

PART I

TRIBUTARIES OF CHANGE

1. The diaspora intercedes: between Belfast and Manhattan

THE MACBRIDE PRINCIPLES

The New York City Comptroller is the custodian of the great city's finances. His office is housed in downtown Manhattan, in the early twentieth century neo-classical grandeur of Number One Centre Street, crowned by a gold-plated monument to civic virtue. In the 1980s the Comptroller's portfolio included pension funds worth $50 billion dollars, rising to about $85 billion at the end of the millennium. In 1984 Comptroller Harrison J. Goldin resolved to use his guardianship of vast investments to promote social responsibility and equal opportunity in employment. This was eventually to have far-reaching consequences for sectarian workplace practices in Northern Ireland.

The story of the city's engagement began with a local newspaper that circulated around the marbled corridors of Goldin's office. New York attorney Dennis McMahon wrote a column in the *Brooklyn Spectator* ruminating on the campaigns by opponents of apartheid to engage US corporations with operations in South Africa. Corporate America should now address discrimination against catholics in their Northern Ireland workplaces, he wrote. Nothing would affront protestants across the Atlantic more than the suggestion that their state was akin to the apartheid regime in South Africa. But the analogy was suggestive to Irish America. According to the 1971 census, unemployment among catholic men in Northern Ireland was 17.3 per cent, compared to 6.6 per cent among protestant men. After the first decade of the armed conflict, catholic unemployment had almost doubled, to 30 per cent, compared to 12 per cent among protestant men. In the commanding shipyards of Harland and Woolf in 1970 only 500 catholics were employed; there were 10,000 protestants. Twenty years

later there were only 500 catholics among 6000 protestants in the factories of the state-owned aircraft manufacturer Short Brothers. Was there
something about making ships and aeroplanes that catholics couldn't
do? The Comptroller's Office resolved to adapt the anti-apartheid
strategy to Northern Ireland.

There were 40 million Americans of Irish origin who, though often
alienated from the armed struggle, were interested in interventions that
could detonate the national and international inertia that had for so
long shrouded the old country. Irish Americans had tried since the
nineteenth century, mostly unsuccessfully, to persuade the US government to intervene in the politics of Ireland.[1] But they now took
inspiration from the international anti-apartheid movement's use of
economic pressure on South Africa.

The Sullivan Principles, drawn up by black civil rights campaigner
Rev Leon Sullivan, had provided an alternative to divestment and
boycott as a strategy for US corporations operating in South Africa. The
idea behind Sullivan's principles was to use investment, shareholder,
pension fund and consumer power to promote equality between black
and white employees, rather than to withdraw investment. This idea was
attractive to Irish Americans who were interested in intervening posi-
tively in Northern Ireland, but reluctant to pull out of the place. The
principles offered a model that appeared positive and relatively unthreatening; they allowed investor activism to appeal to people who needed
reassurance that any principles were within the law, with a narrow focus
on inviting corporate investors to sign up to affirmative action.

The attraction of the Sullivan Principles to the Comptroller's Office
was that they did not threaten its fiduciary duties as a fund-holder: he
would not have been able to promote public disinvestment or any
other approach that might damage funds. The Sullivan model was relatively unthreatening to Americans, and in any case none of the
protagonists in Northern Ireland was promoting withdrawal.[2] The idea
was to promote equality of opportunity, access, security, transport,
training, a working environment free from sectarian political provocation, and the appointment of managers to affirmative action timetables.
These principles transcended the limits of typical equality legislation
by making big power – rather than the victims – the active agent in
reform; and they addressed not only the economic effects of discrimination but also the cultural context that created it.

Comptroller Harrison J. Goldin was a popular guardian of New York
City's finances – in 1986 he was voted the best Comptroller in America;
that year, too, he helped found the Council of Institutional Investors. He
was by then already known for campaigning to make the corporations

take responsibility for their stake in apartheid. In 1984 his office resolved to come up with something similar to the anti-apartheid campaign for Northern Ireland. The New York City Comptroller's Office was well placed to institute this process: as trustee for city pension funds, it held $250 million shares in Northern Ireland, in half of the 24 main companies, who between them employed 11 per cent of the labour force.

The task of drawing up a proposal fell to the only person of Irish descent in the City Comptroller's office, Pat Doherty, a young lawyer specialising in international relations. His mother's people came from Fermanagh and Galway, and his father arrived in New York when he was a toddler with Doherty's grandfather. Doherty senior had been a member of the IRA Derry Brigade during the 1920s, but republicanism, home rule and partition had faded from the family's conversation during the lifetime of young Pat. Only when the little boy noticed a stamp bearing the head of Queen Elizabeth II, and asked why the Queen's head was on a stamp on a letter from the north of Ireland, was he told the story of partition.

The Comptroller's office began to research the problem and the potential solutions.

As part of the Comptroller's quest, the Irish and British governments were invited to give evidence. Diplomats were polite, they swiftly supplied data. In time the data was supplemented by British government explanations for the enduring unemployment differential between catholics and protestants. 'You see,' the Americans remember being told, 'catholics lack the protestant work ethic.' If the Comptroller's office needed confirmation that the state itself was part of the problem, the state's own 'common sense' seemed to supply it.

The solution they came up with was to draw up a set of principles, based loosely on the Sullivan Principles, which would form the basis of a campaign to persuade employers in Northern Ireland to change their discriminatory practices. In the autumn of 1984 the veteran Irish diplomat Sean MacBride, founder of Amnesty International and winner of the Nobel Peace Prize, agreed to be the sponsor of the principles. The MacBride campaign went on to mobilise support for the Principles, drawing on two existing traditions: the shareholder movements' targeting of corporations, and the Irish National Caucus's pressurising of legislatures. The AFL-CIO signed up to the MacBride Principles in February 1985 – to the chagrin of the British government and to trade unionists still anguished by its clear description of discrimination and its potential resolution.

The MacBride Principles now focused the collective mind on the political economy of sectarianism, which they addressed as a civil rights issue. Sectarianism had been frequently exposed, though scarcely addressed, since the beginning of the armed conflict in the North. In 1969 the government had appointed the Cameron Commission to investigate the cause of the alarmingly violent reaction to protests against injustice in Northern Ireland earlier that year. The commission was unequivocal: 'abuses of political power' created discrimination against catholics and ultimately created the demonstrations and disorders that were designated the Troubles. The commission was followed by the Van Straubenzee Working Party, which proposed a direct attack on discrimination against catholics by adopting 'deliberate programmes under which equality of opportunity may be achieved.'[3] The result of these reports and the affirmative action they recommended was the genesis of employment law and an agency to enforce it. They were not implemented, however. After the hunger strikes of 1981 there was an empty space in the Northern Ireland polity where there should have been a political arena. The MacBride Principles, which elaborated the spirit of the early consciousness expressed by Cameron and Van Straubenzee, were to fill that political vacuum.

The organisers assembled four prominent protestants and catholics to be the Principles' signatories. One of them – and the most persistent of them – was Inez McCormack, in many ways a surprising figure in Northern Ireland.

McCormack had grown up in a protestant household. Men in her family had staffed the security services with enthusiasm. However, as a student in the mid-1960s she had supported a campaign to locate Northern Ireland's second university in its second city, Derry. The campaign had failed: the campus was located in protestant-dominated Coleraine. But through her involvement McCormack started to become familiar with the 'interesting and perplexing mixture of political radicalism and social conservativism in catholic culture'. She was ecstatic when she witnessed the flowering of the civil rights movement, and never forgot the state's readiness to shed 'real blood' in response to it. It was police officers from her own protestant background who brutally ambushed non-violent civil rights marchers at Burntollet Bridge; and she was there. It was her own community who commented on her bruises, 'if you hadn't been there it wouldn't have happened'. It was her catholic father-in-law putting on his good suit to join a protest against the police invasion of the Bogside that taught her about dignity.

McCormack's working life began as a social worker, in third world conditions in Northern Ireland, where 'poor people's efforts to preserve some vestiges of self-respect in the face of universal contempt' were compounded by the war between the emerging Provisionals and the British Army.

She later became an inventive trade union organiser in the public sector, one of the few places where protestant and catholic women and men were recruited. In the wider labour market, fair employment legislation had hardly disturbed the differential between the religions or the genders. First the civil rights movement and then the women's liberation movement defined McCormack's politics, and she was convinced that the influence of both made her public sector union uniquely effective during the slough of Thatcherism – her union was the only one to emerge at the end of the 1980s with more members than at the beginning. The crux, she said, was to 'believe that people can be agents of their own change, and to put the institution at their service'.

Though in the 1970s these new liberation movements had winded traditional politics on both sides of the water, the 1980s had inaugurated the claustrophobia of counter-revolution. By that time the civil rights ethos had little room for self-expression – politics was overwhelmed by armed conflict. After the 1981 hunger strikes McCormack had come to the conclusion that 'no remedies were acceptable to the state'. Michael Farrell, a celebrated contemporary in the civil rights movements, who went on hunger strike during internment, and later became an eminent human rights lawyer in Dublin, wrote many years later that McCormack's journey had been 'a long and often lonely battle against both religious and sex discrimination'. [4]

Though trade unionists had been influential at the beginning of the civil rights movement, and the Irish Congress of Trade Unions officially opposed the attempt to bring down the deal, at a rank and file level loyalist workers and militias, in alliance with conservative unionism, had broken the back of the first power-sharing agreement in 1974. Sectarianism and sexism ran as faultlines through the trade union movement.

McCormack represented the unions on the Northern Ireland Equal Opportunities Commission and the Fair Employment Agency during the late 1970s. Towards the end of the decade, two young women who worked at the Northern Ireland Equal Opportunities Commission knocked on her door. One of them, a small woman with long blond hair and high heels, said, 'do you know who I am?'.

This was Patricia McKeown, a clever working-class catholic who'd gone to grammar school, whose family had been 'put out' of its home at the beginning of the conflict, during the biggest forced migrations in Europe since the end of World War II. The McKeowns thought they'd be safe in south Belfast, only to find themselves in a murder zone. 'It is startling to think of just how many of the boys I grew up with were arrested or killed. Too many to list.' Her family 'talked and talked about politics'. Those conversations shaped her. 'My daddy made it clear I could become an astronaut or an engineer or whatever I wanted.' What she wanted was to work for equality. In her adult life she grasped her mother's joy, the 'discovery of rights to stand up about'. McKeown was working for the Equal Opportunity Commission, but from day one realised that the Commission felt that its function was to sit on the fence. For example, one major public body that had been the subject of a complaint had been invited to the EOC and entertained to tea, with nothing more ever being heard of the complaint. 'We weren't expected to identify women as the group most likely to be disadvantaged, we weren't expected to challenge discrimination, or promote the EOC and certainly not to be imaginative.' McKeown and her colleague began to publish circulars for employees to explain the law, but employers complained to the commission. The two were then alerted to the fate of women who were making contact with the Commission – they were being berated by bosses who had apparently been forewarned. The two women had aired their worries. They'd been ignored. They wanted something to be done.

They had noticed that one of the quango's commissioners had made frequent comments in public criticising the EOC for not doing what it was set up to do. So they asked Inez McCormack for a meeting. McCormack listened to all this and cautioned that 'they could apologise for their temerity and keep their jobs, or press on and be prepared to lose their jobs'. Together they put together the jigsaw which showed that women who had turned to the EOC had 'been dismissed by us or suffered a penalty for reporting to us. We disturbed a corporate can of worms'. The Belfast journalist David McKittrick exposed the scandal. McCormack asked the trade unions to withdraw her; and the EOC lost legitimacy. The women's decision cost them their jobs, but they forced an independent investigation of the commission, which recommended radical re-structuring. McKeown's experience clarified something structural about Northern Ireland: 'our public sector was completely controlled by quangos and the Northern Ireland Office civil service – there was little or no democratic accountability'. Employers would not be made to change by agencies lacking the power of enforcement. McKeown's campaign to clean up the NIEOC took her into the union. With her long blond hair and stiletto shoes – 'she had a stiletto mind', commented McCormack – she scoured for opportunities to expand the equality agenda, and acquired a reputation as a risk-taker who really loved the members. Together, McKeown and McCormack created one of the great political partnerships in Northern Ireland.

Before the MacBride Principles campaign had begun, the Irish National Caucus had already mobilised in the US to put pressure on Short Brothers. The public company's great cathedral of aero-engineering was located in the loyalist hinterland of East Belfast, where its massive hangars dominated a landscape of brick terraces, its boundaries marked by red, white and blue kerbstones – a foreign country to the catholics of West Belfast. Less than 8 per cent of the skilled workers there were catholics, and only 6 per cent of apprentices had attended catholic schools. The Joint Shop Stewards Committee of the Confederation of Shipbuilding and Engineering Unions categorically denied that Short Brothers had pursued a policy of discrimination, and stated that 'we would not now or historically permit Shorts or any other company in our jurisdiction to operate religious, sexual or trade union discrimination.'[5] But in 1980 the workforce had gone on strike to protect the right to display the loyalist paraphernalia and slogans that defined the factory as a protestant place – untroubled by the 1976 Fair Employment Act guide to equal opportunity, which required both management and unions to 'discourage the display of flags and emblems which are likely to give offence or cause apprehension'. This was a company owned by the state. But Short Brothers rewarded massive state support with minimal reform.

In 1983 the US government, encouraged by Irish American congressmen, placed a contract with Short Brothers, and the Irish National Caucus launched their campaign. Hitherto Short's had seemed impregnable. Although the Fair Employment Agency had criticised the company's hiring practices, according to Christopher McCrudden, an Oxford scholar who had been part of the process of evaluating change there, it had had 'great difficulty in getting any response from the company'. But on the very day that the INC issued the first statement about the US government contracts, the company contacted the FEA to arrange a meeting with Short's managing director. Faced with the loss of a massive order book, Short's agreed to implement an affirmative action programme.

THE MOVEMENT FOR CORPORATE RESPONSIBILITY
Other campaigners were opening up other fronts. Sister Regina Murphy, of the Sisters of Charity in New York, was an ethical investment activist involved in the Intercommunity Centre for Justice and Peace, and later the Interfaith Center on Corporate Responsibility. Her people came from the farms of Mayo. They weren't radicals. Her mother kept a portrait of Queen Elizabeth on the family's dining room

wall – she felt kindly towards England, where every year her father had trailed to find work.

The Interfaith Center was born after the speech by the great black civil rights campaigner Martin Luther King from the steps of New York's Riverside church at the time of the war in Vietnam, in the spring of 1967. King called to account church and state, faith and capitalist communities: for 'the prophesying of smooth patriotism'; for the recruitment of the poor to wage war against the poor; for the production of napalm to burn the bodies of the Vietnamese; and for building an edifice making 'peaceful revolution impossible by refusing to give up the privileges and pleasures that come from the immense profits of overseas investment'. The impact on America's mainstream protestant churches, which held immense property and shareholding portfolios, was to generate an ethical investment initiative sponsored by the coast-to-coast National Council of Churches. This was joined in the early 1970s by catholics. This, finally, was to have a transforming impact on US relations with South Africa.

Sister Regina belonged to a generation of women in catholic orders whose values, work and self-esteem had been energised by the radical reformation of catholic theory and practice articulated by Pope John XXIII, and by the liberation theology of revolutionary Peruvian priest Gustavo Guttierez. Pope John had issued an historic decree to the clergy to look beyond *charity* towards social *change*. This went to the heart of many women's vocation; many were, so to say, re-born in their church by Vatican II, the modernising congress convened by Pope John between 1962 and 1965. When Pope John urged the religious to place themselves in the service of the third world, women suffering ugly servitude in their own religious orders seized the time. 'We discovered the theological and lived reality of what power can do to those poor people who are powerless,' said Sister Regina. 'I'm a Sister of Charity. We realised charity would be needed forever and that our work needed to be a combination of social justice, structural change and charity. Those of us who were into structural change had to work with those involved in feeding the people on the streets.'

Sister Regina immersed herself in the catholic campaigns for corporate responsibility and ethical investment that had attracted almost twenty orders to the Intercommunity Center for Justice and Peace. They were already seasoned religious activists in shareholder and stakeholder movements when they wrote to the 31 American corporations operating in Northern Ireland expressing concern about discrimination. A call from Pat Doherty in the Comptroller's Office in 1984 united the religious orders with the municipal fund-holders.

The US labour movement's biggest confederation, the AFL-CIO, was also involved in the campaign. Joseph Jamison reflected on a crucial difference between US and Northern Ireland unions:

> ... only the mildest civil rights approaches could be tolerated. We in the American labour movement were often more backward than in Europe – a lot of our creativity came out of desperation – but in one respect we were not: we'd struggled against the notion 'don't raise equality because you'll split the working class'. That was something we'd already faced because of the African-Americans' civil rights movement.

Like many Irish Americans, Jamison felt constrained in what he could do. The Congressional voice of Irish America, from Ted Kennedy to Speaker Tip O'Neill, tended to take its line from the British government. The Irish Northern Aid Committee set up in 1969 to support republicanism (NORAID) did not attract everyone, and the civil rights movement had faded in the incinerating armed conflict. Jamison had been active in the US anti-war movement, and he was convinced that 'democracy and equality were primary, they were the way change could be effected, rather than throwing bombs at cops'. But what was to be done? The MacBride Principles allowed people to move from the margins to the mainstream. Most important, the principles encouraged people to challenge the interpretation of the core of the conflict as primarily an attack on national security and on the state itself. 'What it drew attention to was that this was not a security problem, it was not a nationalist problem, it was a problem of social injustice and inequality, and that took off in Irish America.'

In 1983, in the wake of the Short Brothers controversy, the AFL-CIO's stately Secretary-Treasurer Thomas R. Donahue took a high-powered delegation across the Atlantic. Donahue had grown up in the Bronx, and began his trade union career in New York Local 32B, representing black and white janitors and lift attendants in offices and apartment blocks. He identified with the stream within the labour movement that was supportive of civil rights. His own heritage reached back to the Irish famine. His grandfather had arrived in America from Wexford in the 1850s:

> I believed in confrontational rights – the right to confront. The British people I had contact with always worried that as a catholic Irish American I would be naturally sympathetic to the IRA. I made it clear that I was against violence but that I understood confrontation. Confrontation was necessary to bring about change. In my discussions

with British Embassy or government officials I would usually be required
to condemn violence. I refused initially. I thought it was a demeaning
entry into the conversation – I didn't have to show my bona fides.

For Donahue the South African analogy made sense. 'That used to
annoy the British greatly, but there was clear discrimination against
catholics in the North'.

Jamison recalled that when Donahue heard the 'don't split the
working class' case in Northern Ireland in 1983, he recognised it as 'a
bogus position'. The delegation met the TUC in London, and found
them 'for the most part unsettled, and rather silent on the subject'.
When the delegation went to Northern Ireland, they attended a dinner
hosted by the Secretary of State Jim Prior. (Trade unionists were not
the sort of people that the Thatcher government usually entertained,
but the visiting Americans were known to have influence.) Donahue
remembered that Prior had introduced him to a catholic chief executive: 'I was supposed to see that a catholic could rise to a high position.'

When the Americans met Northern Ireland's trade union leaders –
all men, except for Inez McCormack – they heard passionate resistance
to intervention. What the Americans witnessed confirmed Chris
McCrudden's observation that pressure to stiffen the fair employment
legislation was sparse, coming from relatively fringe pressure groups
and only a few trade unionists. Among the political parties only
Unionism seemed interested – it 'strongly opposed the legislation and
its enforcement, alleging anti-protestant bias at every turn.' [6]

The Americans listened solemnly. Then Donahue, the suave envoy
from Washington, spoke. He too was a white labour movement man,
and he knew all about prejudice, but if American trade unionism had
once resisted employment equality for women and black people – as he
reminded them – 'today I'd go to jail for it'. He could not have been
more surprising to the brothers.

When he returned to the US in July 1983 his delegation reported to
the AFL-CIO a landscape festooned with religious and revolutionary
murals, where sectarianism was all pervasive and 'the root of the political issue'. 'We believe strongly that until the problems of employment
discrimination and all other forms of discrimination currently practised in Northern Ireland are forcefully and forthrightly addressed,
there can be little hope for a reduction in the level of violence', said
their report. The AFL-CIO was ready for a new challenge: this report
recommended targeting corporations and legislators with an equality
strategy. In February 1985 they signed up to the McBride Principles.
The Principles ignited like forest fire across corporations with invest-

ments in Northern Ireland, pension funds – including the massive New York Employees' Retirement Scheme – and dozens of state legislatures.

One who lent his endorsement was the black Bostonian Byron Rushing, the Massachusetts State Representative. He had been a civil rights organiser in the 1960s, and at the beginning of the 1980s was elected to the Massachusetts State Legislature, where he remained a progressive legislator into the new millennium. He recalled that the churches already had a long history of shareholder activism that began before the civil rights movement; it started by repudiating investment in alcohol, tobacco and gambling, 'what we called the "sin stocks"', said Rushing. 'These were conservative religious groups. But when investment was raised about left-of-centre issues, people argued about the issue not the tactics. Lots of people knew about the Sullivan Principles in South Africa.'

Although Irish America had not embraced the black civil rights movement, its language had been appropriated by catholic resistance back home. 'Irish Americans in Boston had worked very hard *not* to identify with black civil rights,' said Rushing. 'But when civil rights people from Northern Ireland came here we could have real conversations with them.' The most dazzling envoy was Bernadette Devlin, whose youth and eloquence signified something new – a radical, urbane modernity that connected proudly with Irish anguish and stamina. She embodied a new politics: Irish pride. When she arrived in the US in 1969 she was adored, but the longer she stayed the more unsettled Irish America became by her analogy between the black civil rights movement and the new civil rights movement in Northern Ireland. The mantra of many Boston Irish was still: Blacks out of Boston, Brits out of Belfast.[7] When Irish Americans tried to exclude African Americans from her Detroit rallies she refused to speak until they were admitted. So angry was the Ancient Order of Hibernians at this that it recalled its donation to the civil rights movement and gave it to the catholic church instead.

But although the black civil rights movement had not attracted their solidarity, Irish America had been engaged with the anti-apartheid movement, and this created links to black Americans. When the MacBride Principles were published, African American legislators responded to that history by reciprocating. In 1985 Rushing supported an AFL-CIO-sponsored motion to his legislature. Massachusetts was one of the first states to endorse the principles.

Sister Regina and the Sisters of Charity, together with several catholic orders and other faiths, pushed a MacBride resolution at General Motors' annual meeting in Detroit, where she challenged an increasingly irascible director about the failure to analyse the employee profile in its factories in Northern Ireland, and the continuing display of loyalist flags there. The company was reminded that in 1981 loyalist workers had gone on strike rather than remove anti-catholic slogans from the workplace. Comptroller Goldin, representing New York City pension funds with more than a million shares in General Motors, with a market value of $110 million, cautioned that it was time that American head offices intervened to guarantee equal opportunity. They didn't win but they secured sufficient votes to bring the issue back to the General Motors meeting a year later. 'That was enough to keep the conversation going,' said Sister Regina, who followed up that Detroit outing by a meeting with the bosses in New York at their New York HQ in 59th Street. 'I remember how little they knew,' she recalled. 'They didn't know that there were two separate school systems, they didn't know how everyone would know you were a catholic or a protestant. We learned how little these corporations become part of the places they were using.'

Insofar as the corporations cared about corporate responsibility it was, she said, because they cared about their image, 'we were getting at people who wanted to save the image, and our great strength was that we could damage their image.' The head of General Motors was another scion of the Irish diaspora: Thomas Aquinas Murphy. He and Sister Regina already knew each other, she'd put GM under pressure over apartheid, and GM had signed up to the Sullivan Principles, 'he was a fervent, conservative catholic, and very respectful of the Sisters.' That helped, but it did not stop General Motors and several other corporations mobilising a challenge to the Principles' legality. The template might be legal in the US, where companies were by then familiar with affirmative action, but was it lawful in another jurisdiction, in the UK?

The Comptroller's Office, on behalf of the New York Employees Retirement Scheme, followed with a resolution at American Brands. Its Gallagher's tobacco factories in Northern Ireland employed very few catholics. American Brands, too, decided to challenge the Principles' legality.

BRITAIN'S COUNTER-ATTACK

The official British response to the Principles was that they were consistent with government policy and therefore not necessary. That was the line when Prime Minister Margaret Thatcher visited Washington early in 1985. 'It was a way to "yes" you to death,' recalled a staffer. But over time the line changed: the principles were not only not necessary, they were counter-productive and illegal. Dublin, too, was hostile. The Fine Gael government was opposed to them, and its Labour Party partner denounced them as a campaign to 'force American money to be withdrawn', by people 'with a vested interest in the total destruction of society in Northern Ireland'.[8] By now all three governments, in the US, Dublin and London, were opposed to the MacBride Principles.

When their advocates tried to put them into practice they were met with an impressive burst of coalition-building orchestrated by the British government. 'People were forever coming through Washington expounding to people like me why we should not support the Principles', recalled Tom Donahue. Michael Farrell was living in the US at the time and campaigning for the Principles, and he remembered how striking it was that trade unionists were arriving in the US to oppose them. McCormack was 'the only prominent trade unionist to support them'. The Conservative Northern Ireland Minister at that time was Richard Needham, whose people had been landowning grandees out towards the lovely coastal town of Kilkeel. In his memoirs he blithely revealed the British government's cynical confidence that it need do nothing so inelegant as to take to the hustings itself; it could protect its *hauteur* as an adjudicator between two tribes by fielding the natives to campaign against the Principles. 'We spent a lot of time sending local catholic politicians and civil servants around American state legislatures counteracting the republican propaganda which was clamouring for the Principles to be adopted.' [9] He found allies among trade unionists, social democrats and nationalists – as well, of course, as Unionists. It was an unsavoury time and the counter-attack dramatised the difficulty of dealing with discrimination that was simultaneously practised and denied. UK government opposition to the principles relied on fastnesses of resistance in the culture. In nationalist circles this was manifest in pessimism about the reformability of the state, pre-occupation with state power, borders and sovereignty, and indifference to equality and human rights as a non-violent agenda for change (perhaps derived from exclusion); in the wider population it was manifest in a general demonisation of any people or parties that were challenging the protestant state and its history of discrimination against catholics and women; and of course it was also manifest in outright protestant defence of the Unionist state and protestant privilege.

SDLP leader John Hume, who was hugely influential among Irish American legislators in Congress, was unreservedly opposed to the Principles. Hume's priority was jobs rather than the equality agenda. He argued that inward investment itself should be seen as an 'affirmative action approach', and one that would be faster and fairer than equality legislation and fair employment policies. His answer to the MacBride Principles was 'you cannot have fair employment if you do not even have employment.' [10]

Progressive champions of the Principles in the US were taken aback when trade unionists and nationalist politicians turned up at state legislatures to give evidence against them. Republicans in Northern Ireland argued that the Principles were reformist, and Joseph Jamison recalled an SDLP politician heroically proclaiming his socialist credentials before Pennsylvania legislators, including Republican politicians sympathetic to the MacBride Principles, as a benign initiative against injustice – seemingly oblivious to the impact the 'S' word would have on American politicians.

There was support for the Principles, but it came from the opposition parties to all three governments. In the UK, although the Labour Party's reputation had been damaged in the 1970s by its draconian practice of direct rule, by the mid-1980s the party's spokesperson for Northern Ireland was Peter Archer, a quiet, meticulous barrister who was one of the founders of Amnesty International. Archer was located in the centre of the party ideologically, and was a lay preacher (Methodism was perhaps the defining branch of moral socialism in the Labour Party). His mother had been a cleaner, and he retained a faithful commitment to the well-being of the majority classes; he was open minded, and interested above all in change. His decision to support the Principles broke with Labourism's traditional deference to the securocrats.

In Dublin the MacBride advocates sought the support of the Fianna Fail opposition. New leader Charles Haughey's adviser was Martin Mansergh, who saw the potency of the Principles. He was a shy, subtle Oxbridge-educated intellectual, whose gimlet-eyed reading of the political landscape in the North was unusual for a member of the political establishment in the Republic; politics there had averted its gaze from the North for half a century, as if it was simply somewhere else. Mansergh acquired a reputation as a humane, creative political presence, whose personal modesty belied his importance as one of the principal agents of the peace process. Mansergh's endorsement of the Principles became decisive after 1987 when Haughey was again elected Taoiseach.

The Principles and Irish American pressure finally acquired strategic 'legs' in the 1992 US presidential election campaign: Bill Clinton and Al Gore, the Democratic challengers to George Bush, became subscribers; their support was part of their election campaign. Nothing could be more influential – now the Principles had advocates in the most powerful politicians on the planet, whose participation in the peace process was to be definitive.

Meanwhile, in the 1980s, the Principles became the subject of legal action. American Brands and General Motors challenged the legality of the Principles in the courts in 1986, assisted by two eminent British lawyers, Alexander Irvine and Michael Lavery. Alexander Irvine QC, on behalf of American Brands, cited the Fair Employment Act 1976, which made discrimination – treating a person less favourably – unlawful. He noted that the Act did not distinguish between acts of discrimination against majorities or minorities. Since the MacBride Principles proposed increasing the representation of under-represented communities, this envisaged 'an employer treating applicants from overrepresented religious groups less favourably'. Thus: 'If an employer is to increase the representation of one religious group, he must therefore reduce the representation of another religious group.' This, he said, would be illegal. (During his later reign as New Labour's Lord Chancellor Irvine would be challenged on a number of occasions by women and black lawyers, for his perpetuation of the old-boys and words-in-ears system of judicial appointment – more reminiscent of the Vatican than a modern state.[11])

Northern Ireland lawyer Michael Lavery QC represented General Motors. He argued that there was 'no lawful way' that the under-represented could be more equally represented 'by means of positive discrimination'. He should know – he was a former chairperson of the Fair Employment Appeals Tribunal. The equality legislation introduced by the British government in 1976 was thus mobilised by both men against a remedy against discrimination.

The academic lawyer Christopher McCrudden argued for the Principles. He was a scholar whose career thereafter specialised in finding rigorous, feasible and useful – and legal – instruments to focus on structural inequalities, and seeking ways to expose them and then change them. He became the most influential scholar involved in the development of the equality strategy, and put himself at the service of the people who needed it. A fastidious, quiet man, he was an unlikely gladiator. Positive action policy, he said, aimed to 'provide *equality* of treatment rather than preferential treatment'. In a New York City courtroom on 12 May 1986 Judge Robert Carter agreed.

American traction was scaring the British government. This was a critical time for the British. The government's shoot-to-kill military strategy was the source of international scandal and the state was under unprecedented international pressure to address the socio-economic causes of the conflict. It therefore decided to concede the need for an equality strategy in employment. A White Paper on fair employment was published in 1988 and new legislation presented in Parliament in 1989. The legislation was weirdly contradictory, however, bearing all the scars of a government endlessly bending and buckling under conflicting cajolery. But it did at last concede employers' duty to monitor their workforce and to promote equality of opportunity, appearing to abandon its hatred of the MacBride Principles. Employers could now pro-actively organise outreach training, and the banning of offensive flags and emblems in workplaces.

THE BATTLE OVER THE FAIR EMPLOYMENT BILL

Secretary of State Tom King told the House of Commons on 31 January 1989 that the Fair Employment Bill was a response both to international pressure and the MacBride Principles, and to a report by the government-appointed Standing Advisory Committee on Human Rights. He acknowledged that the previous 'system did not work'; lack of compulsion had licensed inertia; and there was no doubt that 'to some extent higher catholic unemployment has been caused by discrimination'.

The SACHR report published in 1987 was a breakthrough. The committee had commissioned an expert and novel study of employment that examined evidence from censuses and household surveys between 1971 and 1981.[12] Its analysis of the 'community differential' between catholics and protestants was damning. During this tumultuous decade 100,000 jobs had changed hands – a serendipitous chance to encourage equal opportunity. But catholic unemployment had reached 35 per cent – two and a half times greater than the rate for protestants. The study concluded that unemployment was 'substantially higher' among catholics 'no matter what are the other characteristics of the person'. Higher catholic unemployment was not caused by people's character as catholics; it was caused by the inhospitable ecology of the Northern Ireland state and economy (which was itself heavily steered, if not directly subsidised, by the state). This was a political problem that demanded a political solution. The SACHR report represented a direct challenge to the drift of government policy.

The hegemonic narrative at the time was: republicanism is the problem, therefore the defeat of republicanism is the solution. In 1987, the year SACHR published the evidence of discrimination, this government paradigm became expressed in new political and military priorities. International pressure had discredited shoot-to-kill tactics. In 1987 the government streamlined covert military operations against republican politicians. In 1988 it abolished defendants' right to silence. At the same time the government sought to control civil society by political vetting, and by setting up a new unit within the civil service, the Central Community Relations Unit; this body's solution to sectarianism was to place integration – not equality – at the centre of policymaking. (This was an approach that the government was reluctant relinquish even after the Agreement.) However, the government's own specialist advisers in SACHR counselled that, since part of this divided society was being determinedly disadvantaged, justice had to be a condition of good relations.

When the House of Commons debated the bill at the end of the month, unionism mischievously looked across the water from its garrisoned parish to remind the government of the failings of the virtuous metropolis: whilst it was promoting religious equality, it had not embarked on the reform of relations between women and men, and blacks and whites, in the rest of the country. During the debate Mid-Ulster's loyalist MP, the Rev William McCrea, complained that the concept of the community differential was 'the propaganda of the Provisional IRA'. In any case, he wondered why anti-discrimination legislation was considered good for Northern Ireland's catholics, but not for 'coloured people this side of the water'. Unionists invoked the parallels between catholic dispossession and black people's disproportionate unemployment in Britain – not to argue for a general assault on inequality, but to deny Northern Ireland's undoubted specificity. Read-across was what the government dreaded. MacBride's supporters in the Commons, in contrast, were worried that the Bill was another rhetorical gesture designed to head off its critics, that it was another case of the government responding 'to a perception ... rather than a recognition of the reality.'[13]

A line-by-line textual struggle took place in Parliament to push the new law to a level beyond previous – failed – legislation. The new duties gave the government and public bodies themselves responsibility for implementation. But herein lay a quandary. Responsibility was entrusted to a civil service that had already been criticised by the Fair Employment Agency for being unreformed. (This, too, was to remain an enduring problem before and after the Agreement made promotion of equality a legal duty.)

The MacBride proponents scented a trap: the legislation was to be implemented by a civil service that didn't believe in its necessity. They decided that they had to open up another front. Legislation, by itself, was necessary but not sufficient. Implementation had to be steeled by enforcement, and monitored and tested against the law's intentions. Initially the new front took the form of a battle over targets and timetables and measurement – the means by which everyone would learn whether or not the law was being used to address or to avert the duty. The government conceded what came to be known as the McCormack Amendment: a review.

This was the outcome of a dense parliamentary struggle. There was granite resistance, despite the virtually unassailable evidence that merely confirmed what the government already knew from the Van Straubenzee report commissioned at the beginning of the armed conflict. Furthermore, the fair employment proposals were hardly radical, they were feasible and reasonable, they required no one to lose face or lose ground. Resistance relied, of course, on the myth that the cause of the conflict was not disadvantage but hostile tribes. In parliament the word-by-word textual struggle was semantic, nuanced and technical. It may have seemed instrumental and institutional, closed and lawyerly. But the MacBride proponents believed that without a review there would be no knowing, there would be no record, the society could not know itself, nor could it contemplate its own capacity for change; the review would be the first serious act of reconnaissance. This was about the process by which a society discovers itself. The SACHR research published in 1987 had, after all, shown that employers had scarcely felt pressured by the 1976 fair employment legislation. So what would make it confront rather than conceal the evidence of compulsive sectarianism?

The answer was always external pressure. The extent to which British ministers could bring themselves to address the 'community differential' had always been compromised by an etiolated relationship to its little rogue state across the Irish Sea. Somehow Britain never needed to explain the necessity of its presence because it had an alibi: the Orange brethren who just wouldn't let go. Viceroys from London maintained an elitist estrangement from the local governors, whose incompetence had caused all this trouble, whose bigotry affronted the more ecumenical manners of the English Establishment, and whose parochialism and vulgarity irritated their more cosmopolitan tastes. All of this allowed the British to acknowledge the maladies of the state that they subsidised, without ever taking responsibility for them.

Direct rule minister Sir Richard Needham embodied this tradition. His ancestors were the Needhams of Shavington Hall in Shropshire, a mighty estate with a circumference of seven miles. The Needhams had been among King James's chief cohort of planters in seventeenth-century Ireland. For four hundred years his family had profited from their extensive estates and their gracious 55,000-acre Mourne Park in the lovely foothills of the Mourne mountains. The park was famously encircled by a granite wall – the 'famine wall' – built to give labour to the starving population in the 'great calamity' of the 1840s famines. Richard Needham was the sixth Earl of Kilmorey – seventeen generations of Needham men had been barons in Ireland since the house of Kilmorey had been established by King Charles 1 in 1625.

Sir Richard did acknowledge the 'insupportable arguments' of Unionist recidivism, but this distaste was not what finally animated the government. It was the MacBride Principles and international pressure. Richard Needham later admitted that the government's expeditions to head off the MacBride Principles in the US had failed. The legislation had been introduced 'to show the world, or rather Irish-America and Dublin', that equal employment opportunities existed. 'The very existence of new legislation showed the power that a combined Dublin-Washington alliance had over a British government.'[14]

NOTES

1. Kevin McNamara, unpublished paper, 'Give Us Another MacBride Campaign'.
2. Kevin McNamara, op cit.
3. Lord Cameron, *Disturbances in Northern Ireland: Report of the Cameron Commission*, Cmnd. 532, HMSO 1969; William van Straubenzee, *Report and Recommendations of the Working Party on Discrimination in the Private Sector of Employment*, HMSO 1973.
4. Michael Farrell, *Thirty Years On*, Brandon 1994.
5. Report of the AFL-CIO Delegation to Northern Ireland and to the Republic of Ireland. 9 August 1983, Boston, Mass.
6. Christopher McCrudden, 'Human Rights Codes for Transnational Corporations: What Can the Sullivan and MacBride Principles Tell Us?', *Oxford Journal of Legal Studies*, Vol 19, Summer 1999.
7. Andrew J. Wilson, *Irish America and the Ulster Conflict*, Blackstaff Press 1995.
8. British Information Service, British government note to General Motors, 3 March 1986.
9. Richard Needham, *Battling for Peace*, Blackstaff 1999.
10. John Hume, letter to the *Irish Times*, 12 April 1987.
11. During his time as Lord Chancellor in the Labour government elected in 1997 Lord Irvine was the subject of a sex discrimination case, supported by the Equal Opportunities Commission. It was said that in appointing his personal adviser he drew on a clique of mainly white, male, lawyers. In 2001 the Court of Appeal rejected the claim, but warned that Lord Irvine's practice 'may infringe the principles of equal opportunities'.
12. David Smith, *Equality and Inequality, Part 1: Employment and Unemployment*, Policy Studies Institute 1987.
13. Vincent McCormack and Joe O'Hara, *Enduring Inequality*, Liberty 1990.
14. Richard Needham, op cit.

2. 1989-1994: change and resistance

NEW MAN IN THE CASTLE

Colonial and cold war geo-politics took the world by surprise at the turn of the decade. Walls were tumbling down, and though fortifications proliferated in Northern Ireland, it became a busy time; there were manoeuvres above and below ground. In July 1989 a new man was installed at Hillsborough Castle. Peter Brooke, the new Secretary of State, was a dynastic Tory but he became one of Hillsborough's most creative tenants. He, more than any other Conservative politician – and like Mo Mowlam almost a decade later – understood that the British state was not neutral and that the government had to be seen to intervene pro-actively for peace.

Apparently an avid reader of the republican weekly, *An Phoblacht*, Brooke was actually interested in the place and in peace talks between Sinn Fein, the SDLP, and the British and Irish governments. He believed it was time to 'be imaginative.'

There were structural blockages, however. There was no contact with nationalism, he said: 'were it not for the catholic church it would have been almost impossible to interface with the nationalist community, so the only console on which we could play was the catholic church.' And contact with unionism was vexed.

It was a very low ebb, the AIA had caused total breakdown between unionism and the government. Unionists were going into a self-imposed exile and retreating into a constitutional cul-de-sac and you had to get them out into open country. The unionists were not writing to ministers at all. My two principal objectives were: to communicate to Sinn Fein that there was a way out of where we were; and to get the unionists out into open country. In 1989 the Berlin Wall had come down, South Africa was making progress, the Middle East was making progress, there was a faint sense that Northern Ireland might be the last unsolved problem.

Brooke felt a personal responsibility. 'I did take the view very early on that if we had a stalemate, and if brave men – in all aspects of the

Troubles – were risking their lives in a stalemate, then it was a waste of lives.'

Immediately Brooke's stewardship was confronted by the UDA's revelations in August 1989 that it had been targeting people on the basis of secret files distributed by the UDR and RUC. He was soon due to meet with the Irish Foreign Minister as part of their regular cycle of contact. The calumny over collusion seemed set to be a major setback. He believed that the crisis provided the Irish government with 'an issue on which they could hit us on the head'. But it provided Brooke with 'a genuine opportunity to create an opening'. The first meeting was the longest ever; it 'lasted six hours, the next four hours'. Thereafter the Irish government was 'a vehicle for raising issues for the nationalist community. That was a good thing. It gave both of us the opportunity to decide to trust each other.'

Brooke had also been given something else to work with – other people had been using their imaginations. He was aware that, on the nationalist side, Gerry Adams had enlisted John Hume in dialogue, supported by the Redemptorist priest Alec Reid. They were developing a new paradigm, a constitutional settlement based on consent within both communities. When he was urged by John Hume to offer reassurance to nationalists by clarifying Britain's stake in Northern Ireland, Brooke agreed. It was through a new link, introduced to Sinn Fein by a letter signed personally by Brooke, that the Secretary of State's decisive speech, known as the Whitbread speech, was flagged up to Sinn Fein. On 9 November 1990 – the day that Mary Robinson was elected President of the Republic – he made the watershed announcement, *pour encourager* the peace process: 'The British government has no selfish strategic or economic interest in Northern Ireland'. That was, of course, contrary to the strategy and spirit of partition, and it was hardly consonant with London's re-invigoration of covert military operations. Martin Mansergh recognised in Brooke's historic formula the template that could be found in a revolutionary discussion paper authored by Alec Reid in November 1987. This paper became an early route map for the pan-nationalist front's theory of self-determination by consent in both communities, and the renunciation by Britain of any colonial interest; it was 'a remarkably prescient document', wrote Mansergh, and it 'anticipated Brooke's statement'.[1]

Going much further than would be expected of a minister serving the intransigent Margaret Thatcher, Brooke re-activated long-dormant secret service conduits to Sinn Fein, on the advice of the intelligence man in Northern Ireland, Michael Oatley.[2] Brooke said that he had barely known about the link: 'I wasn't asked to approve it while

Margaret was Prime Minister. I was asked by John Major. I didn't know about it in detail. I effectively knew nothing about it until spring 1991.'

Brooke had recognised that a settlement was impossible without engaging with nationalism and republicanism. They were the only source of a constitutional initiative. He also believed that in the context of these manoeuvres the primary causes of the conflict also had to be addressed. 'If the objective was to restore peace then you had to be moving on all fronts at once,' he said. 'I don't want to exaggerate its capacity to influence events but you had to ensure that the pattern of policymaking was mutually consistent, you had to make the totality of public policy homogenous. Socio-economic policy had to be of a piece.' Crucially, Brooke decided that equality and social need had to penetrate all policy-making, and in 1990 he put out equality guidelines on gender and religious and political affiliation, to be applied to all policy-making.

Brooke's equality protocol had extended to Northern Ireland the government's response to a European directive on gender. This was a defensive Westminster initiative in 1990, designed to 'reduce the risk of legal challenge' under the European Convention on Human Rights; it had come from the government's Ministerial Group on Women's Issues. But when the guidance was introduced into Northern Ireland, it was expanded to include religion and political affiliation. Civil servants may very well have expected it to dwell undisturbed in departmental drawers. No one could have predicted what subsequently happened, that these policy initiatives would be drawn into the dynamism of parallel peace processes, and that their participants would alight upon seemingly dehydrated protocols and circulars to try to transform them into tools for change. But the forensic mentalities of the equality protagonists, and their stamina, alliance-building, and research and development capacities, made them formidable operators.

Activists and academics in the disability, trade union, and human rights movements in Northern Ireland saw the guidelines as instruments of institutional change. They roundly criticised the NIO for minimising their application, and insisted that these instruments should be refined into something really useful. Under pressure from the MacBride movement, in 1991 Richard Needham, Brooke's number two in Northern Ireland, agreed to improve them. They saw this as not so much a victory as a caution: the government was responding to pressure rather than wanting to do the right thing.

Although catholic disadvantage was part of the guidelines, their origins as a gender initiative gave the government the opportunity to deflect protestant sensitivities. And the span of constituencies was widened to include not only religion, politics and gender but also disability and age; and they utilised the more positive language of equality and human rights. This may have been intended to make the guidance more acceptable.[3] It was certainly intended to be internal – and across the water it did snooze in the drawers. But the equality movement in Northern Ireland forced the government to make them public and thereby useable.

In 1991 Brooke introduced a new policy that represented another break with conservative orthodoxy, Targeting Social Need, aimed specifically at reducing the unemployment differential between catholics and protestants. It was also to be a 'public expenditure priority'. He was explicit in his purpose: the aim was to address social need *and* 'reduction in community differentials'.[4] He believed that policy had to direct funds to address the geo-politics of disadvantage. This meant giving not equally but differently; in order to redress the community differential and focus on those in greatest need, 'we deliberately decided, in terms of the expenditure of public money, to build in criteria on TSN'. Brooke was not blind to the geography of disadvantage. West of the River Bann (Northern Ireland's longest river, running from the south east to the north west) was predominantly catholic and poorer. Derry, the biggest town in the west, had been the site of the civil rights movement's most vigorous challenges to Stormont against sectarianism in the voting system, housing and the economy. Thirty years later Brooke was aware that differential disadvantage was unchanged, and that investment had to be drawn to the areas of greatest disadvantage.

If the wider focus was intended to defuse the impact of such measures, it did the opposite. It galvanised the most vigilant constituency concerned with equality: women in the workplace. At that time neither nationalism nor republicanism yet had an institutional equality agenda, and neither modelled their project on the most dispossessed in all communities – women. Yet it was women who breathed life into them.

The public employees' union had prioritised the interests of the most disadvantaged workers: catholic and protestant part-time women. It was in the interests of these groups that the impact assessment guidelines were ultimately tested. But first the union insisted that they had to be transformed, toughened, enlarged and emboldened. The Northern Ireland Council of Voluntary Organisations later observed that, though Brooke's promise to address deprivation and disadvantage was 'the most significant policy initiative', it would remain 'a nice idea', unless the government found forms of law enforcement.[5]

This initiative was stalled after Brooke's tenure was cut short in April 1992, when he injudiciously agreed to a vaudeville sing-song on RTE's *Late, Late Show* on the day of a bombing. His exit left social need and equality in policy-making orphaned, doomed to wander around the labyrinth of the inhospitable bureaucracy in the NIO.

But Brooke had, at least, 'achieved his ambition of starting political talks between constitutional parties on the totality of relationships'.[6] Unusual among Tory politicians, Brooke grasped the synoptics of the social, the military and the political, and he manoeuvred between peace processes: one level concerned constitutional relations between states, and states of war; another concerned relations between citizens, and between citizens and states. In these parallel peace processes there was a presumption that the equality discipline should be inscribed in a constitutional settlement.[7]

It would be another two years before his successor, the patrician Sir Patrick Mayhew, finally presented the long-awaited equality protocol, Policy Appraisal and Fair Treatment (PAFT), which stipulated that equality 'must condition and influence policy-making in all spheres and at all levels of government'.[8] 'We got the guidelines by staying stubborn', said McCormack. 'And all along, the debate enabled us to keep arguing that it was the system, not the people, that had to change.' As McCrudden noted, yet again the timing of PAFT was not accidental. Bill Clinton, a MacBride Principles supporter, was now in the White House. The peace process was one of his priorities. After a period of prevarication, the British government understood that it had to show its commitment to equality.

INTERNATIONAL PRESSURE

Brooke had tried to find ways through the impasse in Northern Ireland, both in the conduct of the armed conflict and in the institutional processes. But his demise meant that, once again, external efforts were necessary; for the next few years the peace processes were dominated by international pressure.

Albert Reynolds succeeded Haughey as Taoiseach in 1992, and, working with the adroit Fianna Fail adviser Martin Mansergh, secured his government's support for the prototype peace plan that had been proposed by Gerry Adams and John Hume. This specified the right to self-determination for the people as a whole, with a specific commitment to consent by the people of the north. The plan had been encouraged by Brooke's 'no selfish interest' formula. However British

Prime Minister John Major's precarious majority after the 1992 election led him into an 'informal alliance' with the nine Unionist MPs – a peculiarly conjunctural 'selfish interest' – in order to preserve his government. The Adams-Hume proposals – or Hume-Adams as the document was known, in deference to the SDLP leader – was, for the moment, doomed. As if to seal its demise, the secret communications sanctioned by Brooke were leaked by the irrepressible William McCrea, and not only denied but disowned. Major said that it would turn his stomach to do business with republican terrorists. Dublin and Washington watched aghast. The peace process faltered, confidence in politics ebbed and the equality and social need initiatives, so important to the impoverished ghettoes that fielded the foot soldiers, faded.

Somebody had to do something surprising. And that someone was also a surprise: the President of the Republic of Ireland, Mary Robinson. At Aras an Uachtarain, the presidential residence in Dublin, a light was kept permanently at the window to pay tribute to the trauma of famine and dispersal, and to welcome Ireland's people everywhere: here was home. The tone of her presidency had been defined by her inauguration; it would 'promote the telling of stories', it would sponsor 'celebration, conscience, social justice', and 'extend the hand of friendship and of love to both communities in the other part'. No President had ever shown such rapport with the island.

Robinson was a socialist, a feminist, a human rights lawyer, a modern woman who would not be in sync with the manly but corrupt cleverness of previous Taoiseach Charlie Haughey, nor the ripe melancholy of a culture under the church's surveillance. In the 1980s she had made a bold gesture towards the North: as a Senator in Dublin she had resigned from the Labour Party in protest against unionists' exclusion from the processes that produced the Anglo-Irish Agreement. She brought both her values and her Irish erudition to a process of collective self-discovery that during the 1990s made Ireland one of the most interesting societies in Europe.

But she had not been to West Belfast. Nowhere felt the pain of the busted peace process more than the largely catholic constituency where electors had voted en masse for Gerry Adams. It was a place that wore the scars of civil war. It was also, however, one of Northern Ireland's busiest civil societies: when the state had walked away, West Belfast organised itself; and when it organised itself it was often subjected to political vetting by the NIO and deprived of funding. Like all working-class neighbourhoods West Belfast had a talent for disappointment – hope for the best, expect the worst. It was an ailing place, here you died younger than in Bangor or Basingstoke. But it also had talent –

expressed in sheer staying power, bonhomie and a cultural renaissance that, for all the poverty of the place, resonated with the cultural revival down south. A visit by the President of the Republic to this den of the demonised was mooted. This was dynamite. The NIO argued against it. The British government was opposed.

But didn't the demonised deserve her attention? The governments were talking to republican leaders, why couldn't she meet the people of West Belfast? Weren't they citizens of the island of Ireland, weren't they entitled to be republicans, and weren't they necessary participants in peace-making? President Robinson was going. The British warned the Irish government: they *could not* – by which they meant they *would* not – guarantee the President's safety. So the community groups themselves guaranteed her safety. They used Inez McCormack, a friend of both the president and of community activists in Northern Ireland, as her escort.

The planned locale for the visit was a massive municipal gulag, Whiterock, housing catholics re-located to the edge of the city, and ranked as one of the most deprived neighbourhoods, [9]an area where the RUC was unloved and unwelcome. A large security presence would convert a community visit into a confrontation. So, apart from a small police presence, the President's safe passage was dependent on the goodwill of what the NIO described as a 'terrorist community'. There was something else that would test the residents. There would come a moment during the visit that everyone would want to witness, when their man Gerry Adams met Mary Robinson and they would shake each other's hand. At that time Adams was still censored in the British press; he was invisible and inaudible, an un-person. The mass media also wanted that handshake. But West Belfast would not allow either themselves, or their presidents, to be exploited for someone else's propaganda purposes. They knew that the President's visit was a tribute to them, to their right to recognition. But the encounter was also reciprocal – it was their tribute to her position to keep that encounter between themselves. They brought to that moment an emotional and political largesse: they not only banned the press, they banned their own cameras. There would be no snaps of their two presidents for the people's mantelpieces because they knew that the photograph would be broadcast not to celebrate them but to accuse them. A community longing for visibility had the discipline to efface itself to protect the President.

President Robinson was met by children from Irish language schools – Irish language teaching had been denied state funding – and by music from the virtuoso pipe and fiddle player Sean Maguire, the great McPeake family of singers and the award-winning St Agnes Choral Society. 'Up the Aria', somebody whispered to Gerry Adams. He greeted President with a welcome in Irish, 'cead mile failte', and they shook hands. Beside him was standing an elderly woman blinded by a paratrooper's plastic bullet in 1971, Emma Groves. Support the campaign against plastic bullets, Ms Groves asked the President. Robinson also met Terry Enright, whose son had been murdered by someone carrying a gun that had belonged to the RUC. Enright was a loved, long time activist in cross-community regeneration campaigns in West Belfast, well-known for his passionate campaign to regain open access to Belfast's Black Mountain, a no-go area appropriated by the military during the armed conflict, 'Come up the Mountain', he asked her. This was the 'terrorist community'. Robinson's visit could not have exasperated Unionism more, not least because the demons were revealed as decorous and disciplined.

NEW MAN IN THE WEST WING

In 1992 Northern Ireland had also returned to the American agenda. In the US Primaries Irish Americans had galvanised around the Arkansas governor Bill Clinton, and Clinton consulted Irish American movers and shakers about what they wanted from an American President: wearied by the effect of the special relationship between the US and the UK that seemed to silence the White House on this issue, they said they wanted change. Clinton was urged to appoint a peace envoy, and grant a visa to Sinn Fein's banned President Gerry Adams.

Another of Clinton's sherpas was a law school buddy, former Congressman Bruce Morrison, a lawyer whose pioneering Bill to legitimise the status of almost 50,000 Irish migrants who had left the old country during the bleak 1980s – thereafter known as the Morrison visas – made him much-loved among Irish Americans. Morrison had been to Northern Ireland and had met protagonists from all sides of the conflict. Rights! That was Morrison's mantra: 'democracy isn't votes it's rights'. When Clinton appeared at an Irish Forum in Manhattan in April 1992 he had decided on a new approach. He promised to endorse the McBride Principles, to dispatch a human rights envoy, and grant Gerry Adams his visa. 'The New York primary in April 1992 sealed his nomination,' said Morrison. Morrison's activity in the 'Irish Americans for Clinton' campaign later metamorphosed into Americans for a New Irish Agenda. As well as Morrison the powerful lobby included Joe Jamison from the American labour movement, the billionaire Chuck Feeney, Bill Flynn from Mutual of America, which specialised in pensions and insurance for non-profit organisations, and Niall O'Dowd, a maverick and influential publisher who had left Ireland in the 1970s. Many of these people were already familiar envoys to Northern Ireland, with good contacts, people who had reconnoitred the political landscape in search of an inclusive settlement.

A couple of weeks before Clinton was elected that autumn, Morrison worked with the Clinton team to prepare a presidential statement. The statement became Clinton's manifesto for Northern Ireland. On jobs it stated: 'We believe that the British government must do more to oppose the jobs discrimination that has created unemployment rates two and a half times higher for catholics than for protestant workers'. And it argued that human rights must be asserted 'against the wanton use of lethal force' and 'collusion between the security forces and Protestant Paramilitary groups'.[10] This manifesto, as he expected, 'sent London crazy' and, according to Morrison, no sooner was Clinton elected than Downing Street briefed the press that it would make Clinton jettison such excesses.

However, although Clinton appointed a vigorous member of the Kennedy clan, Jean Kennedy Smith, to be his Ambassador in Ireland, in the early days little emanated from the White House to vindicate his presidential promises. Stuff had to be sorted out in Washington – the new administration was, after all, proposing an entirely new diplomatic discourse. Northern Ireland was no longer to be zoned as a British sphere of influence.

In the mean time Bruce Morrison's Americans for a New Irish Agenda were planning a delegation to Ireland. Niall O'Dowd floated a ceasefire with the Republicans to open a space for the envoys. The IRA agreed. Sinn Fein believed that 'the Irish American community provided us with our best chance of internationalising the issue of peace in Ireland ... unlike the Irish anywhere else, Irish America had considerable influence – not just in politics but in the business world as well'.[11] And the MacBride Principles were an exemplar of what was meant by internationalising the quest for a settlement. Clinton's election now raised the prospects of international influence snipping the cordon sanitaire thrown around republicanism.

In September Morrison's powerful delegation arrived in Ireland, in the context – as agreed – of an undeclared ceasefire. They met protagonists from across the political spectrum, including loyalist leaders close to the combatants, who offered enlightening observations on the class conflicts within unionism. Gusty Spence told the Americans: 'We had nothing but contempt for mainstream unionist politicians' – because 'These people will fight to the last drop of our blood, and they'll lead from the usual position – the back.'[12] The Americans' encounters with working-class protestants and catholics were decisive, said Morrison. The IRA had been as good as their word, and when the delegation returned to the US they encouraged the White House, with support from Congressional Representatives on Washington's Capital Hill, and Taoiseach Albert Reynolds in Dublin, to give Adams a visa.

The White House was not diverted by a subsequent outbreak of sectarian violence. Reynolds had convinced Clinton that Adams should get his visa. On 2 January 1994 he got it. A few days later he arrived at the Waldorf Astoria with John Hume, his collaborator in the peace process, and Alliance leader John Alderdice, to participate in the National Committee on American Foreign Policy conference to which all of Northern Ireland's political leaders had been invited. At this, the Unionist leaders withdrew.

Nationalist and republican eyes were not on the equality and poverty duties. They were focused on the constitutional arrangements being addressed in the Downing Street Declaration that had been signed between Reynolds and Major in December 1993. During this time British eyes were on the White House, where the Adams visa had aroused a crisis. And Dublin's attention was on keeping Downing Street committed to the peace process. Unionism was in and out of Downing Street, holding the Prime Minister in its dour thrall.

During 1994 the pan-nationalist front was choreographing a historic leap, and on 31 August the IRA announced a complete cessation of military operations. This created a problem for Unionism, which could not conceive of itself outwith war against republicanism: its identity depended on a devil. UUP leader Molyneaux therefore met the ceasefire with dismay. It was not an occasion for celebration, it was quite the opposite, he said, it was 'de-stabilising the whole population'. Catholic neighbourhoods had been ecstatic – they, presumably, were not part of the 'whole population'. Complete cessation was also not enough for John Major. He demanded clarification: what did 'complete' mean?

Six weeks later the loyalist paramilitaries announced their ceasefire. This was written and presented by Gusty Spence. It affirmed the union, but also the right 'to seek constitutional change by democratic, legitimate and peaceful means'. Though thousands of loyalists had fought and died for their state, the loyalist leaders would not tolerate 'a return to the exclusive, divisive, abusive and corrosive political institutions of the past which were an affront to, and a blight on, the democratic embodiment and equitable concept of our country'. Bill Flynn of Mutual Life of America was there for the announcement, unobtrusively waiting in a back room, and a week or so after the Loyalist cease-fire he welcomed a loyalist delegation to the US.

At the end of the year, however, the process was gravely wounded: Albert Reynolds' folksy but unyielding leadership was brought to an unexpected and untimely halt. His resignation was provoked by the failure of his Attorney General Harry Whelehan to process an extradition order concerning a priest accused of sexually abusing children north of the border. By now Ireland was undergoing a cultural revolution that had both church and state reeling, about the endemic abuse of children by the church under the blind eye of the state. It wasn't Reynolds' fault, but the Attorney General had been his appointee. Ireland had become perhaps the only state in the world where the abuse of children could bring down a premier.

In spite of this, Dublin was still assiduously following up the Downing Street Declaration, and on 22 February 1995 the Irish-British Joint Framework Document was published, believed to have been drafted by the artful Dublin diplomat, Sean O'hUiggin, a poet known for his intellectual elegance. It outlined the skeleton structure of future relationships across the islands of Ireland, and was a prototype of the 1998 Agreement. It did not address the statutory equality and human rights duties – they were not yet in the pan-nationalist blood. But the document prescribed that all institutions of government would become directly accountable to all of the people, and capable of attracting their wholehearted support. An 'appropriate and equitable role for both sides of the community' would be guaranteed; electoral arrangements (proportional representation) and departmental power would aim to avoid 'any entrenchment of the main community division.' For protestants this meant the end of their majoritarian dominion, but it also offered a guarantee to protestants fearful of future demographics that might make catholics the majority. The new political culture would be based on 'the greatest possible degree of parliamentary scrutiny and public accountability'. Political institutions would give expression to identity, but the constitutional project would seek to avoid 'any entrenchment of the main community division'.

Again the British Prime Minister confided in the detached Molyneaux (Unionism had exiled itself from all of this), who recalled a meeting in Number 10 where Major pushed the Framework Document across the cabinet table, 'and I put my fingertips to it and stopped it'. Molyneaux didn't want to see the document. [13] Neither he nor Major could, therefore, be accused of complicity. When the document was leaked, Major mustered every conservative MP he could find to reassure the ranks that the peace process was not 'going green'.

Only decommissioning would satisfy him – and, of course, the Ulster nine.

The year of the ceasefires had ended badly. The peace process was now adrift: it had lost its great champion in Dublin, and its enemies in London were refreshed.

NOTES

1. M. Mansergh, 'The Early Stages of the Irish Peace Process', in *Conflict Resolution*, December 1999.
2. Ed Moloney, 'IRA-MI6 Relationship Protected Spy HQ', *Sunday Tribune*, 24.9.00.
3. C. McCrudden, 'Mainstreaming Equality in the Governance of Northern Ireland', *Fordham International Law Journal*, Vol 22, No 4, 1999.
4. Peter Brooke, speech to CCRU Equality Review Conference, February 1991.
5. NICVA, 1994.
6. Michael Mansergh, op cit.
7. Mary Holland, doyenne of the *Irish Times*, was the first to describe the equality movement as a parallel peace process.
8. C. McCrudden, op cit.
9. Northern Ireland Statistics Agency, Northern Ireland Deprivation Measures, 2005.
10. C. O'Clery, *The Greening of the White House: the Inside Story of How Irish America Tried to Bring Peace to Ireland*, Gill & McMillan 1996.
11. G. Adams, *Hope and History*, Brandon 2003.
12. Roy Garland, *Gusty Spence*, Blackstaff Press 2001.
13. E. Mallie & D. McKittrick, *Endgame*, Hodder & Stoughton 2001.

3. Back to basics

The crisis caused by Reynolds' resignation left enthusiasts in the peace process feeling wretched. So near and now so far. But it had become clear to the MacBride proponents that the equality agenda was not entirely contingent on the constitutional question. It was not – despite the government's propaganda – a republican front. Indeed it had hardly attracted the attention of the nationalists and republicans in Northern Ireland. This parallel peace process made demands of the *British* state, and of any state that might in future govern Northern Ireland. Though the equality agenda was an opportunity to break out of constitutional confinement and pre-figure new times, this had not excited the pan-nationalist imagination. However, this was what animated the equality movement: it was a way through the political impasse to effect material change for disadvantaged catholics *and* protestants.

The public employees' union, now named Unison after a merger of manual, managerial and professional public sector workers, and therefore one of the biggest trade unions in Northern Ireland, had always represented both protestant and catholic workers. It promoted the utility of PAFT to both communities of workers and their clients. Proponents of the MacBride Principles and the New Agenda in the US had also made contact with loyalist leaders, and the MacBride campaign had taken on board loyalist complaints about protestant exclusion from some catholic workplaces. During the 1980s Goldin and Doherty had met the UUP's Molyneaux and the DUP's Gregory Campbell, who had been invited back to New York City Hall. The MacBride Principles did not mean discrimination against protestants.

In October 1994 the MacBride proponents celebrated the tenth anniversary of the Principles in New York, with a conference that heard that by now American corporations' employees in Northern Ireland were more representative than those of British companies. The MacBride Principles were working. The data was a gift to the peace process.

In Washington, Clinton's Department of Commerce hosted an economic investment conference in 1995. The Americans had invited all the business and political interests, and it was to be an opportunity to focus British attention on its equality duties.

It was preceded by the St Patrick's Day festivities at the White House in March – a social must. Secretary of State Patrick Mayhew was uneasily contemplating his visits to Washington. But his mind was on another mission: to lobby the Americans to block Gerry Adams' visa, banish him from the White House celebrations. He failed. The Speaker, Newt Gingrich, carefully choreographed manoeuvres: John Hume would take Adams to meet the President himself. When the trio met they shook hands and the crowd around them gave them a round of applause.[1] Gerry Adams had metamorphosed from pariah to star, a politician with as much presence and ease as Clinton. But this was only a beginning; the eloquence of the handshake was not yet matched by the words on equality coming from the President's mouth.

Britain's boycott had only added to Adams's exoticism. The lanky figure of Mayhew loitered in the wings, making breakfast appointments with the press. He had something else on his mind. On 7 March he presented them with three principles that must be met before Sinn Fein's admission to all-party talks: decommissioning (and by that he meant a formal commitment), a gesture and a timetable. This ultimatum – known as Washington Three – took months to sink in. This was in part because people could scarcely bring themselves to take it seriously. Seamus Mallon warned John Major that this was a hole Mayhew would never get out of. Reynolds reminded the Prime Minister that 'my party went into power, went into government, and went into Parliament first – and they didn't hand over their guns to anybody. In fact, some of them brought their guns in their hip pockets going into Parliament'. He failed to persuade the Prime Minister. [2]

Washington Three had not yet been assimilated, however, as Britain's last word. In May, Mayhew and Adams returned to the US for the economic investment conference hosted by the Clinton government. Patrick Mayhew had still not met Gerry Adams. He was warned: you can't come to this event and not meet the man. At the last minute, as Adams was about to arrive at the same city and settle into the same hotel, Mayhew agreed. The two men had a brief private encounter. [3]

Mayhew and Adams were soon in the same room again, this time at a crowded meeting to debate what was, according to Pat Doherty of the New York Comptroller's Office, still 'the most controversial issue' for Irish America, discrimination and the MacBride Principles. The event was billed as an irresistible showdown between supporters and opponents – too important for either to miss. This was a meeting where Inez McCormack shared a panel with church leaders who had been campaigning against the MacBride Principles, with the British government's support. Two years earlier these church leaders had met their colleagues in America's corporate responsibility movement and told them that the MacBride Principles were divisive: campaigners should trust the fair employment legislation; they should be sensitive to the unionist majority. The Presbyterian Reverend John Dunlop – who had a reputation as a protestant moderniser – warned that there were 'undesirable elements' on the 'MacBride train'. [4] Sharing the panel was Queen's University scholar Eithne McLaughlin, who was at that time collating research on the impact of the new equality and social need initiatives.

The audience expected fireworks, said Doherty, 'but they didn't happen'. The opponents of the Principles were the guests of a White House that had signed up to them, and they weren't going to win an argument with the most powerful politicians in the world, and furthermore their resistance would have 'allowed them to be seen as being against equality':

> it would lose them points among influential people in the audience. Many people in the US saw discrimination as analogous to black-white issues in the US, so they already had the cards stacked against them. And many British and Unionist arguments had echoes of segregationist arguments in the southern states during the '50s and '60s.

Eithne McLaughlin quietly offered some stark statistics on the community differentials. McCormack's style was soft as brushed steel. The woman unsettled her enemies. She had received death threats during her political career. But nothing in her audience, whether it was Patrick Mayhew standing at the back, or their holinesses on the panel, could be as eerie as a life lived as a feminist organiser of poor workers in a place crossed with front lines. She agreed with the churchmen that, yes, of course, investment was vital, but insisted that the peace had to be disciplined by equality and social justice, and that the people who *needed* peace had the right to participate in the production of it.

Mayhew knew the evidence. He knew what worked. But it would soon dawn on the Americans, on Dublin and the peace process that his answer was unyielding: it was Washington Three as the terms of republicans' entry into talks.[5] The disarmament orthodoxy, as Fionnuala Ni Aolain, Christine Bell and Colm Campbell have described it, presented the conflict as 'the response of the liberal-democratic state to politically motivated violence and terrorism.' This discourse not only denied the link between state action and the causes of the conflict, but also the fact that security powers 'were not simply a response to the conflict but in fact partly constitutive of it'. [6] The point was that the equality matrix clarified what was concealed by the disarmament orthodoxy.

MAKING PAFT INTO A VERB

It was women who put the government to the test (aided and abetted by scholars whose interest was not primarily gender but discrimination and disadvantage). Unison members, feminist trade unionists, not republican or nationalist politics, brought PAFT to life. They had asked McCrudden: how do we discipline the state, make the marginal visible, allow anyone affected by policy to participate in its production? His reseponse was that it was not equality law as such, but environmental impact assessment in international development practices, that provided a model. It was a model with which the government was already becoming familiar, as a way of ensuring compliance with obligations. [7]And Unison members, in any case, regarded the guidelines as promising fairness, and making policy available for assessment, and behaved accordingly.[8] This was what the government had feared – that the people would take them seriously. The right to participate in policy-formulation could effect a quiet cultural revolution in the everyday business of an estranged state. 'And then wouldn't we be citizens!' declared Patricia McKeown. She argued that direct rule breached the people's access to political institutions: 'there was no means of putting checks and balances on the administration of the state before PAFT'.

Unison knew that it could invoke the guidelines – precisely as had been intended – to oblige the health trusts to measure the impact of the government's privatisation strategy on women, and weigh their duties towards equality and social need against privatisation policy. That's what they thought they were doing – PAFTing the government and the institutions. When the Down and Lisburn Trust proposed privatisation of hospital hygiene and kitchen services, Unison calculated that the people likely to suffer negative effects were Downpatrick catholics and Lisburn protestants. But the trust would not analyse the impact on these communities, so the union organised its own audit. The results showed that the workers most likely to suffer were women in the most deprived wards, in both Downpatrick and Lisburn. The union took the trust to a judicial review. Mr Justice Kerr, later Northern Ireland's premier judge, rejected the union's case on the technical ground that the Department of Health had failed to send the PAFT guidance to health trusts. But he agreed that there was 'not a little force' in the union's submission. It was to be expected, said the judge, that the trust would provide evidence that it had considered the PAFT provisions.

He warned that, had PAFT been issued properly, the employer would have had to take them into account. This seemed to give 'legal status'. The government therefore had a pyrrhic victory; the case had cemented the status of a tool the government had expected no one to know about and no one to use. [9] Participation and impact assessment had arrived. Unison spread the word. 'An obscure set of government guidelines became common parlance in the union', said Patricia McKeown. 'People grasped that it was something they could use.' McKeown alerted neighbourhoods where health services faced privatisation, and where, by now, terse impact assessments were dutifully – rather than seriously – being done, usually without engaging with those likely to live with the consequences. The union was uniquely positioned to engage both workers and communities of clients.

The importance to working-class protestants was palpable. 'I saw it as promising awareness and equality, and monitoring that, which is really important', recalled Dawn Purvis, a loyalist and later a Member of the Assembly. 'You have to understand, Northern Ireland was governed for so long by civil servants.' Dawn Purvis had been attracted to the new, left-wing, voices in the Progressive Unionist Party. PUP leader David Ervine had begun to ask public questions about PAFT and trust privatisation policies. 'Promoting equality, monitoring and awareness, that is what the peace process was all about, and any agreement should be about', added Purvis. The deployment of PAFT in relation to privatisation was dramatic. 'It so frightened the entire NHS in Northern Ireland that it stalled market testing for more than two years', said Patricia McKeown. This tranche of privatisation was the first equality-proofing test of PAFT. The shrinkage of powers and public services directly administered through the local and national state that is brought about by privatisation has been described by the eminent human rights scholars John Morison and Stephen Livingstone as 'fugitive power' – functions privatised and detached from the state and thus from public accountability. For Morison and Livingstone, policy appraisal and impact assessment implied a larger democratic potential for the new times, by enforcing democratic values throughout the proliferating agencies and powers.

The women at Unison found an ally for the popularisation of PAFT in the Committee on the Administration of Justice. CAJ's director was Martin O'Brien, a man whose politicisation began when he was boy. 'I was 12, and people from the Peace People knocked on our door and said "do you want to come on the peace march?". So I went with my brother and sister.' After that O'Brien formed a forum, Youth for Peace, which invited political parties to address teenagers, created opportunities for protests against violence, and offered support to young people being harassed or intimidated to leave their homes by paramilitaries. 'I got exposed to the ideas of Martin Luther King and Gandhi, and I found out that not everybody had a life like mine: I wasn't routinely harassed by police, my home wasn't raided, we didn't have relatives locked up for things they hadn't done.' Then he began to change:

> I started out thinking that prejudice was what was wrong. But I realised that it wasn't just prejudice – there was a structural discrimination and injustice. Two things were important to me: building relationships – the soft community relations stuff – and structural inequality, the harder stuff. I felt that if you wanted a peaceful society you had to have a fairer society. That led me to CAJ.

O'Brien became a major international mover and shaker for human rights and for the equality ethic. He acquired a reputation as a gentle but unyielding advocate, 'nice but dangerous'.

Working with Unison, CAJ organised briefing sessions for non-government organisations and community activists – and thus, noted Chris McCrudden, a 'loose coalition was born'. The equality agenda was acquiring critical mass in the trade union movement; equality and social justice was bridging the community divide; and human rights activism was acquiring a socio-economic discourse. John Morison and Stephen Livingstone saw in PAFT, and the movements around it, something big: 'certainly this seems set to be *the* significant idea which will underpin post-ceasefire public policy'. Martin O'Brien reckoned that 'what gives it bite is the commitment to engagement in a process. It is participation that challenges power – the idea of equality on its own doesn't.'

This period in Northern Ireland's intellectual life revealed the great pressures that had obscured the evidence that was there for all to see. The struggle to make sense of the society, the struggle for knowledge, showed that evidence is always dependent on the work of interpretation. And interpretation was always framed by ideology. Evidence does not speak for itself. Evidence, like beauty, is in the eye of the beholder. Northern Ireland's institutions had always known that there was disproportionate disadvantage among catholics – it was organised, it was intended. That much had been acknowledged in the first official dossiers of the armed conflict. The question was always: how could that be made to matter. That was the importance of the 1989 Fair Employment Act. Through the provisions it made for review of progress, it had opened up a new flank in the conflict: knowledge itself. Robert Osborne believed that it was the failure of the legislation in the

1970s and the 1980s that had opened the door for evidence-based research that could influence policy.

The academic discussion about the Act mattered to the marginalised, because the review was about *them*. They had a need to know. And the debate mattered to unionism, because it would challenge or confirm the practices of the protestant state, whose hand steered its economy. It mattered to nationalism because it would vindicate or discredit its case against Britain. It mattered to women because they experienced themselves as the objects of multiple oppressions; they were the poorest and the most put-upon. Finally, the review process was implicated in the reform – and reformability – of the British state.

HIGH NOON IN THE ACADEMY

The review politicised the academy. Scholarship itself was annexed to the conflict zone. Some of the researchers commissioned to investigate disadvantage and discrimination in the 1990s commented that the process not only brought to a head 'the academic proponents of the competing perspectives'; it also led to academic perspectives themselves being 'perceived as becoming closely aligned to political perspectives'.[10]

It was high noon in the academy. The review of the 1989 Act produced two completely contrasting hypotheses. Unionism's alibi for the 'community differential' was that there were simply too many catholics. The problem was breeding. And they didn't have the sense to leave the place.

Graham Gudgin, director of the Northern Ireland Economic Research Centre, together with Professor Richard Breen, director of Queen's Centre of Social Research, offered unionism an unusually scholarly endorsement, in a report commissioned to assess the legislation's impact. Their research was regarded by some as 'elegant';[11] but some of its academic admirers felt queasy when the report's authors told a seething seminar in Belfast in 1996 that, in effect, catholics were the cause of catholic disadvantage. The problem was catholic migration (too little) and birth-rate (too much). The unemployment ratio 'cannot be used to infer the presence or absence of fair employment'. They added a political expletive: 'any Act aimed at decreasing the unemployment ratio by combating systematic discrimination in Northern Ireland is unlikely to succeed, unless it was intentionally to introduce an element of discrimination against protestants.'

The economist Anthony Murphy was caustic: the two men's claims about lower catholic migration and higher birth-rate were wrong. The rate of Catholic migration had been 50 per cent higher than that of protestants during the two decades of the armed conflict. That Catholics were less likely to succeed in job applications – whatever their qualifications – was more to do with their religion than anything else. Two thirds of the differential was caused by religion.

Gudgin's report had not reviewed the law, it had rendered it redundant. His critique was so extreme that he was exposed – he'd gone too far. And the implications of his research, though reassuring to the unionist establishment, did not necessarily attract those protestant politicians for whom class remained an important category. The government had no alternative but to commission new research. That did not do Graham Gudgin's career any harm, however; it recommended him to the top man. After the Good Friday Agreement Graham Gudgin became adviser to the Office of the First Minister, where he counselled David Trimble on the statutory equality duty that he had so passionately opposed.

Queen's University social policy expert Eithne McLaughlin was commissioned to do the new research. She was joined by three members of SACHR, including the UUP's equality spokesperson Dermot Nesbitt. Three volumes emerged. They were as decisive as the 1987 SACHR report, which had propelled the 1989 Act.

Five years after the Act was passed a wide-ranging review of the legislation revealed that senior civil servants managing the Northern Ireland state had swerved away from the obligation to change themselves. The new research suggested that unemployment had become – contrary to Gudgin's conclusion – 'a more significant indicator of labour market inequalities than in the past'. Contrary to myths of protestant work ethic and catholic fecklessness, catholics were still more than twice as likely to be unemployed, but were significantly more inclined to take any job. Women, too, were more inclined to take any job, however low the pay, but access to education, training and employment opportunities were undermined by the lack of child care. In West Belfast, long-term unemployed catholics 'were in many respects more "flexible" and less "discouraged" than protestants'. Yet catholics were less likely to be alerted to jobs by the benefits office (fewer than 4 per cent). A third of workers had experienced intimidation in previous jobs, and these were overwhelmingly catholics. Most catholic and protestant workers said they would not venture into areas of past intimidation, despite the ceasefires.

There was thus 'little comfort' for those seeking to explain unemployment differences 'in terms of the characteristics and behaviour of the unemployed themselves'. Intimidation remained 'the most important finding for fair employment policy'.[12] So, equal opportunity in the labour market required an assault on sectarianism throughout the society.

What was the impact of PAFT? The government's economic strategies could not be evaluated, because Departments displayed 'an unwillingness to expose evidence to scrutiny or an unwillingness to collect the necessary evidence'.[13] An institutional sulk infused government Departments. PAFT had been designed 'to provide a clear mechanism to ensure that public policy is adjusted for equity' *for both communities*. Failure, said the researchers, would 'confirm long-standing suspicions' about the entire political process.

The flow of European funds into Northern Ireland's dispossessed neighbourhoods made them a clear candidate for PAFT and TSN. Indeed the Fair Employment Commission had proposed that businesses receiving European funds should be subject to PAFT. Oh no, said the Department of Finance. In a dramatic commentary on the failure of PAFT to 'enter the bloodstream' of the civil service, the researchers found themselves, unintentionally, cast in the role of action researchers, whose very presence seemed to focus the bureaucratic mind, and whose questions seemed to prompt officials to give 'significantly more thought to implementation' than they had done during the stewardship of the Central Community Relations Unit (the body initially commissioned to implement PAFT). [14]

The fate of TSN, described by Peter Brooke as one of the government's three policy priorities, was also entangled in political appeasement of protestants; at best it met ambivalence, and at worst truculent inertia. Again the official review's first difficulty was to reap a response from government Departments. None met their deadlines. The Northern Ireland Office itself never responded. [15]

The Department of Finance was characterised as unaccountable, obscure and conservative. So impenetrable was it that 'TSN would never be capable of objective assessment'. Its approach called into question 'the entire role and value of public expenditure priorities'. The Department of Economic Development, it transpired, did not do religious monitoring. How, then, could it target the religious differential? Under the NIO's cynical eye, these equality instruments had become emaciated; they needed life-support from 'political leadership at Ministerial level'. But the Ministers weren't bothered, and so TSN languished – 'a principle awaiting definition, operationalisation and implementation'.

Dermot Nesbitt, the UUP's equality spokesperson, had attended the seminars and workshops organised by the researchers during 1995-6. But just as their report, *Building for the Future*, was to be published, in

June 1997, he astonished the team by springing on them a minority report. It was a deft manoeuvre – it arrived too late to be considered by the researchers. Nesbitt's *Note by a Dissenting Member* reprised Graham Gudgin's claim that doing something about catholic disadvantage would discriminate against protestants. The problem, he said, was breeding. His conclusion was brazen: 'It is surely not equitable to ask the Protestant community to sustain for such a long period of time a possible diminished right to employment because of sustained higher natural increase in the catholic population.'

EQUALITY AND MO MOWLAM

In the dog days of John Major's government, Brooke's breakthroughs, which energised the peace process and offered opportunities to show the reformability of the state, had been squandered. Washington Three, more often known as the demand that the IRA decommission or disarm, became hegemonic. This provoked consternation even in some fastnesses of the secret services. The MI6 mandarin Michael Oatley, who had been sent to Northern Ireland in the 1970s by Prime Minister Edward Heath, and who counselled Peter Brooke to re-open the secret channel to Sinn Fein in the early 1990s, described the Major government's behaviour as 'an example of picadorism at its most provocative'. Decommissioning was just 'a new excuse to avoid the pursuit of peace'.[16]

But if Washington Three had ruptured the peace process, the equality and participation matrix was already pre-figuring a new experiment in democracy that ultimately became inscribed in the Agreement.[17] It has come to be recognised – by those who notice it – as a dynamic exemplar of reformed democracy for the twenty-first century. In the mid-1990s John Morison and Stephen Livingstone had seen the radical potential of a legal duty for equality; they regarded it as a 'significant constitutional principle' in the organisation of government in Northern Ireland.[18] This potential lay in the infusion of *values* in the practice of government – 'come what may in the wider peace process'. There were values that ought to appear on 'any roster of democratic values' – equality, transparency, accountability, participation – and these should discipline the practice of any government.[19]

This 'significant constitutional principle' was rightly suspected by its enemies (even though they insisted, wrongly, on assigning it to republicanism), and they met the movement to give it legislative force with 'a sustained attack'.[20] They recognised the atomic power of the idea: this 'effectively constitutionalises the equality aspiration', protested David Watkins, a senior civil servant, later a director of security services in the NIO. 'Arguably this law would seek to dictate the socio-economic policies of future governments, irrespective of electoral mandates or budgetary constraints.'[21] That, of course, was exactly what made it so alluring to its advocates, among them Peter Archer, the former Labour shadow minister for Northern Ireland. For him the attraction of the Policy Appraisal and Fair Treatment guideline when it surfaced in 1994 was that it proposed governance 'based on human rights'.

For David Watkins and the NIO securitariat, human rights conjured demons – 'highly motivated lobby groups' that would usurp elected representatives, and 'frustrate the wishes of a democratically-elected government'.[22] Yes, Archer acknowledged, with a smile, as if he enjoyed the paradox. 'It is anti-democratic in a sense: you are saying there are certain ground rules that you cannot break even if you have an electoral majority'. Northern Ireland in its unreformed state embodied, for him, 'exactly what Lord Hailsham would have called an elective dictatorship'.[23] The whole point of human rights was that 'They are not subject to elections. They are almost constitutional.'

After the 1997 general election Mo Mowlam, who already had been persuaded of the case for a *statutory* equality duty, became the Secretary of State in the new government. Mowlam was at the time hailed by all sides, from the unionist establishment to Sinn Fein, as an unusual if not unprecedented politician: she was inclusive; she made herself available to all parties, including those close to the conflict. Everyone anticipated a new impetus to the peace process after Labour's massive election victory: here was a government no longer dependent on the Unionists in parliament.

New Labour came into office with an agenda of constitutional reform and devolution, and a renewed energy in tackling the impasse in Northern Ireland. Those on the ground took the opportunity to seek to embed a new egalitarianism into the constitution. Their previous years of battling for equality placed them in a potentially crucial position in influencing any agreement that was reached, and for contributing to its success through their innovative approaches. The appointment of Mo Mowlam was a major bonus for this strand of the peace process (for more on Mo Mowlam see pp216–8). Within months of taking office she had restarted meaningful peace talks. She also facilitated the restoration of the IRA ceasefire and the inclusion of Sinn Fein in the multi-party talks. These eventually led to the Agreement.

In March 1998 a White Paper had been published honouring her pre-election commitment on equality, making it obligatory upon public bodies to carry out their duties with 'due regard' to the promotion of equality of opportunity. Of course, and quite appropriately, the critics of the equality duty also had the ear of government, and the White Paper exemplified the attempt to reconcile the two positions; it floated 'for consideration' the possibility of a legal duty to promote reconciliation between different religions and political aspirations.

The government's legislative ambition was oddly diluted, however, in the draft offered to the parties involved in the peace talks in 1998: the *'Heads of Agreement'* paper did not refer explicitly to a statutory equality duty, indeed it didn't use the word equality at all. Instead it offered softer, vaguer *'equity* of treatment', a term not used thus far and therefore a term that suggested a shift in emphasis, an approach that implied even-handedness and impartiality rather than a concern with outcomes. Whether or not the two terms amounted to a significant shift mattered less than the fact that the E word that everybody had used hitherto was being erased. But if the drafters thought no one was watching they were wrong: the effect was to galvanise the Irish government's vigilance, it gave 'much greater concentration' than it might have to the equality agenda during the talks on the Agreement in 1998 in the knowledge that failure to honour the parallel peace process could be de-stabilising. [24] The manoeuvre had concentrated the collective mind. In the final days of the talks, the equality agenda became increasingly central to the whole success of the negotiations.

However, the importance of the Watkins critique of the equality duty was that it came from the highest echelons of the NIO securo-cracy and the community of civil servants (sometimes interchangeable). Whilst politicians came and went, the NIO remained, burnishing a reputation for pride that they, and not their political masters, really ruled. These were the people and systems tasked with implementation of a duty that was a critique of their management of the place. This was to cause problems for Mowlam. The ceaseless quarrel with the evidence reassured a unionist conscience that was determined to live in a world of its own. Their scepticism made no impact on the Agreement when it was eventually negotiated: they were irrelevant to it. But the sceptics contributed to its de-stabilisation in the new times that followed. Gudgin, as we have seen, was rewarded with a place at the highest table: once devolved government was restored he became economic adviser to the Office of the First Minister at Stormont. And the NIO man who launched the 'sustained attack' on the fair employment and participation initia-tive, David Watkins, became the NIO's director of security – effectively the commissar of the securocrats. The status quo would be in safe hands, guaranteed life after the Agreement.

NOTES

1. E. Mallie & D. McKittrick, op cit..
2. Ibid.
3. Adams, op cit.
4. Interfaith Center for Corporate Responsibility, record of 12 February 1993 meeting.
5. Mallie and McKittrick, op cit.
6. C. Campbell, F. Ni Aolain and C. Harvey, 'The Frontiers of Legal Analysis: Reframing Transition in Northern Ireland', *The Modern Law Review*, 66 (3) 2003.
7. McCrudden, 1999, op cit, p1709.
8. Ibid, p1714.
9. John Morison and Stephen Livingstone, *Reshaping Public Power: Northern Ireland and the British Constitutional Crisis*, Sweet and Maxwell 1995.
10. R.D. Osborne and Ian Shuttleworth, 'Fair Employment in Northern Ireland', in Osborne and Shuttleworth (eds), *Fair Employment in Northern Ireland, A Generation On*, Blackstaff Press 2004.
11. P. Bew, P. Teague & H. Patterson, *Between War and Peace: the Future of Northern Ireland*, Lawrence and Wishart 1997.
12. P. Quirk & E. McLaughlin, 'Long-Term Unemployment in West Belfast', in P. Quirk & E. McLaughlin (eds), *Policy Aspects of Employment Equality in Northern Ireland*, SACHR 1996.
13. John Simpson, op cit.
14. Robert Osborne, Anthony Gallagher, Robert Cormack & Sally Shortall, 'The Implementation of Policy Appraisal and Fair Treatment Guidelines in Northern Ireland', in Quirk and McLaughlin (eds), op cit.
15. Padraic Quirk and Eithne McLaughlin, 'Targeting Social Need', in Quirk and McLaughlin (eds) op cit.
16. Michael Oatley, 'Forget Weapons and Start to Trust Sinn Fein', *Sunday Times*, 31 October 1999.
17. The case for infusing policymaking was finessed in a document published by CAJ in 1997, *Mainstreaming Fairness*.
18. John Morison and Stephen Livingstone, op cit.
19. John Morison, *Reconstituting Politics, Waiting for the Big Fix*, Report No 3, Democratic Dialogue 1996.
20. McCrudden, op cit.
21. David Watkins, quoted in McCrudden op cit.
22. Watkins, quoted in McCrudden, op cit.
23. Lord Hailsham, a maverick Tory, coined the phrase in 1976, to describe the power of governments with slight majorities to resist the opposition and control legislative programmes.
24. McCrudden, op cit.

4. Doing the deal

The deadline was looming. Good Friday, 10 April 1998, was the day determined by President Clinton's special peace envoy Senator George Mitchell to be the day of agreement. The text had been delayed. It didn't appear until Monday night on 6 April. There was less than a week to go. Inside Castle Buildings, a dull office block in Belfast, delegations were crowded into their quarters. The unionist parties were located on the first floor, the nationalists and the Women's Coalition on the ground floor, and the British Prime Minister in a suite at the top. The coffee bar was there, too. Everyone had to pass the Women's Coalition office on their way into the building and the women exploited that to maximise their influence. Everyone seeking refreshment had to gather at the coffee bar on the top floor. If Sinn Fein people were in the coffee bar, the UUP evacuated it. Republicans were not yet out of their de-contamination zone, it seemed. Other delegations developed 'hanging around' into an art. This didn't mean doing nothing, it meant doing diplomacy. The Women's Coalition organised a division of labour: there were analysts, scribes, and people whose job it was to make friends, to loiter creatively around the corridors, the bar, the photocopier, listening, chatting checking out. Creative loitering was adopted by Dawn Purvis, who had become a familiar face of the PUP during the previous couple of years. She was seen to be scurrying, loitering, listening, organising. 'It was useful for the party to have someone to run about, sniff about, and I was a known face, so I could approach people from the other parties. I built relations, I was organising documents, I was the co-ordinator.'

During the talks, delegates were aware that while they were sending out their own listeners and talkers, Martha Pope and Mo Mowlam were also among the 'sniffers' moving around the delegations, scenting what was, and wasn't on. Martha Pope was Senator Mitchell's assistant, and was regarded as his 'backbone': 'she was always there, always briefing him, always briefing the parties'. Contrary to some accounts, which represented Mowlam as marginalised by Tony Blair during the final week, she was seen by many of the delegates as an assiduous presence, and instrumental on the prisoners' issue. She discarded her shoes and her wig and moved informally among the delegations. Neither ministers nor special envoys felt sure that everyone was going to sign up to the final document, and nothing could be taken for granted. Their sniffers' reconnaissance was vital.

For delegations closest to the combatants and closest, therefore, to what was deemed low life, this interaction with Senator Mitchell, Martha Pope and General John de Chastelain, the head of the decommissioning body, was experienced as their first sustained, respectful encounter with the upper classes. 'I wouldn't have met people like this before,' said Dawn Purvis. 'The only people I'd have met from a different class would be doctors, and they'd treat you as if you were daft anyway.'

Purvis was a working-class loyalist who lived in an area where 'there were bombs going off, shootings going on, we were living in the thick of it, but it was never talked about': 'we never heard the news, it was switched off or turned over; the news was irritating, interrupting the flow of life'. Her neighbourhood was poor, but 'the unionist and loyalist people said "we can't complain because it's *our* government"'. This class reticence had produced a community that held its tongue. 'You didn't speak out, you didn't have much but you didn't speak out. The people who spoke out were catholics, they were subversive!' She only got involved in politics after the 1994 ceasefires. 'It was wonderful, we started discussing what kind of Ireland we wanted.' She was attracted to the tone of the new loyalism voiced by Billy Hutchinson and David Ervine. She'd read Sinn Fein literature during elections and noticed that they advocated better living conditions whilst unionists proclaimed 'keep the union safe.' The new loyalist voices were now talking about 'bread and butter issues'. 'I remember wondering: what are bread and butter issues?'

Women had had to put up with men who were involved in paramilitary organisations, 'fighting for their country' while women worried about feeding their families; domestic violence was common and often 'if a woman didn't have his tea on the table she'd get another hiding'. Hutchinson and Ervine were talking about women's rights too and – bravely in Northern Ireland – supported women's right to choose and control over their own reproduction. Dawn Purvis started listening to the news and offered to work for the PUP. She'd known about the civil rights movement in 1969. 'It was all seen as a papist plot, or a nationalist uprising. It wasn't – it was British citizens asking for British rights, and if the protestants had joined that fight then we wouldn't have ended up where we did.' Like many protestants who *thought* their way into the peace process the journey demanded that they re-interpret their own history, and now, immersed in the work of creating a settlement, she believed that the equality agenda and the politics of PAFT offered protestants and working-class men and women in general an approach that 'sums up what the peace process was all about, and what any agreement should have been all about.'

Purvis was a member of the PUP delegation, who crammed around fifty people into their quarters, and symbolised the class of unionism that brought some candour and creativity to the making of the deal. The intimacy of the interaction between the delegations disturbed the visceral distaste and brittle class and cultural insecurity that infected the place. The presence of the parties close to combatants, which also included former prisoners, was vital to its durability. They had helped finesse the text, they felt it was theirs.

When the text appeared on Monday it was showered by refinements and compromises that would for the time being resolve the national question, the jurisdiction of the British and Irish governments, the shape of power sharing government and its values. The terms of relations between the citizens of Northern Ireland, its democratic institutions, and the participation of both Britain and Ireland in the new jurisdiction – Strands I and II – represented a new historic compromise that cleverly unsettled the symmetry of nation and state and sovereignty. Consent and constitutional safeguards gave recognition to both nationalist and unionist aspirations not as *ethnic* but as *political* ambitions. Indeed when the British government in the last lap of the talks offered a formula on 'ethnic communities' (during a session on language rights), implying that nationalists were an ethnic minority, it was thrown out. It would have been inconceivable to represent unionism as an ethnic majority.

The width of the electoral system, the size of the assembly, and the composition of executive government, aimed to make politics irreducibly inclusive. These themes, too, provoked heavy bargaining. Would the electoral system favour the fantasy of a sensible centre composed by parties that felt themselves to be above the squalid fray, or would it embrace all the protagonists and smaller parties that had been marginalised by British electoralism? Would unionism stomach north-south institutions and Dublin's presence with London as an interlocutor? These questions exercised the delegates for much of the week. And though the status of combatants, prisoners and victims was scarcely addressed in the initial text, they commanded hours of tumultuous negotiation because they symbolised the interpretation of the conflict itself and the prospects for political legitimacy. The talks were stalling on issues that refracted the rhetoric of conflict – including the border, the span of representivity to be allowed in the new Assembly, the status of prisoners and resources for victims.

Under the terms of the Agreement, Unionism traded majoritarian rule for consent. As we have seen, the reassurance that there would be no change in constitutional status without the consent of both communities had been the decisive contribution contained in texts emerging from the pan-nationalist front since 1987. However, in return for an admission that this cross-border treaty inevitably involved the surrender of absolute sovereignty, the UUP sought to minimise the north-south institutions included in the Agreement (a parochial obsession in the context of Europeanisation and globalisation).

Prisoner release was also totemic. Without the support of the prisoners, the deal would fall. And without recognition of the prisoners, the parties close to the armed struggle could not be expected to sign up to any deal. In 1998 there had already been a mutinous reaction to the peace process among loyalist prisoners. Mo Mowlam decided to talk to them in person. Her famous prison visit was indicative of her relaxed humanitarian approach, but her gesture also acknowledged that the prisoners were political. It followed: no prisoner releases, no deal, no peace. But it was one of the touchy subjects kept for last; it agitated and finally split the UUP delegation only hours before the deal seemed to reach consensus. However, it also united Sinn Fein and the loyalist PUP and UDP, and, strongly supported by the Women's Coalition, they worked for an early release date. 'People could say the three parties had a vested interested', commented Avila Kilmurray, a seasoned political activist and member of the Women's Coalition team. 'But nobody could say that we did. It was fought tooth and nail – we argued that there was no provision for people on the run; some people would say "But they're murderers", but we wanted to create normalisation around issues that could be seen as extreme. The big difference was between those who recognised Northern Ireland as a deeply divided society, and those who thought it suffered from an aggravated crime wave.'

On the morning of Good Friday, Sinn Fein had still not yet formally decided to accept the agreement. The PUP went to see the republicans around 10 o'clock to ask them to accept it. By then the UUP, which lacked a majority at the talks, had been compelled to do business with one of the smaller loyalist parties and the PUP had insisted: no agreement unless there is an agreement on prisoners. Sinn Fein struggled hard and tried to hold out for release within one year. Release within two years was the compromise after the NIO persuaded Tony Blair that releases within a year would jeopardise a yes vote among unionists.[1]

So, it was now clear, there would be an agreement.

Meanwhile, the parties wrapped around the prisoners also found themselves together on the electoral arrangements. The UUP, SDLP and Alliance preferred a smaller assembly: the smaller the assembly, the more secure their dominance. 'We knew the UUP, the SDLP and the Alliance Party didn't want anybody but themselves in the Assembly,' said Dawn Purvis. Tony Blair was lobbied for a larger assembly and top-up arrangements that would guarantee a place for the small parties that had contributed greatly to the Agreement. But the Women's Coalition sensed that neither the British nor Irish governments were really interested. What was at stake for the Women's Coalition was not merely space to ensure greater representation for women, but a guarantee that all the major protagonists in the conflict would find their place in the arena. Their argument drew on other experience of post-conflict arrangements, and on the debates within feminism on representation and marginalisation.

Presence – the opportunity to give voice, to be seen and heard, to change the priorities of politics by changing the composition of the legislators, by being *present* – had already been vindicated by the presence at the talks of the most marginalised groups: former prisoners and women. In her defence of women's admission to the assemblies in proportion to their presence in the population, Anne Phillips offers the eloquent mantra: 'embodiment matters'. It mattered enough in the talks to arouse chauvinistic ire. One of the UDP negotiators Davy Adams, a loyalist councillor, reckoned:

> They were very determined, very sincere, very capable. It was difficult for some of the older members of the establishment to deal with them: 'good god, women aren't supposed to be in this role!' The women's treatment by some individuals made us say, 'christ, that's no way to treat anyone'. From our position it was also like watching friends being insulted, because our relationships had developed on personal terms. And most of the people like us came from homes where the mother was the rock. It soon became obvious that the Women's Coalition were putting forward ideas that were really positive.

The women wanted an electoral framework that topped up the constituencies with another ten seats allocated on the basis of overall votes. This would guarantee the presence of parties such as the Women's Coalition, which might not muster enough constituency votes to secure elected members, but might gather a significant poll across the country – more than, say, a single successful constituency candidate might get. 'We said every party to the talks should be given a chance at least for the first term. Without the small loyalist parties, for example, there would not have been an Agreement,' said Monica McWilliams. But the PUP failed to persuade the UDP to hold the line. 'Thursday night we were up to all hours trying to keep the loyalists with us on this.' She also nobbled SDLP leader John Hume to berate him about the electoral system, but he was implacable. 'At about 5 o'clock we knew we'd lost it.' They were sickened.

All of these themes were huge and contested. But they still did not address the really big question: through what prism could such a polarised society see the deal? How could the society come to know itself and change? Would the institutions redress the causes of the conflict: injustice and inequality? Would the institutions and ideologies inscribed in the Northern Ireland state be stabilised, its sovereignty restored? *Would power-sharing mean power shared in the service of social justice, or the status quo?* Would the deal change everything?

By Thursday the talks were stuck on issues that polarised the 'constitutional parties' – the release of prisoners, disarmament, the scale of north-south joint activity. The anxious interregnum was well used by the equality advocates. Here was an apparent paradox – an alliance between men connected to armed combat and non-violent women. Furthermore, the Women's Coalition included people from both unionist and nationalist backgrounds. What united these parties was that they all *needed* the equality agenda, they all represented communities of interest who needed change. The Irish government saw itself not only as the guardian of nationalist interests but of a strong equality duty. They had already made contact with loyalist prisoners. And the Women's Coalition had nurtured regular contacts with both the republicans and the loyalists for two years. The coalition's office was one of the most efficient and focused; it mounted flip charts listing priorities right up to the final few hours. The SDLP were 'a big disappointment' to the Irish government however. 'They contributed almost nothing,' complained one negotiator. Even after being offered an Irish government briefing on the equality and rights themes they didn't respond.

The parties relied upon their access to both governments to push their agendas. Broadly, the Republic of Ireland was the guardian of the nationalist interest, and the British government was perceived to be the protector of the unionist interest. The equality agenda was uniquely cross-community. The Equality Coalition could not rely on the British government, despite Mo Mowlam's goodwill: it had already sensed that Britain's interest in equality was merely tactical.

The British government had decided that everyone had to benefit from the deal and it understood that it had to 'deliver something to Sinn Fein' – and that something was equality. This was supposed to keep Sinn Fein in the talks, and reward republicanism for its historic compromise over the national question – its accommodation to partition. But the Irish negotiators knew that the civil service 'might not want the principle to mean much in practice'. And all of those with an interest in the equality duty were alive to its fitful presence in government texts over the years. So, it fell to the Irish government, which was simultaneously co-signatory with the British government to any deal, and also interlocutor to the nationalist parties and the Women's Coalition, to press the equality duty. The Irish government was already aware that there was anxiety about the precarious commitment to equality in the text. 'We were determined that the Agreement would not be criticised,' commented an Irish diplomat, 'because inequality was a material contributing factor to the outbreak of the Troubles. Addressing it was especially important to the most disadvantaged communities because that was where the paramilitaries came from.' Whilst admitting that it was 'probably not the case that our government felt strongly about it,' he said, 'we knew that others did'.

The 'others' were an alliance across all the parties closest to the dispossessed among both nationalists and loyalists, and the Women's Coalition, which maintained links with both. The parties affiliated to militias and the feminist party with a stringent critique of the militarisation of Northern Ireland shared some progressive priorities; the equality agenda bridged the polarisation between disadvantaged catholics and protestants. That did not mean it was soft. On the contrary, said a member of the Irish government team, it was 'very subversive, because it subverts the power'. The document initially produced for the final round by Senator Mitchell included only one sentence on equality, said a senior Irish official; and despite pressure on drafters to expand the equality section, it remained shallow. 'I accused them of bringing back desiccated sentences.' Everybody knew what had not worked in the past. The Irish government, assiduously briefed by the Equality Coalition, toiled to locate at the centre of government the *statutory* duty, engagement of those with an interest in the process of policy-making, so that this 'commitment could not be marginalised'.

Only in the last 36 hours did the combined pressure of the Women's Coalition, Sinn Fein and the loyalist PUP and UDP get all this into the text. The gap opened up by the difficulties swamping the talks was what gave them their opportunity. By Thursday negotiations were trailing through the night. Hungry delegations bivouacked in the cold and otherwise empty building. But while the talks were strung out the equality section was enhanced – it was the beneficiary of 'extra time'. 'We wanted it to be a document that women could be proud of, so that women could see women being specifically acknowledged,' said Monica McWilliams. The Women's Coalition pinned down a senior civil servant during a drafting session. He wondered, he told them, what women had to do with conflict resolution. 'It's simple,' replied Avila Kilmurray. Quoting Kathy Harkin, the much-loved Derry civil rights activist who had founded the city's first refuge for battered women, she told him, 'We've been living in an *armed patriarchy* for the past thirty years'. The text was amended. The Women's Coalition not only wanted women in; they also wanted the violence women endured as women to be recognised as a human rights issue. And they wanted the civil servants to stop referring in the text to the Secretary of State as *him*. 'We wanted Mo acknowledged as a *her,*' said Monica McWilliams.

Late on Thursday night civil servants briefed the parties lobbying for the equality section and they could see the fruits of their input: the span of identities and interests that came within the equality duty's radar was now wide; it ranged from religion and ethnicity, to gender, marital status, disability, age, carers' responsibility and sexual orientation. It became known as the Nine Grounds. This was so pervasive as to imply a generally egalitarian culture. The talks had got stuck on the constitutional issues that had undone every attempted agreement since the beginning of the armed conflict, but the Irish government slogged through Thursday night on the equality duty.

The equality advocates, including the Irish government, struggled hard to get an Equality Department at the centre of the new government – to oversee implementation, to diffuse the new ethic through the administration, and, as McCrudden put it, to get it into the blood-stream of governance, and pre-empt 'quangoisation' by departments buying in consultants – a practice that would leave the culture of the bureaucracy unchanged. They failed. This was a bridge too far for Britain, which was guarding itself against 'read across' in Britain itself. But in the final hours they succeeded in tagging the text with a special pledge: 'the British government intends, as *a particular priority*, to create a statutory obligation ...'; it would attract '*due regard*'. The equality duty would be mandatory and an over-arching priority.

The UUP, the SDLP and the Alliance Party were at an angle to the equality debate, though that did not imply opposition. The UUP, with a gay man – Stephen King – among its senior negotiators, found itself able to accept the text rather more comfortably than might have been expected. A member of the UUP team thought that unionism had invested too much in fighting Strand 2 (the Strand on North South Institutions): 'We over-estimated Strand 2, because it was the most critical thing for Sinn Fein – and the most critical thing for us. We put too many resources into fighting that one.' The party's problem was that it came into negotiations scarcely able to read its adversaries: 'between the Sinn Fein ceasefire and Sinn Fein in the talks we had to try to educate our members in a whole new way of thinking'. The unionists had been encouraged by the British government to believe 'that SF were into an agreement heavily loaded on equality'. But they 'didn't really believe Sinn Fein would go for an agreement that was limited on the constitution. We thought Sinn Fein would get fed up and leave. But none of this happened'. The UUP kept watch on Gerry Adams' writings before April and registered that he was giving great space to the equality issue. 'This was clearly much more important to them.' UUP thinkers therefore expected that they could do a trade off with Sinn Fein.

When the initial document arrived on Monday 6 April some read it, some went home. By Tuesday, the UUP delegation was absorbed in its own divisions and disappointed that the equality and human rights principles went further than they had expected, further than elsewhere in Europe. A UUP negotiator told me: 'we had thought: settle the border and make sure people have ethnic equal rights'; but already there was a difficulty – the UUP conceived of equal rights as 'minority rights', whilst the equality advocates' agenda was precisely not contingent on the constitutional question.

However, the UUP still saw everything through the filter of the constitutional question, and conceded 'any human rights you want' as long as republicans agreed to 'secure our constitutional position'. The party put up stiff resistance to Sinn Fein's efforts on the Irish language, and the notion of equality of treatment for the identity and culture of the two communities – 'we tried to get rid of it'. The language campaign seemed to unionism to be backward and divisive. But the Nine Grounds, that was different. Stephen King negotiated equality on the UUP's behalf and when a civil servant came to him with a question, 'you don't wanted sexual orientation removed?', he said 'oh no!': 'When I reported to the leader he raised his eyebrows but I said don't worry, people will think we're lovely'. King's own position within unionism – as an economic liberal and social libertarian – signalled adhesion to the UK's modernity compared to the historic catholic conservativism of the Republic, and distaste for socially-conservative nationalism in the north. He didn't necessarily relish the prospect of 'anti-progressive power-sharing at Stormont where the only thing that is agreed is how to make this a reactionary place'. After all, said King, direct rule might have been undemocratic but at least it was modern. The equality duties in respect of the Nine Grounds were nothing if not modern. And so this part of Strand 3 attracted relatively relaxed consensus.

'The Agreement is an unprecedented jump in human rights', commented one of the Irish government negotiators: 'In the last 36 hours people got rid of the initial document. The last and final document was much stronger. The final document was the parties' document. There was very little resistance to it. People had accepted that there would be an agreement, so they were coming out of their trenches.'

The Irish government perceived in the final text two agreements: one addressed the equality of national allegiances; the other concerned equality between citizens and relations between citizens and the state. This second part was the section regarded by some of the drafters as the 'sundries', reckoned Dawn Purvis. 'They were put at the back, but they should have been at the front.' This section had been a shadow until the Equality Coalition lobbied the two governments to get something more substantial into the talks and the text. 'This was their contribution to the peace process', said an Irish diplomat; 'then the parties magnificently built on it and made it their own'.

This was a poignant moment for Chris McCrudden, the human rights scholar who was among the architects of the words and ideas that got into the Agreement: 'It is one of the few documents I've read over the last twenty years that I'm almost completely happy with,' he commented. Why? 'Because it is unambiguous that equality is the central theme.'

Almost as soon as the ink was dry, however, there was a suspicion among Dublin diplomats that it was only a matter of time before Mowlam would be evicted from Hillsborough Castle. And then what?

'The big question,' said an Irish diplomat, was whether the 'central theme' would be honoured – would it be implemented, 'will it take?' After all, the NIO had not been 'adept or enthusiastic about equality policies in the past'. Would they tolerate them in the future, he wondered, would they finally do what they'd always refused to do? 'Will the new heart take to the new body?'

NOTES

1. Dean Godson, *Himself Alone, David Trimble and the Ordeal of Unionism*, HarperCollins 2004, p349.

5. The struggle over equality

LOST IN TRANSLATION

The Agreement's journey into real life began with a great promise. The negotiators had proposed in their text a transcendent duty: to produce more than peace, to begin the millennial work of transforming the sectarian and sexist power relations that structured their society. If this argument seems grandiose, beyond any imaginable prospectus of an Agreement hailing from a people whose politics tend to elicit a supercilious yawn on the other side of the Irish Sea, we need only remind ourselves of what the negotiators thought they were doing. The adversaries were present: the deal was not crafted by distant diplomats. And these adversaries were not political primitives, mad, bad Paddies; they were sophisticated protagonists, who – for good or ill – had tested the wit of what John Morison calls jaded 'Westminsterism' for three decades. The armed conflict, sovereignty and statehood had dominated their political horizon. But it had not entirely obscured their line of vision. It had also exposed, in extremis, the sectarian and sexist power relations that structured their society. The Agreement was an outcome not only of a de facto civil war, but also of ingenious movements and interests that were not included within the arc of the conflict. [1]

However, from the beginning the Agreement had to struggle for survival. The 'central theme' was lost in translation between two texts: the Agreement, and the Bill that subsequently appeared before the British Parliament early in the summer of 1998. The drafters of the British bill had tried to re-instate in it the orthodox view of the conflict, by giving priority to good community relations as the condition of the peace and diminishing the status and processes concerned with the equality duty. The lure was, of course, that this erased the role of the state as a contributor to the armed conflict, and therefore as itself a transitional subject.

The recidivists did not prevail that summer. The Agreement's spirit was restored during a dense schedule of nearly forty meetings, between the drafters and the champions of the equality duty – Inez McCormack, Martin O'Brien and Christopher McCrudden, and in the Lords Peter Archer and Anthony Lester, barrister and Liberal peer.

'I don't think we could have had an agreement that didn't cover those areas', commented Paul Murphy, the British minister responsible for the legislative work during the summer. But, amazingly, he admitted, 'it was a tough job to get it on to the statute book, we had to do a lot of pushing. I was given a broad remit to ensure that happened'. It was as if it made no difference to the drafters that the Agreement had already been affirmed by referendums in two countries.

The Agreement's advocates found themselves in a protracted defensive struggle that summer, 'they're unpicking the Agreement', said a seasoned human rights organiser involved in the process: 'it is a constant process of attrition. You see a nasty mind at work putting this package together'. Amidst the torrent of detail, the consuming battle was to protect the primacy of equality in the Agreement from sly textual manoeuvres. The issue, according to McCrudden, was 'how to translate what appeared to be a breakthrough at the political level into legislative text'. This translation was to prove a difficult task. It was best expressed in that hot three-letter word: *due*. On 6 July the Secretary of State circulated among the campaigners and parties the draft legislation. This said that public authorities were required only to 'have regard' to the promotion of equality of opportunity. 'Due' had disappeared. But 'due' gave the duty its primacy. By the time the Bill was presented to Parliament a few days later the three-letter word had been restored to what was to become Section 75 of the Northern Ireland Act. *Even* market forces, which had by then acquired biblical status in British policy-making in the public sector, had to have *due* regard. There was also introduced 'a priority between the equality duty and the "good relations duty"'.[2] Priority was strengthened when the Bill went to the Lords: the good relations duty was made specifically subject to the equality duty. This was of the greatest political importance not only to the future but also to the narration of the conflict: it gave the burden of responsibility for the problem to the state, rather than the people.

There was an important process shift, too, in the journey from the Commons to the Lords: public authorities had not only to assess the impact of policies on the Nine Grounds, they had to prepare and publish their assessments and they had to consider alternatives; and the duty applied not just – as people usually assumed – to equality policies themselves but to the 'general run' of all decision-making. Consultation meant engaging those with an interest. The legislation intended the equality duty to apply across Northern Ireland Departments and to UK government Departments.

By the time the Bill moved to the Lords from the Commons there was still much to do to rehabilitate the spirit of the Agreement. But government ministers were not generally unsympathetic to the intense lobbying and textual activism of Lords Peter Archer and Anthony Lester.

Ultimately the legislation succeeded in going beyond the negative limits of typical Western equality laws, to 'weave the politics of equality into the fabric of decision-making across *all* spheres of government'. The approach was 'anticipatory' and 'participatory'.[3]

This amounted to an 'internationally unique' constitutional commitment.[4] The novelty was expressed in various flanks of the deal: the equality and participation matrix; the 'creative ambiguity' around national aspirations, sovereignty and jurisdiction written into the power-sharing architecture of the Assembly and the executive;[5] and the politics of recognition expressed in the identities and interests inscribed in the demands made of both state and citizens.

I have argued that, most importantly, it positioned the state not as a neutral arbitrator, an agent of change, but as a subject itself. The legislation gave to the state a specific duty to mediate the work of transformation and to transform itself. The Agreement's guardians lay not only in the Northern Ireland state, however, but in other states – in London and Dublin – and in the civil society that had an interest in it, that *needed* it and had so cleverly contributed to it. Therein lay an aspect of the constitutional originality – as the begetter of both a state in transition and identities in transition.

Professor Christine Bell argues that the deal breaks with British constitutional tradition. It sets out values to be promoted by the institutions: 'the Belfast Agreement and the Northern Ireland Act 1998 do not codify an existing consensus but aim to effect that consensus'.

DISSENT FROM THE 'CENTRE'

The Agreement had numerous enemies among those who felt betrayed by the historic compromise (though on the island of Ireland they were a small minority). It had sceptics and enemies, too, among Northern Ireland bureaucrats and securocrats, who felt criticised by it, burdened by it – or thwarted by it. After all, peace had not delivered the defeat of their enemies. And there were also embittered critics in the 'narrow ground of the purported political centre.

The unionist fellow traveller Paul Bew – later Lord Bew – scoffed that the Agreement was merely an 'ethnic bargain' that had been on the table since the 1970s.[6] He was wrong. It was precisely not the resuscitated cadaver of Sunningdale in 1973 or the Anglo-Irish Agreement of 1985. This was new. What was entirely new was the palpable presence of civil society in talks and in the Agreement's ideas. This was neither an elite stitch-up nor an ethnic carve-up. Bell, who has provided invaluable insights into late twentieth century peace agreements, argues that 'in a divided society civic society plays a crucial role in mediating the positions of political elites. It provides a space for creative thinking … it provides an agenda which goes beyond traditional divisions'. This thinking is vindicated in the Agreement. The equality duty, so appealing to both disadvantaged protestants and catholics – and to those suffering unfair disadvantage in general – addressed socio-economic issues at the heart of the conflict.

The focus on equality originated in feminist endeavours, and brought into view the thoroughly gendered division that is typically marginalised in peace treaties.[7] It refined a template through which diverse oppressed or disadvantaged groups could make their presence felt in the policymaking process. In other words, an experiment in democracy crafted outside the purported 'ethnic conflict' provided a decisive instrument for its resolution. But this contribution of the parallel peace process is unnoticed by Bew – perhaps a case of sexism unmasking sectarianism.

Among purportedly progressive academics there was a reluctance to acknowledge prejudice as structural and causal, and also therefore to support positive duties to redress it within a reformed political process. The influential – and purportedly progressive – political theorists Paul Bew, Henry Patterson, Paul Teague and Peter Gibbon exemplified this tradition. Bew and his colleagues denied that discrimination was causal; they denied that it had permeated the state; and they denied that redress was critical to the peace process. For them, the biggest problem of the critics of the state was that they exaggerated the 'the role of politics in defining labour market outcomes'. [8] So, by analogy, women's economic disadvantage in economies where their participation has been heavily regulated by the state appears as an effect of evolution rather than political struggle. For Bew et al egalitarianism could not 'operate as a mechanism to encourage communal integration'. For them integration – rather than equality – was the point of the peace process. [9] Ultimately, in their account of inequality, they relied on misty allusions to catholic under-development and the birth-rate shibboleth: catholics' relative poverty was caused by 'the laws of arithmetic and not discriminatory practices'. [10] This group was important because it lent its intellectual authority to the interpretation of sectarianism (and for that matter sexism) as neither structural nor systemic. That is, they apparently lent endorsement from the left to the conservative, sectarian and sexist resistance – at a point in

Northern Ireland's history when the peaceful reformability of this failed state was being tested.

According to one of their critics, Paul Stewart, Bew et al translated sectarianism as merely 'a motive of particular unionist regimes', rather than as being 'inscribed in the very practices of the state'. They positioned the state and the protestant working class as only opportunistically sectarian. They interpreted the social alliance between protestant capital and labour as 'wrought out of mutual dependence': it allowed protestant workers to profit from Britain's welfare state, while the Stormont state 'secured working class support in the form of sectarian advantage'. This approach depended on an outdated view that working-class economic militancy was capable of offering a progressive antidote to what was viewed as retro Irish nationalism.[11] Political struggles could be understood in purely economic terms.

This economism serviced another political priority – anti-republicanism. The sectarianism that Bew et al sought to minimise was iron in their own soul. It was revealed in their complaint that the fair employment project was *politically* suspect because it 'has been prone to sectarian capture'. This echoed the familiar slur that the equality agenda was a Provo front. They complained that republicans had made a 'take-over bid for the Irish left'. [12] Not only did they ignore the implications of the exclusion of catholics from the economic covenant they described; they also ignored the force of sectarianism as a 'structural component of the state, reflecting all the institutions of domination, including labour itself'.[13] (This sectarianism echoed the misogyny of the British left, which had also celebrated the economism of the men's labour movement as synonymous with socialism.) The economic disadvantage of catholics (like that of women) was an effect of their evolutionary failure, it seemed. Economism thus masked sectarianism and sexism – it was vested in a mournful longing, a parochial and sentimental attachment to a form of class politics that had, in fact, been ruined by both.

What could make purported progressives cross the line and align themselves to the class enemy? What would encourage their endorsement of such extreme advocates of the status quo? And to whom did they give responsibility for their society's difficulties? These questions had a particular pertinence after the 1994 ceasefires, when the vaunted 'social alliance' was ruptured by a new *progressive* unionist politics among former combatants, the foot soldiers who had been prepared to go to war for that 'social alliance'. They believed that that the protestant working class had benefited from the 'social alliance', but had also been betrayed by it. 'We had nothing but contempt for mainstream unionist politicians', said Gusty Spence, because of their indifference to the 'squalor and poverty that we were born into'.

The equality agenda constituted the basis for a new 'social alliance' – between catholics and protestants, women and men, human rights campaigners and a host of community networks. It was that critical mass, sealed by the commitment of the former combatants, that later guaranteed its presence in the Agreement.

In Northern Ireland it was not uncommon to represent 'the Troubles' as a miserable diversion from the 'real struggle'. But sectarianism went to the core of the place, and the challenge to it could sometimes make people lose their political minds. A similar thing often happens to progressives challenged by anti-racism or feminism; they find it difficult to look at the world in a new way, to empathise with the most marginal; they give themselves to the enemy rather than make themselves the subjects of challenge and change.

Bew's censure was indicative of another lament, a kind of mourning heard not among those from whom it might have been expected – those loyalists who stood with Ian Paisley Snr outside the process – but amidst the liberal intelligentsia who had played little part in its concepts, whose longing for 'normal politics' and alienation from the conflict now articulated itself as scepticism about the settlement. Their concerns may not be important in themselves, except insofar as they sapped enthusiasm in a place burdened with more than its share of depression and shame, but their critique invites a riposte from contemporary debates about identity, difference and democracy.

DIFFERENT NARCISSISMS
Robin Wilson and Rick Wilford have also been persistent critics of the Agreement, summarised by their quip that the settlement epitomises 'the narcissism of minor differences'.[14] These two cannot be claimed simply as rejectionists. Robin Wilson strongly affirms himself as left-wing, and he was for some years the director of the progressive think tank Democratic Dialogue. He also served on the Community Relations Council and promoted his approach to equality and reconciliation in European Union arenas. And the two men's research into the workings of the Assembly gave them unusual access to its life and times. Their critique therefore merits some response.

Wilson and Wilford argue that the specification of identities, interests and communal affiliations in the Assembly, the executive and its departments increased sectarianism; and that the requirement to register communal affiliation should be abolished. Their view is that in the

Agreement identities and interests are addressed not as individuals but as collectivities, whereas modern governance should address citizens as individuals. For Wilson and Wilford, attention to identity and interest has pre-empted the normalisation of Northern Ireland's politics: extremism has defeated the 'moderate middle'. The equality duty in Section 75 is a sop to the republicans – it is procedural and has made no tangible difference.

Instead of prioritising equality, the Agreement should have made reconciliation and integration its objective. They were in favour of the approach outlined in *A Shared Future*, a government commissioned report that promoted reconciliation as Northern Ireland's priority, as an alternative to socio-economic equality.[15]

Wilford and Wilson argue that the Agreement is 'a Faustian pact with sectarianism and even paramilitarism'.[16] They note that sectarianism increased – the number of peace lines/conflict zones increased – following the ceasefires and the Agreement. However this is not surprising. The experience of post-conflict regions more widely is that violence rarely abates; militarism and tyranny bequeath violence to post-conflict societies. As it turned out, by the twenty-first century violence had declined in Northern Ireland, though – typically – sectarianism found expression in other forms. It is also common in post-conflict societies for violence against women and street violence to be endemic; violence by young men – as a strategy of masculine dominion over women, other men and social space – tends to flourish. But Wilford and Wilson engage in none of the international comparisons that might have helped them analyse these phenomena. [17]

In their wide-ranging analysis of the workings of the executive and the Assembly they spotlight the disintegration of cordial relations between the Assembly's Unionist First Minister David Trimble and his SDLP Deputy First Minister, his partner in leadership of the Assembly and the society:[18] the relationship was polarised, personal and unsustainable. But this was conjunctural rather than systemic – less a symptom of an unreasonable obligation to function as equal partners than of Trimble's irascible, intemperate manners. Trimble was notorious as a leader who had somehow never acquired the social skills of leadership,[19] a man who operated not as society's top man but as his party's top man, a figurehead unable to represent the society – an insecure *Unionist* First Minister, glancing over his shoulder at unionist enemies inside and outside his party. This conjunctural crisis was evident not only in tantrums in the OFMDFM but in the disintegration of Trimble's party, and its ultimate defeat by Ian Paisley's DUP in 2007.

Guided by the commentariat, the world expected spontaneous combustion when the DUP's veteran leader Ian Paisley was anointed First Minister, and the man who had spent a lifetime saying No and Never agreed to share power and space with Gerry Adams and Sinn Fein, the people he'd vowed to die rather than do deals with. Wilford and Wilson predicted that republicanism was 'too totalitarian' to render Sinn Fein an acceptable power-sharing partner for most protestants for the foreseeable future. They were wrong. A year later Paisley, Adams and McGuinness were performing genial partnership. The authors had underestimated republicanism, but, less credibly, they had misread Paisley – this spicy, populist troublemaker was Northern Ireland's most successful politician in 40 years. If that didn't make him nice or honourable, it was testament to his zest and his intuitive reading of the zeitgeist. By standing outside the peace process – every peace process – by picketing the talks he had merely done what unionist fundamentalism had always done, give nothing. All he had to do was wait. Inevitably, the centre couldn't hold. The work of radical constitutionalism and peacemaking had been done by others, and it had been done well enough to engage all the parties, including Paisley's. Without the interventions of British secret services that toppled the sovereign Assembly in 2001, the partnership would have happened earlier. Wilford and Wilson should have known this. Despite their somewhat supercilious commentary on the Assembly, they did acknowledge that the devolved administration – populated by historic adversaries – was working rather well, and actually 'making some notable policy differences'. Its committees, where enemies gathered in crowded rooms, were productive and co-operative; their chairpersons were professional and consensual and avoided sectarianism.[20] DUP and Sinn Fein Members were already doing business in the Assembly years before the election that made them the most powerful parties. Above all, they had for a decade been local government's most adroit tenants. Whilst the purported centre was exposed as a shadow, these parties were embedded.

Wilford and Wilson resent the requirement that Members of the Assembly register their communal affiliation: it should be removed.[21] In their view the Agreement's 'terrible beauty' was that it cemented 'unreconstructed communalist aspiration'. Perhaps – but for the moment it was a peaceful and appropriate antagonism. The most tormenting grit for Wilford and Wilson seems to lie in the requirement to *show oneself*. From within the longest armed civil conflict in Europe since World War II this seems like political *hauteur*, an attempt to stand above the sordid strife, as if they were present and yet agnostic. They thus exemplify Susan Bordo's ravishing critique of 'post-modernism and gender-scepticism':[22] they are animated by the fantasy of attaining 'an epistemological perspective free of the locatedness and limitations of embodied existence.' (Women might have wished that the electoral and constitutional ambitions expressed in the Agreement had added gender to the registration of communal affiliation.) The faultlines of gender offer insight into the impossibility of being simultaneously nowhere and everywhere in a conflict: to paraphrase Bordo, in a society that is divided (constructed by both sexism and sectarianism), 'one cannot simply be human'. The appeal to deny difference tends to assert itself when power is challenged; it emerged in gender politics, for example, when the reigning propertied, white, male, western hegemony, 'located at the very centre of power', began to be dismantled. The lament 'why can't we just be people' is aired 'when the marginal assert themselves'. And so it was in Northern Ireland when the majority could no longer rule as both a protestant and unionist yet un-identified majority. That un-identified presence resists self-awareness, it has no imperative to scrutinise its bias or privilege, whereas the marginalised have no escape from their location and their history. Though often experienced as threatening or overwhelming, the marginalised are not located at the centre of power. To renounce their identification would be to renounce the source of their own 'transformative facilities'.

In any case Wilford and Wilson ignore a prime case of political wit in the Assembly, when the Women's Coalition – the only genuinely cross-community party – resolved to re-designate its elected Members for the sake of the Assembly's survival. In October 2001 unionism split over its response to the IRA's decision to decommission weapons, and thus to the resumption of the stalled Assembly. Although the First Minister had secured 70 per cent of Members' support, he had not secured a majority among unionists – by one vote. This produced a crisis. The Women's Coalition had designated its Members as Inclusive Other, and its two elected Members were the unionist, feminist journalist Jane Morrice and the nationalist, feminist academic Monica McWilliams. Amidst bilious derision, they now proposed to the Assembly a motion allowing re-designation – Morrice as Unionist, McWilliams as Nationalist –which would add the extra vote needed to secure Trimble's election. The DUP accused them of 'political cross-dressing'. But when Morrice proposed the manoeuvre she said: 'We have not been persuaded to change our identity ... we are a coalition of unionists, nationalists and "others". We draw on membership and our votes from all three designations'. She reminded the Assembly that the

Women's Coalition had never attempted to persuade one another of each other's cultures or national affiliations – they embraced rather than denied their diversity. It became an unhappy footnote that the Women's Coalition, having initiated the re-designation to save the Assembly and the Agreement, was then written out of history; while the Alliance Party, purportedly cross-community and centrist, after it reluctantly came on board and re-designated three of its members as Unionist, won acclaim – or derision – in equal amounts, as Trimble's saviour.

Citing Bobbio's affirmation of the 'individualistic concept of society', Wilford and Wilson insist, '"Normal" liberal democracies do not routinely dissolve into open antagonism between stereotyped identities. Rather citizens are created as individuals'.[23] But this is a concept derived from classical political science, the figure of the unencumbered individual. Wilford and Wilson ignore the global debates among feminists and others that have not only discredited this conception but have queried some of the more deconstructionist ideologies of identity,[24] which resist the recognition that 'one is always somewhere'.[25] As Bordo reminds us, 'there is no view from nowhere'. To foreswear talk of collective realities structured in sexism or sectarianism is to forfeit an opportunity to organise, to voice the experience of marginalisation, to have it heard, to call power to account, to see our standpoints as potentially transformative; it is, as Bordo suggests, to give up the messy, practical struggle to 'create institutions and communities that will not permit *some* groups of people to make determinations about reality for *all*'.

Wilford and Wilson's critique of collectivities relies on what they regard as regressive ethno-national conflicts. But their torrid rhetoric is wordless about the inequalities endured by specific groups within and beyond ethno-sectarianism, including, most remarkably, women – though gender equality was the inspiration of the equality duties. Indeed they bury the feminist imagination that prefigured the participation obligation that contributes to the Agreement's constitutional novelty. They are mute about the potential of a 'transitional constitution'.[26] And they prize the 'normality' of liberal democracies – as if the Agreement were not a peace treaty composed in the context of many other, more or less ingenious and more or less successful, international treaties. They promote an alternative to the Agreement's proposed duties in the form of a 'moderate-middle coalition' that would be voluntarily 'ethnically-egalitarian', based on reconciliation and integration: 'Integration offers a more viable model of power-sharing based on a moderate-middle coalition'.[27] However, this proposal seems more

regressive than the Agreement – an opaque, inert prospectus that imag-
ines no transformation of power relations. Their notion of
reconciliation contains no requirement for redress, no change in the
balance of power (or at least in the public's *management* of power), no
truth-telling, no resolution; just niceness. (John Morison cautions that
however representative in 'the classic sense' the new regime may be,
Westminsterism had failed to release Northern Ireland from democratic tyranny; he also argues that the 'normal' classic sense 'may well be
an outmoded concept'. However, he sees the value-driven constitution
implied in the Agreement as offering the 'raw material' for enforcing
basic democratic values.[28])

Wilford and Wilson seem to locate power among the paramilitaries,
not the state, though neither the republicans nor the loyalists were
located at the centre of power. They became, however, a proxy for
extreme Big Power, against which the moderate-middle could position
itself as the centre. 'There is no such thing as the centre', comments
Monica McWilliams. As the Women's Coalition had reminded the
Assembly during the re-designation debate in 2001, 'We are not a party
of the centre'.

It was not the 'moderate middle' that mobilised civil society around
the equality duties that invited citizens to become active subjects who
'collaborate in the exercise of government, shape it and inform it.' And,
as we have seen, during the talks the moderate-middle was disengaged
from civil society's gift to the peace process.

Many of the otherwise ingenious peace treaties written towards the
end of the twentieth century continued to constitute their populations
as 'passive subjects' rather than 'active power-holders'.[29] The Northern
Ireland deal did not.

EQUALITY VERSUS INTEGRATION

The Wilford Wilson critique pits integration against equality. Wilson
represents the equality movement as republicanism *manqué*. He
follows the NIO line, insisting that the government should place
'reconciliation above rights'. He argues that 'community relations
should not be subordinated to the equality agenda', but nowhere does
he explain why. It should be noted that between 1995 and 2006 €1488
million were distributed in Northern Ireland for regeneration,
renewal and reconciliation, through the European Community's Peace
I and Peace II initiatives, but these, given Wilford and Wilson's lament
about embedded segregation and worsening sectarianism, have apparently had no effect. Wilson offers a model of 'community relations'
with the spiffy aura of a pleasurable cafe society and the civic city:

cosmopolitanism and the 'politics of civic principles'. The proposal
echoes the 'civic city' debate promoted by Amitai Etzioni and David
Putnam, and adopted by the centurions of New Labour, only to fade
along with the short-lived Third Way. The notion of cosmopolitanism
is alluring, but it, too, has been subject to unsparing analysis, for
example by the eminent English student of popular cultures, Beverley
Skeggs, who has explored its class, space and global connotations, and
not least its exclusivities: 'to be cosmopolitan one has to have access to
forms of knowledge and generate authority from this knowing. It
relies on access to cultural capital'.

Most important, however, the Wilford-Wilson project offers no
redress: by assigning the equality agenda to republicanism they merely
let their own sectarian slip show; indeed they re-sectarianise the issue,
oblivious to the transformative potential of all the Nine Grounds.
Their argument involves a stealthy redistribution of blame: the recon-
ciliation/integration and reconciliation not rights discourse, for all its
saintly worthiness, requires of the state no redress. In contrast, the
equality discourse in the Agreement locates blame with the state and
not the people; and it places responsibility on both the state and the
people for the reformation of relationships; in that sense it vindicates
the reading of rights not just as the re-distribution of resources but also
as relationships.[30]

GENDER AND IDENTITY: BEING AND BECOMING

The history that Wilson ignores – as does Paul Bew's theory of the
social alliance – is the journey that began with the search by Inez
McCormack and Patricia McKeown in the early 1980s – even before
the MacBride Principles began to define the equality project – for some
way to deliver change in which poor women and part-time working
women, catholic and protestant, could participate, for an approach that
reached the parts that hegemonic politics and the equality laws could
not reach. What they had realised was that an equality strategy didn't
work if it expected riches to cascade from the privileged to the poor, or
if it expected women to profit from proximity to men's relative privilege, or if women were expected to wait until somebody or other was
elected to power, or if the recourse to law was constrained by the
narrow templates of equal opportunity and anti-discrimination law.
Everything they had learned from the new social movements had
confirmed what did *not* work for those who had been humiliated and
harmed the most; they knew what did not disturb the institutional
sexism that also bulwarked sectarianism; and they had discovered that
nothing changed power relations without their intervention.

One of the great ideological innovations of the women's movement that emerged at the end of the 1960s was that – in addition to its great seismic challenge to the polarisation of public and private in the concept of 'the personal is political' – it re-interpreted gender as a social system, not determined by biology: gender 'exists precisely to the extent that biology does not determine the social'.[31] But Britain's equality laws had been scripted just as the women's liberation movement was swirling on to the scene. The equality legislation implemented in the 1970s did not, therefore, assimilate the new knowledge. It modernised an older aspiration – equality as women's evolutionary trek from the private into the public realm, equality as a comparison between equivalents in the workplace, equality as aspiration towards the pinnacle of human excellence, masculinity. But the women's movements of the world were imagining the metamorphosis of gender relations, in which both men and women were transformed. Certainly, women had transformed their access to the public realm and to the professions. They had invited men and the institutions to co-operate in revolutionising the domestic and public divisions of labour. But, though they had not been defeated, they had been disappointed.

By the end of the century this long march had been detoured: a new historic settlement had indeed settled, but nowhere had masculinity as a *social* subjectivity – and as institutions – been radically reformed. The new global settlement was not the old patriarchy, but we now entered what I call a new historic settlement, the new era of neo-patriarchy. Somewhat surprisingly, however, the Agreement's novel approach to equality and disadvantage could conceivably enable this new settlement to be challenged.

The ingenuity of the Agreement's negotiators during those last few sleepless days before the Easter deadline was that they defined an equality agenda that addressed the cause of the conflict, but was not exhausted by the conflict. This stemmed from their critique of sexism and sectarianism as a synergy that had produced the old politics of the place. The equality movements' congregation of interests in sexism, sectarianism and other causes of disadvantage and oppression therefore released the equality agenda from the constraints of the conflict. By naming categories of disadvantage with an interest in the impact of policy-making, the Agreement was more disruptive and innovative that might at first appear. In specifying the Nine Grounds it named denigrated and disadvantaged groups not merely as objects but as agents of social change; the advocates of the equality duties insisted – despite British efforts to reduce the categories to individual interests – on the Nine Grounds as group identities and interests. This was vital – it transformed them from clients or complaints to complex communities of interest, and it thereby shifted the burden from the victim to the system. The Agreement offered them a constitutional entitlement to emerge from marginality into the policy-making process; by pledging access to assessment and appraisal, it ventured beyond opportunity to outcome. Therein lay another of the radical – albeit arduous – potentials of the process. How come? As Anne Phillips puts it in her polemical contribution to international feminist debates on equality – with the elegance of simplicity – when outcomes across society are manifestly different and unequal then individuals' characteristics, choices, luck or circumstances become less relevant, and 'the better explanation is that opportunities were themselves unequal'. When equality of opportunity is the prime objective, 'equality of outcome is the best test for identifying whether the objective is achieved'. A preoccupation with the idiosyncrasies of individuals' characteristics may feature compellingly in individual complaints, but 'group disparities are best regarded as *prima facie* evidence that opportunities are not equal'. [32]

In a society transfixed by embalmed identities, the diversity of the Nine Grounds creatively unsettled the identity issue that the Agreement appeared to address. How did it do this? First, by describing not the *properties* of those identities, but their *problem*: structural disadvantage. It, therefore, did not so much define an identity as offer a response to collective experiences of disadvantage. Identities were conceived, therefore, not as fixed, but in flux. Nor did the Nine Grounds presume single identities; on the contrary they could be imagined as multiple and mobile, moving across time, place and relationship. No one would only be a protestant, a nationalist, masculine, heterosexual, single, young or disabled. Identities were to be emptied of their privileged status: the Nine Grounds were attached only to positive commitment to doing something about disadvantage and social need. This then implied their transitional status: by the very release from their relations of subordination.

The success of the equality agenda in the talks came from its capacity to engage protestants whose multiple identities – most importantly their experience of *class* and *gender* – had failed to find political expression. Protestant dominion may have constituted protestants in general as 'the power', driven to defend the old order, but there were pauperised protestants, gay protestants, protestant women exhausted by the care of their men, children and relatives, and by their poverty; there were protestant women beaten by men, and protestant men ashamed of the excesses of protestant and patriarchal power: these were all people who were able to find their interests articulated by the equality agenda.

By specifying the interests of women *generally*, the Agreement not only offered women the possibility of constitutional space, it also created the conditions in which gender as a social relationship predicated on the subordination of women could be addressed at all levels. Crucially, the approach to women in the context of the Nine Grounds also positioned men as participants in a gendered culture. Women insisted on their visibility in the Agreement, and if the dominant definitions of the conflict had concealed women in general, it had also concealed gender in general – and therefore masculinity too. This concealment obscured the ways in which 'gender regimes' penetrated sectarianism and social class. Eilish Rooney's invaluable insight is that this approach to gender relations challenged the idealised appearance of women as *peace people* during the conflict. In the Agreement women appear not as saints encouraging everyone to be nice to each other – to *bury their differences* – but as demanding contenders. Their demand of the settlement was that the transition from war to peace be transitional for women too, as a group disadvantaged by everything – social class, sectarianism, sexism, and war. [33]

The negotiators had crafted a template that established women as the lightning rod: their experience *'generally'* achieved a special place in the text, but the naming was also indicative of the Agreement's radical approach to the limits of a politics of identity. Furthermore, this was exemplified in the categories' non-equivalence: caring for dependents is a responsibility, blindness is a circumstance or capacity; travellers are – like settled people – an ethnicity; political affiliation is a choice; sexual orientation is to some a choice, to others a destiny. But naming, in effect, positioned everyone: everyone was young or old; everyone got through everyday life by taking care of themselves or being taken care of (and the Agreement named that work not as neutral, but as a source of disadvantage); everyone was structured in relation to gender, sexual orientation, religious or ethnic heritage. But the clear intention in the naming of the Nine Grounds was to imply that people's subjectivities were not in their DNA: they only existed across time and in the system of relationships that produced them. Everyone however, was something, some time – which was no doubt irritating to those who disowned themselves amidst difference, and for whom a politics of difference was merely divisive. [34] Usually their complaint focused on the electoral arrangements and the principle of proportionality that regulated the formation of the executive, the appointment of ministers and the distribution of departmental powers among the parties. But even here, the process of naming was not exclusive to the dominant political divisions. And in any case, the commitment to consensus in the Assembly, though distasteful to those who preferred 'normal' party polarisations, was an attempt to address the history of majoritarianism that had produced Northern Ireland as a failed polity.

The sponsors of the equality duties intended to make space in policy-making for interests and identities that might vary from moments in a life-cycle – identities expressed as choice, identities derived from birth, identities invented by their enemies – all of them structured not by individual idiosyncrasy but by social systems. The purpose was to re-design the political process so that policy-making did not confer privilege, respect and resources *without thinking*. The duty conferred a legal obligation to consider, to consult, to decide. This aspect of the Agreement is routinely edited out of mainstream histories of the peace process, but it was this that contributed to the Agreement's novelty and attracted an enthusiastic consensus (rather than reluctant acceptance of compromise) around those radioactive words, *rights* and *equality*.

The Agreement deftly composed categories that were united not by their status, or by their equivalence, but by their relation to power, denigration or exploitation. The differences between the Agreement's Nine Grounds provided a clue to the creativity of their sponsors – they had been interested in more than the distribution of resources and rights between the iconic identities of the conflict on the one hand, and on the other the contemporary fixtures in the discourses of difference – race, class, gender. In the design of the executive and ministries, and the constitutional duties, they were interested in the reform of relationships, in the drama of power and powerlessness, in transitional processes and life-cycles, and ultimately, therefore, in *becoming rather than being*.

DISAPPEARING ACTS

When the new administration took over in Stormont, the Office of the First Minister and Deputy First Minister had a large reservoir of women's organisations with whom to work out a gender strategy. How did it engage those with an interest, enable them to map their priorities? What thinking did it bring to a policy-making project that would realise a new deal between men and women?

It didn't. It did not convene those with a stake in it to brainstorm together, to map the priorities and commission research based on those priorities. What it did do was enlist a couple of experts to write a report, and then push it out for consultation. The outcome, *Gender*

Matters, published in 2005, pre-figured the Westminster government's gender strategy in its 2006 Women and Work Commission report, *Shaping a Fairer Future.* Both represented a crisis for women's enlistment of the state as an ally for the advancement of pro-woman policy-making.

Taken together, these documents were a watershed. Their underlying theme was a repudiation of mainstream feminist theories of gender as a social system. In these documents gender doesn't matter, it isn't a system. First in Northern Ireland and then in Westminster a historic break was being attempted from the thinking that had prevailed, more or less, since the equality legislation of the 1970s – that women suffered from socio-economic sexism. Now that was effectively denied.

According to *Gender Matters,* women's relative poverty was an effect of feminine choices – from jobs to parenthood. This analysis attracted uncharacteristic protest from the Equality Commission in Belfast, the new body set up to guide and monitor the equality duties. So, it asked with an unprecedented sarcasm, women were choosing 'to have no value attached to their attributes and take on a large proportion of domestic and caring work for no pay or recognition'. The Commission also criticised the report for ignoring the interaction between gender and other regimes of discrimination – ethnicity and disability, for example – and for ignoring the impact on women of the armed conflict. [35]

What was significant about the way the term gender was used in Northern Ireland (and later Westminster) was that it emptied 'gender' of the problem of power. Men suffered, too, it said. Boys did badly at school; men didn't heed testicular cancer. Thus gender differences were here, there and everywhere. The indicators of disadvantage were re-interpreted merely as difference, bad luck and bad choices. Choice was the problem, not power. And thus was born a new political problematic: the choice paradigm replaced the power paradigm.

Gender Matters is 'not a gendered analysis', commented the Equality Commission. This could not have been more embarrassing – assuming the government had been available for embarrassment – because it was the Equality Commission, not the government, that was the invigilator of the constitutional duty. Furthermore, the Equality Commission had itself been criticised for being weak, and for failing to come out fighting for the new constitutional duty. This made this criticism all the more persuasive. The Commission also savaged the budget and priorities for 2004-2008, which were conceived after the dissolution of the Assembly, under direct rule. They criticised it as a 'read-across budget' – a UK format transposed to Northern Ireland without regard to its post-conflict circumstances, and certainly without *due* regard to the constitutional equality duties. The state's approach to gender therefore represented a failure to understand the language and intention of the Agreement, and its continuing subjection to the Westminster agenda

WHAT WORKS – EQUALITY SPONSORS INTEGRATION

Equality at work was another problematic area. The government's practices after the Agreement ignored the evidence of what worked. The world of waged work was the *only* realm that had – in many workplaces – already been radically reformed and de-sectarianised, the only place where catholics and protestants would encounter each other normally and meet each other as equals. It was the only realm where cultural harassment and the practices and emblems and bric a brac that enunciated protestant privilege had been specifically addressed – and erased.

The flags and bunting had been removed from the workplaces and the profiles of the workforce changed, *only* through confident enforcement of the Fair Employment Act, and of affirmative agreements in big companies that had historically been stockades of protestant proletarian consciousness. [36] An attack on sectarian hiring practices and workplace culture had moved them toward appropriate proportional representation in hitherto polarised places. Though this had been ignored by government, companies that had undertaken affirmative action agreements in the 1990s to reform their unrepresentative workforce were demonstrating – contrary to Wilford and Wilson – that integration and representivity were achieved simultaneously. In other words, equality sponsored integration. [37] The Fair Employment Tribunal had developed a 'rigorous enforcement regime'. [38] The implications for strong – rather than soft – enforcement of equality were therefore inescapable. Strong legislation, strong enforcement. That had worked.

So, too, had the MacBride Principles. Among private companies, the most consistently representative employers were the American subscribers to the MacBride Principles. Catholics comprised 43 per cent of their workforces, according to the Investor Responsibility Research Centre, [39] while the rest of private companies only managed a 36 per cent catholic workforce, drawn from a population in which 44 per cent were catholics.

Among British employers, however, it was a dismal story. The biggest British private sector employer in Northern Ireland was the supermarket chain Tesco. Its workforce was only 32 per cent catholic. In the new millennium Short brothers, the aircraft factory that had been the subject of Irish American concern in the 1980s, still only employed 14.7 per cent catholics. The aircraft industries more widely, despite growing exponentially, continued to employ disproportionate numbers of protestants – fewer than a third of employees were catholic. In energy and transport, similarly, the number of catholic employees never rose above a third. [40] The defence and security sector also remained a relative desert for catholics – in 2005 the prison service, the new Northern Ireland Policing Board, and the Secretary of State for Defence all employed fewer than 10 per cent. [41] Research by CAJ revealed that, although employment in the public sector and the civil service tended to reflect the population, representivity declined higher up the hierarchy.

And what about unemployment – the well of disproportionate disadvantage that had attracted a special place in the Agreement? In the new millennium Northern Ireland boasted a boom – unemployment figures were the lowest ever (4 per cent, lower than the UK's 5 per cent). But delving underneath these figures, CAJ found – an invisible multitude, the missing economically 'inactive', who were not on the unemployment register. The non-working in 2005 were *double* the official unemployment statistic, and a majority were catholic. Thirty-three per cent of catholics were without waged work, compared to 24 per cent of protestants. It was worst of all for catholic women, of whom 42 per cent were without paid employment. Workless households were being 'obscured by re-definition'. [42]

FAILURES OF POLITICAL CULTURE

Despite the rhetoric of post-conflict boom this multitude needed the new legislation. The drafters of the Northern Ireland Act had opted for a speedy timetable for implementation of the equality and social need duties. Anything less, they believed, would induce sloth and cynicism and a politically disastrous sense that nothing ever changed. This raised a critical issue: did the society, its civil servants and its activists have the capacity? The pressure on everyone was immense. Nothing less was being asked than re-designing the way that policy was made. [43] The civil servants frequently responded to this by franchising the work out to consultants. That cost the public purse a lot of money, and it also forfeited the opportunity to take staff on a learning curve; and it utterly misunderstood the point of the statutory duty – that it should enter the bloodstream, that it should circulate in the bureaucracy's collective consciousness.

The new Northern Ireland Equality Commission found itself in a blizzard of papers and processes, and during the first few years of the new order it was itself 'in gestation'. The speed of the cycle to produce equality schemes also put the social movements in civil society under great stress. It was the shoestring sector, but it, too, had to deliver, both for the people and for the reputation of the process. Everyone was overwhelmed. There was a pall of disappointment.[44] But the first and obvious failure was that of the party political culture: it was disengaged from the process, it did little or nothing to sow its seeds, as if the participation and assessment process had nothing to do with them. The political parties had not invented the equality duty – its advocates lay rather in civil society. But often these people were in a state of exhaustion. They had given the peace process everything, they were worn out.

There were civil service and managerial enthusiasts. One was Evan Bates, head of personnel at the Royal Group of hospitals in West Belfast, in the middle of the inner-city war zone. He felt that the equality mechanism was bureaucratic and tedious, but that 'if people were minded to do something it gave them a focus'. At the Royal Group, Unison was vigorous and ubiquitous. The union and personnel managers had a long history together and thus they were unusual in making the equality duty part of their institutional life. Section 75, the part of the Agreement that dealt with equality measures, was 'not effective in forcing people who were reluctant,' commented Bates. 'There was in the civil service an antipathy to consultation', and thus the law 'was something to be worked around'.

Most organisations were simply not tooled up to engage seriously in the Section 75 processes unless they were the dozen fortunate beneficiaries of extra resources to fund specialists. This in turn demoralised some of the committed civil servants who wanted the process to work but who 'received paltry, if any response'.[45] However, the interpretation of some community organisations was also mediated by anti-Agreement politicians.

Conversations with activists in a creative loyalist community centre outside Belfast revealed an astonishing ignorance. They'd read the Agreement, that was evident from the copies of it in their offices, in their bags: pages creased, text highlighted, corners curled – it had been read, all right. They tended to disagree with it – the arrangements with the Republic offended them. But somehow their sense of abandonment by the political system – the sense that their community had taken up arms to defend the state, but that their interests were not defended by that state – was untouched by the equality and human rights section. Their political representatives were UUP, and therefore uninterested, and their own eyes had glazed over the text, they'd not noticed it. The suggestion that it might be useful to them attracted a stoical incomprehension.

Their reaction confirmed the larger failure of party politics to field the Agreement as a manifesto for a new society. There was 'little public awareness about benefits that could accrue to society from greater equality', commented Eithne McLaughlin.

EQUALITY DUTY DOESN'T APPLY TO BRITAIN

The law was not optional, but there was widespread non-compliance. And if the devolved government had not yet got to grips with its implications, the suspension of Stormont and the return of direct rule seemed to seal its fate. Suspension of the assembly in 2002 changed the way policy was being made. The first brief encounter with self-government could be likened to a passionate love affair that had metamorphosed into a fling. It wasn't real life. Reality was London, and London had never liked Section 75. Evan Bates reckoned that the main flaw was that big decisions – the work of the annual programme for government – didn't go through the equality assessment process. Most of the things that affected people in Northern Ireland, especially after suspension, went through no screening. Chris McCrudden's judgement in his evaluation of the implementation of Section 75 was that the response of the state had been 'very disappointing' during both devolution and direct rule. This had not been universal, however: some of the ministers in the devolved government, particularly health minister Bairbre de Brun, had been 'very effective indeed in ensuring that civil servants get the message'. But whatever the disposition of ministers, implementation depended upon senior civil servants, and civil service higher grades 'had long seemed to see Section 75 as either an irritant or fundamentally misguided'.[46] Among some there was 'an aversion' to it. Nevertheless, argued McCrudden, as time went on committees in the new administration had been beginning to ventilate the equality duty; they were beginning, 'slowly, and not very surely, to use their powers to probe departments'. Then Northern Ireland's government was taken away. Suddenly new boys – mainly – descended from Westminster, and the committed civil servants were made to feel that their implementation of Section 75 was 'at best quixotic or at worst dangerous to their careers'. [47]

British antipathy was revealed in the difference between the first and second programmes for government and budget of the new millennium. The devolved government's 2001-2004 Programme for Government declared its commitment to the Agreement's principles of 'tackling community differentials, particularly in unemployment'. Furthermore 'ensuring equality and tackling social disadvantage has also underpinned and informed the Programme for Government and shaped departments' priorities'. This was exactly as the constitution required. But in the 2004-2008 programme – during direct rule – introduced by the Secretary of State in 2004, equality was erased. Targeting poverty and greatest objective need was out; and testing the impact of the programme through the duties specified in Section 75 was out, deemed 'inappropriate and impossible'.

And yet in an interview with me, the Secretary of State did acknowledge that Section 75 applied at the budget level of policy-making: 'I certainly thought that it did'. But the NIO thought otherwise, and thereafter designated 'high level' policy-making beyond the reach of the equality duty. The impact of this regression was devastating, not least on the massive £16 billion new investment programme, the biggest in the society's recent history, a once-in-a-generation enterprise. This was subject to no equality impact assessment and no social need assessment.

The Department of Employment, Trade and Industry and Invest Northern Ireland (the agency responsible for attracting and allocating investment) were bound by Section 75, of course. But they decided that it didn't apply to themselves, and they didn't apply it to big distributors either. In Belfast, only 8 per cent of total inward investment assistance was allocated to the deprived – and mainly catholic – West and North of the City. Whilst £208 million was allocated to the middle-class and protestant South, only £56 million went to North Belfast – working-class, mainly catholic and most battered by the armed conflict. Beyond Belfast, the area to the West of the River Bann – declining and predominantly catholic – which had suffered throughout the life of the northern enclave, attracted only 30 per cent of assistance. Instead of using the Agreement as intended, and as its mandate, the government consolidated the old geographies of catholic deprivation and protestant privilege. According to CAJ: 'Invest NI is contributing to increasing inequality, by replicating the pattern of general spending which sees those areas in most need receiving least'.[48]

It was not just the view of the 'usual suspects' that the equality, objective need and participation duties were wrongly marginalized. The Equality Commission, which might be expected to have understood the law it was tasked to enforce, challenged Invest NI, only to be told that 'high level' government policy-making did not 'lend itself' to equality impact assessment.

However, despite the floating 'high levels' exemption, the government was not exempt. A House of Lords ruling was unequivocal: the

Agreement, and the legislation to implement it, amounted to 'in effect a constitution'. It was expected, therefore, that 'the values which the constitutional provisions are intended to embody' had to be interpreted and implemented 'generously', in order to 'create the most favourable environment for cross-community government'.[49] There could be no doubt: big decisions and direct rule were not, and were never expected to be, exempt. But Britain behaved as if they were.

A test of the new arrangements came in 2004, when direct rule minister John Spellar decided to extend to Northern Ireland the Anti-Social Behaviour Orders that were beloved by the Prime Minister and only reluctantly implemented by most local authorities. Stiff opposition to Spellar was organised by a galaxy of children's organisations and human rights advocates. They argued that the policy should be assessed for its impact on grounds of age, gender and political and religious affiliation, and that those with an interest – young people, or their advocates – should have been consulted. The experience in England showed that ASBOs mainly targeted young men, many of whom were incarcerated for failing to meet their ASBO restrictions. The criminalisation of more and more young men carried multiple risks in Northern Ireland. The High Court in Belfast chided the government: the constitutional duty, it found, 'is clearly intended to be a wide and dynamic one.'[50]

HOUSING: SECTARIANISM VERSUS EQUALITY

Another area where inequality remained entrenched was housing and regeneration. Housing in Northern Ireland had for a long time been removed from local authority control and vested in a central agency, the Housing Executive. This was because its allocation had been exposed as blatantly sectarian.[51] The Housing Executive prided itself on its non-sectarian approach, but by the time of the Agreement, Northern Ireland was a more segregated society than at the beginning of the Executive's existence. The Housing Executive camouflaged its management of spatial sectarianism by the notion of choice – catholics would not want to live in protestant neighbourhoods and protestants would not want to give up space to catholics. Simple. Cultural. Consumption. Choice.

But how had the Housing Executive managed the key issues of supply and demand and distribution? The answers were shielded from public scrutiny; the statistics were secret, and only with great persistence were they prized from the organisation. It was not until 2004 that the Housing Executive was forced to break its silence in response to a Parliamentary question by SDLP MP Eddie McGrady: how many catholics and protestants had applied for homes; how many catholics and protestants had been allocated homes. His question went to the heart of the historic conflict and the reformability of the state. The answer was a shock.

Applicants: 60 per cent catholic, 40 per cent protestant. Allocations: 40 per cent catholic, 60 per cent protestant. Allocations were being made in inverse proportion to housing need.

What was the explanation? The Housing Executive felt that to infer discrimination against any group would be 'very misleading'. 'It comes to choice as to where people live'. Allocations depended on availability. Availability, in turn, depended on the area. And availability was converted into choice. In Belfast, homes were available in protestant neighbourhoods that protestants were leaving, but these were not neighbourhoods that were available, that catholics would 'choose' to live in. They would not feel safe. But construction of new neighbourhoods had been restricted by a government limit on new homes – only 1500 per year. And virtually all public housing was segregated: 'There has been debate on how to de-sectarianise housing', said the HE, 'but you can't socially engineer it'.

During direct rule and its aftermath, reconciliation – and its prospectus, *A Shared Future* – was promoted at the expense of socio-economic equality. This was particularly evident in regeneration strategies. These created the opportunity to address the relics of old industrial neighbourhoods, and homesteads that wore the scars of the conflict. These were the distinctive locales where socio-economic inequality and sectarianism found the most dramatic socio-spatial manifestation. Regeneration could have provided the opportunity for redress. But regeneration became the site of a new struggle over the meaning of the Agreement. And this time it was class cleansing that appeared in the guise of sectarian neutrality. The planning process was enlisted to exempt politicians from implementing the equality duty in the remaking of the city. In the name of creating 'neutral' neighbourhoods on prime sites, and working-class people were to be swilled out.

North Belfast was one of the poorest and most battle-scarred quarters of the entire conflict. Everybody knew the Seven Towers – they dominated the horizon beyond Belfast city centre to the north of the city. These tower blocks were thrown up in New Lodge during the 1960s, and were regarded as fortresses of nationalism. They had been given handsome new foyers with concierges. But still they sent people crazy. Pigeons nested in the cladding, droppings carpeted landings, and raw sewage spit into baths and sinks. Asked how she felt living in the blocks, a young woman look astonished at the question. 'Are you serious', she replied, before her hand covered her face and she burst into tears. Her children were among the 63 still living in the blocks – though the Housing Executive agreed there shouldn't be any. These residents wanted out, but they didn't want to leave the community. The Housing Executive wanted to move them out – and away.

The 2000-2007 Housing Executive strategy, *Tackling Housing Need*, set aside a £15 million special fund to acquire land to meet urgent need – catholic need. But since social housing is segregated, there would be no social housing near the city centre.

Of the £15 million allocated, the executive spent only £5.3 million. And it used its power to vest land in only four – protestant – neighbourhoods. The housing strategy laments that there is nothing it can do about segregation: 'surplus lands in one community are not readily available for use by another'.

Social researcher Eoin Rooney discovered that since 2000 loyalists had drawn an Orange Line around territory deemed protestant. His report, *Waiting for Equality*, revealed that the Housing Executive plan to build 2300 new homes between 2000 and 2007, mostly to meet catholic need, had failed. Halfway through, fewer than a quarter had been built, and 28 per cent of these dwellings were in protestant communities with a housing surplus. Rooney noticed that the Unionist vote, in remorseless decline in the North Belfast Parliamentary constituency since the early 1980s, was suddenly staunched in 2005.

Regeneration created unique opportunities for both unionist and nationalist neighbourhoods to enjoy renewal – and, through Section 75, their presence in the planning of the renewal. But these communities that needed so much and suffered so much were once more marginalised by a determination to do a body-swerve on the legal duty. One response to segregated social housing that encircled major regeneration sites was to include *no* social housing: in 2006, a report commissioned by the government, the Grimley report, suggested that since public housing was polarised, 'further housing development has the potential of increased polarisation'. So, in the name of a shared future, social housing would be abandoned in favour of private apartment blocks – just what the Seven Towers parents didn't want. And the Grimley report went further – social housing should be kept away from the main routes in and out of the city – out of sight out of mind.

The notion of shared space was mobilised against working-class residents – protestant as well as catholic – and against Northern Ireland's other significant ethnic minority, the Chinese people who had been settling there since the 1960s, and who by the end of the century constituted a stable and vocal presence in the city – and in the equality movement. The Chinese had endured racism throughout the conflict, particularly in proximity to loyalists around the Ormeau Road area near the centre of Belfast. In the new millennium they planned a new community centre and sheltered housing for Chinese elders. But the Chinese community was again confronted by loyalist racism, and also by institutional opposition: integration could not, it seemed, be served by sheltered social housing specifically for Chinese residents near their own networks around the city centre.

Regeneration offered the promise of imaginative renovation in the area of Crumlin Road gaol and the Girdwood Barracks – iconic sites in north Belfast. The gaol was a Victorian prison that had warehoused thousands of suspected combatants during the armed conflict, while Girdwood Barracks had been condemned as a place of torture. The site was surrounded by both republican and loyalist neighbourhoods that featured at the top of all deprivation criteria. But 60 per cent of the proposed housing on the site was to be private – this was the outcome of a Masterplan published in 2007, initiated by direct rule minister David Hanson. The Participation and Practice of Rights Project – a human rights organisation working with both protestant and catholic residents – noticed that, as it flouted its legal duty, it referred to *A Shared Future* 17 times, equality and inequality three times, and social need once. Pessimistic planning was proposing a new kind of social engineering: spatial sectarianism was being replaced by ethnic and class cleansing.

INVESTING IN PROTESTANTS

Northern Ireland's population was poorer than the rest of Britain, and catholic households were poorer than protestant households – when the Assembly began business the gap was £180 a month.[52] Beyond the workplace, in the neighbourhoods that fielded the foot soldiers, attempts to redress this had been presented to protestants as if they were economic larceny: equality as theft. But Targeting Social Need (TSN) had been designed to address both poverty and the poverty differential between catholics and protestants. The Northern Ireland Council for Voluntary Action (well-placed to monitor TSN since its constituent organisations worked with the disadvantaged) delivered its verdict: TSN had had 'no effect'. Unemployment had actually fallen *more* in non-targeted areas. [53] That, of course, assumed that targeted areas had actually been targeted. It seemed that nothing had made much difference: either policy had not been implemented, or it had had no effect.

But in 2004 John Spellar did something extraordinary: he bypassed the entire effort to address the poverty differential. He decided to target protestant neighbourhoods as a priority. He launched 'pilot community conventions for Protestant Working Class Areas', and later established the Protestant Working Class Task Force at senior civil service level to improve capacity and to channel resources. The Task Force administrators explained this transgression of their statutory duty (which directed resources only at *objective* need): 'protestant community organisation was weak'. Secretary of State Paul Murphy believed that 'in catholic areas there's more of a tradition of community activism; that's not the case in protestant areas. European money was more successfully attracted by catholics'. The 'protestant work ethic' left them without 'the experience of setting up groups'. This was a legend that had been rolled out routinely to explain away bad politics in protestant areas – most notoriously during the Holy Cross debacle.[54] It assumed that catholic communities, in the Rev John Dunlop's words, successfully downloaded resources whilst protestant communities did not. He was wrong. The Secretary of State was wrong. The conventional wisdom was wrong.

It had nevertheless become a settled myth that catholic communities had once been ruled by a monolithic religion and were now organised by a new monolith, republicanism; that they were better organised, better represented and better at securing funds, not least from the coffers of the European Social Fund's special peace funds.

In 2004 NICVA tried to track down the investigation of community capacity that was commissioned after Spellar's announcements. It was interested in whether the government's preferential treatment of protestant neighbourhoods was evidence-based, whether it was a response to *greater* needs: 'The political circle could be squared only if government could come up with some indicators that would serve to benefit Protestant working class areas but which could be defended as relevant, robust and reliable. In short, the minister needed cover.' [55] In short, having prioritised protestants, the minister was in a quandary: how could he justify it? Was it ethical? Was it legal?

'The political difficulty is that government cannot just give money to loyalist areas, any more than it can give it to republican areas. Funding on the basis of religion or political affiliation is discriminatory and unlawful,' commented NICVA. But that was exactly what the government had done.

After much effort NICVA uncovered a scandal. There was no evidence of *greater* need or incapacity among protestant communities. And research that seemed to undermine the myth of weak community capacity in protestant neighbourhoods had been suppressed. In 2004 NICVA asked for the evidence uncovered by Deloitte MCS for the Department of Social Development. The request to see Deloitte's research and report was refused. NICVA eventually managed to get hold of the report in 2005, but only after appealing under the Freedom of Information Act. The results explained why.

Catholics were 57 per cent of the population in the neighbourhoods with the weakest community infrastructure, though they comprised 44 per cent of the total population. So, catholics were not blessed by better community organisation. According to NICVA, the research had 'blown a hole' in the protestant weakness hypothesis. The government's response had been to set up a small group to 'validate' the Department's policy. Even then, however, 'this difficult finding would have to be explained to ministers', who would then have to give the policy their blessing. [56]

The Deloitte research was confirmed by another study, commissioned by the OFMDFM. It was buried on its website in 2004 and showed that in areas of high deprivation there was no significant difference between the social capital of catholics and protestants.[57]

Then research by PricewaterhouseCoopers proved that catholics were *more* likely to live in areas of weak community organisation, and during Peace II, the second phase of European funding, their organisations were *less* likely to attract money. This research was also suppressed by the Department of Finance and Personnel. However, its findings were disinterred and published by NICVA's redoubtable Paul McGill. They showed a different prism of segregation: that catholics comprised fewer than 20 per cent of the 500 most affluent areas, and more than 70 per cent of the 500 most deprived areas. But catholic community grant applications were more likely to be rejected than protestant bids. Fifty per cent of catholic community bids succeeded. Sixty per cent of protestant community bids succeeded. In the 10 per cent most deprived areas, funding per head was £462 for protestants and £314 for catholics. [58]

None of this deterred British Ministers. In April 2006, Spellar's successor David Hanson reiterated that £33 million would be directed at protestant neighbourhood renewal. The money would address educational failure, 'lack of social cohesion, active citizenship and civic leadership'. It would also address 'the transformation of paramilitary organisations to modern society'.[59] (All of this was in fact a bit of a con. The moneys announced were often raising protestant hopes by recycling former spending plans.) There was, however, a significant and deliberate redistribution, away from the always more disadvantaged catholic communities, and towards protestants.

In the first years of the new millennium violence emerged as the problem of loyalism; there was widespread criminality, and feuds between rival paramilitary factions. Bizarrely, the government donated £3.5 million to the Ulster Political Research Group – associated with the UDA – to fund the erasure of loyalist murals, and apparently to give combatants something to do: 'you can't have a load of unemployed paramilitaries running about'.[60] In 2006 the UDA asked for another £30 million to help its transition. It didn't get this, but £1.2m was granted to help the UDA combatants in their transition from violence. Riots and the shooting of a police officer then put that in jeopardy. But this was not just a question of violence: once more, the award had not been subject to the legal obligations.

It was only when the Assembly was restored – and Section 75's equality duties were restored to their primary place in the ministerial mind – that Social Development Minister Margaret Richie decided to withdraw public funding from the UDA.

EQUALITY IN THE POST 2007 ASSEMBLY
Devolution rather than direct rule offered the only hope for the constitutional equality duties. And after the drift and bad faith of direct rule, something big happened, something no one could have imagined. A new devolved government began to pursue equality with renewed vigour.

After the Assembly election in 2007 the DUP sat down with Sinn Fein. The new majorities and minorities had attracted the baleful ire of the commentariat, but they were first confounded when in March Ian Paisley and Gerry Adams had their first face to face meeting and agreed to set up a power-sharing executive. They were confounded again in May when Paisley and Martin McGuinness stood together at the bottom of Stormont's Grand Staircase, flanked by garlands of flowers, Tony Blair and Bertie Ahern, and took the 'pledge of office'.

At the beginning of the partnership Paisley, the grand guignol of politico-religious fundamentalism in European politics, had performed as a willing but unsmiling power-sharer. This was a 'work-in not a love-in', he cautioned. But it soon became a laugh-in, and Paisley and McGuinness performed with such unexpected amiability that their partnership became known as the Chuckle Brothers. The voters witnessed a uniquely genial and collegial culture among its politicians – good manners became *de rigueur* – that would have been inconceivable in Westminster.

The first challenge to the DUP's comprehension and commitment came early. It was about sexuality, and therefore also a test of the cultural modernity of the new times. In May Paisley's son, Ian Jnr, a junior minister in the OFMDFM and a close confidant of his father, announced that he was 'repulsed' by homosexuality, and that gay people harmed themselves and their society. This provoked Paisley Snr's first crisis as the leader of his society. His response was to re-affirm his pledge of office and its commitment to honour equality and human rights. Whatever the Paisleys privately believed, their office obliged them to rise above themselves – a case of the Agreement changing public discourse, creating a consensus where there had been none.

The new intake of Assembly Members brought fresh energy to the process, most visibly through one of Sinn Fein's most articulate advocates, its equality and policing spokesperson, Martina Anderson – a former prisoner. Before her election she had been Sinn Fein's Unionist outreach worker, and once in the Assembly she became the party's leader on equality and human rights. She knew her brief. She had authority. She had been convicted in 1986 of conspiracy to cause explosions. During thirteen years in jail she had experienced routine strip searches, sometimes half a dozen times in a day. But she had also studied and gained a first class honours degree. She had been released in 1998 under the terms of the Agreement.

It was Anderson who began to challenge the administration's escape from the equality duty and its evident preference for the promotion of 'good relations' prescribed in *A Shared Future*. Section 75 (1) 'is a powerful tool for all', she said. 'It is a basis for our common human rights that is not tarnished by division. I support the concept of shared future, but I do not accept a document (*A Shared Future*) that puts the responsibility for the conflict on the most marginalised communities'. She also confronted the notion that 'high level strategy' was exempt from the equality and participation duties, taking her case to the Equality Commission and the Human Rights Commission. Did Section 75 (1) apply to 'high level strategy'? The answer was unequivocal: Yes. In an Assembly question that became known as Question 666, she asked Peter Robinson (DUP), the Minister of Finance, whether 'high level' strategy would be subject to impact assessment. When she met him he conceded that policy would be assessed for its impact on good relations. He didn't mention equality. Nothing could have been clearer. *A Shared Future* and reconciliation were perceived as an alternative to socio-economic equality.

Anderson argued that the best way to operationalise Section 75 was to have it flagged up in the programme for government, to have it featured in the budget. That might encourage unionists to get their own communities to use the law. If they wanted to make a difference, 'the thing that allows them to make a difference is Section 75'; it had clear relevance for poor protestants. For example, education budgets prioritised good relations, but the selection system failed working-class protestants: 'Five per cent of children in Shankill pass the 11 plus. I'd be having sleepless nights over that statistic.'

When the 2008-2011 draft budget, *Building a Better Future*, emerged from the OFMDFM at the end of 2007, however, it was still defined by the 'high level' immunities. It promoted economic growth without specifying where, and for whom; and once more good relations, not equality, prevailed. The budget attracted a big response – about 9500 commentaries, one of the biggest ever. The Department of Finance was forced to accept the need for equality impact assessment. Indeed, without it the budget was deemed to be at risk of losing support within the OFMDFM. And it was agreed that this outcome would influence future budgetary phases. 'This is definitely progress,' commented Tim Cunningham. Ten years after the Agreement, the new beginning was beginning.

NOTES

1. Colm Campbell, Fionnuala Ni Aolain, Colin Harvey, 'The Frontiers of Legal Analysis: Reframing the transition in Northern Ireland', the Modern Law Review, 66(3), 2003.
2. McCrudden, 1999, op cit.
3. Ibid.
4. E McLaughlin & P. Faris, *Section 75 Review, Part One*, NIO, p1.
5. See Christine Bell, op cit.
6. P. Bew, 'At Last We Know the Human Cost of Gerry Adams', *The Blanket*, 4 October 2002.
7. Christine Bell, op cit.
8. Bew et al, op cit.
9. They were not alone – Robin Wilson, the former editor of *Fortnight* magazine, also scorned the equality agenda in favour of integrationism.
10. Bew et al, op cit.
11. P. Stewart, 'The Jerrybuilders: Bew, Gibbon and Patterson – the Protestant working class and the Northern Ireland State', in S. Hutton & P. Stewart (eds), *Ireland's Histories*, Routledge 1991.
12. Bob Purdie, 'The Demolition Squad: Bew, Gibbon and Patterson on the Northern Ireland State', in Hutton and Stewart (eds), op cit.
13. Paul Stewart, op cit.
14. Robin Wilson (2000) The Equality Debate.
15. '"A Shared Future": A Consultation Paper on Improving Relations in Northern Ireland', J. Darby and C.Knox, 2004, http://www.asharedfutureni.gov.uk/exsummary.htm.

16. Rick Wilford and Robin Wilson, *Northern Ireland: a Route to Stability*, Democratic Dialogue 2003.

17. See South Africa Institute for the Study of Trauma and Violence for research into post-conflict violence and gender

18. Rick Wilford and Robin Wilson, 'From Belfast Agreement to Stable Power-sharing', paper delivered to the PSA Territorial Politics Conference, Queens University Belfast, January 2006.

19. D. Godson, *Himself Alone: David Trimble and the Ordeal of Unionism*, HarperCollins 2004.

20. Rick Wilford and Robin Wilson 2006, op cit.

21. Rick Wilford and Robin Wilson 2003, op cit.

22. Susan Bordo, 'Feminism, Post-Modernism, and Gender-Scepticism', in Linda J. Nicholson (ed), *Feminism/Postmodernism*, Routledge 1990.

23. Wilford and Wilson 2006, op cit.

24. C. Pateman, *The Disorder of Women*, Stanford University Press 1989.

25. Bordo, op cit.

26. Christine Bell, op cit.

27. Wilford and Wilson 2006, op cit.

28. John Morison, 'Constitutionalism and Change: Representation and Participation in the New Northern Ireland', *Fordham International Law Journal*, Vol 22, No 4, 1999.

29. K. McConnachie & J. Morison, 'Constitution-Making and the Reconstruction of Society', in K McEvoy & L. McGregor (eds), *Transitional Justice from Below*, Hart 2008.

30. Iris Marion Young's phrase in *Justice and the Politics of Difference*, op cit.

31. Bob Connell, *Masculinities*, Polity 1995, p71.

32. A. Phillips, *Which Equalities Matter?*, Polity 1999.

33. E Rooney, *Intersectionality in Theory and Place*, Queen's University 2005.

34. Among the commentators most exercised by this, Tom Hadden, and Robin Wilson misunderstood the naming of categories as the fixing of identities.

35. Criticism from this source was interesting because the Equality Commission had itself been subject to challenge by Eilish Rooney, for its failure to address the sectarian differential between catholic and protestant women. The explanation offered had been that this would be 'divisive' for the 'women's sector'. The sexism-sectarianism matrix was still dangerous, even in the Equality Commission. See Eilish Rooney, 'Women and Human Rights: Conflict, Transformation and Change', paper delivered to Transitional Justice Institute Conference, University of Ulster, May 2005.

36. Christopher McCrudden, Robert Ford & Anthony Heath, 'The Impact of Affirmative Action Agreements', in Bob Osborn and Ian Shuttleworth (eds), *Fair Employment in Northern Ireland, A Generation On*, Blackstaff 2004, p162.

37. Ibid.
38. Ibid, p165.
39. Heidi Welsh, *IRRC Report on Fair Employment*, Washington 2003.
40. CAJ, Equality Report, CAJ 2006.
41. Ibid.
42. Ibid.
43. Osborne, in *Fair Employment in Northern Ireland, A Generation On*, op cit.
44. McLaughlin and Faris, op cit.
45. McLaughlin and Faris, op cit.
46. C. McCrudden, 'Mainstreaming Equality in Northern Ireland', in *A Review of Issues Concerning the Operation of the Equality Duty in Section 75 of the Northern Ireland Act 1998, Part Two, Annex B*, 2004.
47. Ibid.
48. CAJ 2006, p148.
49. Robinson v Secretary of State for Northern Ireland and Others, 22 July 2002, UKHL.
50. Application by Peter Neill for Judicial Review, 4 May 2004; High Court of Justice in Northern Ireland, 7 October 2005.
51. In 1968 the nationalist politician Austin Curry helped squatters to take over a family dwelling that had been allocated to a young, single protestant whose family was related to local unionist politicians. The squatters exposed as a scandal the power of local authorities to gerrymander elections, by their control over public housing, and the containment of catholics in overcrowded raggy slums.
52. Northern Ireland Statistics and Research Agency, 1999.
53. NICVA, *Ten Years of a Failed Policy*, 26 January 2001.
54. For an account of how the notion of weak protestant community organisation was mobilised during the Holy Cross blockade, see chapter 8.
55. NICVA 2001, op cit.
56. P. McGill, *The Case for Protestant Disadvantage Lies in Tatters*, Scope, NICVA 2005.
57. *Social Capital, Collectivism, Individualism and Community Background in Northern Ireland*, cited in McGill, op cit.
58. Paul McGill, op cit.
59. David Hanson, Minister for Social Development, 13 April 2006.
60. H. McDonald, 'UDA asks for £30 million', *Observer*, 16.7.06.

PART II

PARAMILITARISM, PRISONERS AND PEACEMAKING

6. The journey of the loyalist paramilitaries

Ulster Unionist MP Jeffrey Donaldson's exit from the unhappy seclusion of the UUP's delegation in Castle Buildings on Good Friday 1998 – ostensibly in protest against the negotiators' concessions on prisoner releases, his party's pragmatic resignation to their importance in the process, and to the decision to keep paramilitary de-commissioning out of the talks – was symbolic of the strategic equivocations of unionism: though it condemned the men of the gun, men of the gun were always by its side and violence in the vaults of its imagination. This violence was more than a rhetorical menace. It was a gauntlet to be flourished and a weapon to be discharged not only, nor even primarily, against catholics, but against purported appeasers within the unionist firmament, including the British state. Violence was a resource. Auxiliary armies had augmented unionism's power throughout the twentieth century. Militarism was much more than a defensive fortification against the Irish majority on the island: force had been the decisive discourse within unionism itself. What appeared as a straightforward conflict between unionism and nationalism, protestants and catholics, was also, simultaneously – indeed *a priori* – a conflict within unionism itself: militarism was an answer to any retreat from intransigence within unionism.

But, as Donaldson demonstrated, constitutional unionism was a capricious fellow traveller for the loyalist paramilitaries; while censure was always lying in wait for the combatants, constitutional unionism was always able to put itself beyond scrutiny. The mainstream's link to force was in general disavowed.

If violence is understood as a founding discourse of unionism, then the militias' long march into the peace process has to be recognised as all the more risky and radical. The themes that drive this book – the equality and human rights dimensions of the Agreement, and what their history reveals about the British government's actual interests – had particular salience for the combatants and for their self esteem. Within unionism they were the 'dim, compendious'[1] and neglected mob, and yet they experienced themselves as – or rather they made themselves – necessary. In their thousands they took to the gun to defend the union. And the paramilitaries from the catholic 'other' looked at their society down the barrel of the gun because, in the main, they were men, and because they could imagine no remedy.

Donaldson's sanctity signalled the constitutional politicians' ambivalence about the military men, but there is no doubt that there would have been no settlement without them. My argument is that the equality and human rights duties promised more than peace, and for the combatants they offered a dignified stake in a deal – an historically unprecedented way to address the crisis of class in Northern Ireland. The deal offered men as men an opportunity for the first time to assert their class interest with, rather than against, women. It invited protestant/unionist men to contemplate their class interest with, rather than against, catholics.

The peace process had demanded of the combatants a faculty that scarcely nudged the men of constitutional politics: the capacity to change. Without some combatants' aptitude for personal change – for them the feminist mantra 'the personal is political' had a poignant resonance – and without their readiness to raise their consciousness of their histories both as men and as working-class men we cannot make sense of their long march into the peace process and the loyalist parties' passionate endorsement of the equality duty. Tony Blair would have been wise to pack this secret beside his bible during the Middle East mission that followed his resignation from the British parliament.

In this part of the book I propose that the journey undertaken by loyalist combatants into the peace process was arguably the most creative contribution to come from unionism. The trek did not lead them to disown their part in paramilitary organisations. On the contrary, they were organising a different kind of relationship to both the physical force tradition and to unionism.

The first chapter in this section deals with the routes by which loyalist former combatants and prisoners determined that they wanted to do their loyalism differently; how the prison experience, and their proximity to the enemy, the republican prisoners, influenced their political thinking. Some prisoners of the 1980s found a new incarnation, as community activists, and as couriers between the militias, their communities and the political realm; they deployed their reputations as new kind of social capital to invest in peace, democracy, pluralism and social justice – goals that had so troubled the constitutionalists for more than three decades, and that had been represented within constitutional unionism as loss. But the metamorphoses of the military men was not something that mainstream unionism was interested in. Nor was the state inclined to support prisoners' discoveries – which, if they did not amount to reconciliation, could be described with confidence as recognition and on occasion respect. The prisoners' 'forward march' was interrupted by constitutional unionism's culpable ambivalence about violence and its enduring resistance to power-sharing. The loyalist combatants' trajectory towards a settlement was also detoured by a scandal: the British secret state's re-armament of the loyalist militias at the very moment when they were contemplating peace and power-sharing (see Part V); and after the ceasefires, interest in a pluralist peaceful settlement was greatly compromised by the magnetic pull of macho havoc. As well as dealing with the journey of the protestant paramilitaries into the peace process, however, this chapter also tells the story of the loyalists who remained intransigent, and whose activities did so much damage to the prospects for peace.

The second chapter in this section looks at the decisive role of Republican former combatants and ex-prisoners in formulating a peace strategy. It should be noted, however, that they were not virtuous recanters whose reputations would be based on baddies becoming goodies. Nor is their stance to be confused with a strategy for politics. Republicanism was slow to register the potency of politics as politics – as the public culture of peaceful conflict: although republican prisoners were envied in the loyalist wings for their rigour, discipline and thinking, political strategy was also underdeveloped in republican culture. If working-class loyalism was annexed for another class interest, working-class republicanism was alienated and exiled from political arenas, whether the devolved one-party state, or distant direct rule from Westminster.

In catholic neighbourhoods the political revival of the late 1960s derived not from republicanism but from the civil rights movement and from socialism. Republicanism was by then residual, nationalist and socially conservative. When overwhelming force was thrown at civil rights activism, it was its defeat that re-activated republicanism. But while many of the young men in this profoundly patriarchal nationalism had been locked up, either in their battalions or in British prisons, the women were building community politics. The 1970s echoed the gendered division of political labour retrieved marvellously in Margaret Ward's history of the Land League.[2] When republicanism embarked on a *political* practice in the 1980s, it was adapting activist infrastructures that had largely been built by women. Republicanism as a physical force tradition invented neither the community politics that became a social base for its mantra 'the Armalite and the ballot box', nor the equality agenda. Though the political establishment dubbed the battle for equality provo propaganda, it was only slowly that it gained recognition within republicanism as a peaceful – and important – means to cultural pluralism and economic reform.

LOYALIST PRISONERS AND THE PEACE PROCESS

To appreciate the significance of the loyalist ex-prisoners' participation in the deal we need to apprehend the radicalism, so nuanced and precarious, of their intervention and its implications for unionism's 'social alliance'. Constitutional unionism had always relied upon the unionist militias to assert its relative autonomy from the British government, and it had always fielded armed men whenever its dominion over catholics was in jeopardy. In 1912 Edward Carson raised the Ulster Volunteer Force, armed with German guns, to resist Home Rule for Ireland (and in 1914 bequeathed his men as the 36th Ulster Division to the British Army for deployment in World War 1, in return for the abandonment of Home Rule). In May 1966 the UVF was raised again after two years of raucous fundamentalism directed by Ian Paisley not only against catholics but also the government: Carson's ghost was invoked in response to Prime Minister Terence O'Neill's tentative rapprochement with the Republic and modest retreat from bigotry.

Cabinet papers released after forty years have begun to challenge the prevailing narrative – that the militias were a defensive response to armed republicanism. They indicate that Ian Paisley's politics of schism, backed by militarism, was directed by the unionist establishment. O'Neill's cabinet was briefed by the RUC in 1966 – two years before 'the troubles' began – that Ian Paisley's 'extremist movement' and the UVF were 'one and the same threat posed to the government and to Northern Ireland'.[3] According to Margaret O'Callaghan and Catherine O'Donnell, whether or not this briefing was correct, its impact cannot be exaggerated. Warning that peace was fundamentally threatened, the RUC told the Cabinet that, though 'there is always the IRA', 'an equal or even greater threat is posed at present by extremist Protestant groups'. Already there were believed to be 30 UVF divisions in Belfast and '"a good number" of Ulster Special Constabulary and Crown Forces are active members'.[4] The RUC also concluded that the police and army were the main source of the militias' weapons. But O'Neill's ability to address this intra-unionist crisis was fatally compromised – by his own party and his own colleagues in the cabinet. Thus, by the end of the decade O'Neill was confronted by the armed insurgency of the protestant militias (and security services) as well as the peaceful uprising of the civil rights movement. He warned his cabinet colleagues that his government's response to civil rights had exposed it as an apparently 'sectarian government': by resisting 'this molehill of reform we are allowing a mountain to fall on us'.[5] The mountain fell upon the whole society, which lived in the debris for the next thirty years.

In the early 1970s this loyalist presence in the security services attracted the Army's attention. Military Intelligence was well aware of the many who had joint membership of the UDR and paramilitary organisations, and of the role of the British army, in the shape of the Ulster Defence Regiment, as a major source of weapons for the paramilitaries. The militias were crowded with informers, agents and spies (for a fuller account see Part V).[6] The problem, the British government was warned, was not the collusion itself but the risk that collusion created. The government's concern was about control and reliability – its problem was always the *loyalty* of the loyalists. What if they became – as they habitually did – disloyal? That question was answered in 1974, when unionism took to the streets in protest against the Sunningdale Agreement and power-sharing and a 'provisional government' – Protestant power workers, 'well-armed private armies and extreme politicians' – rendered 'a section of the realm totally ungovernable';[7] and it was palpable again in 1985, after the Anglo-Irish Agreement, when dissenting unionism brought the place to a standstill.

Constitutional unionism did not, however, match the fighting men's capacity, learned in prison, for self-criticism and elements of empathy with the enemy. The combatants' prison experience, in the early days locked up and in close proximity with republicans, had enabled some of them to do something remarkable, to put their brittle political identities at risk by 'the hazard of hearing' the despised adversary. Though they would not be reconciled to the republicans' nationalist project, they often envied their heroism, and they came to recognise and respect what they shared: class and the experience of marginalisation. This, for protestants, had always before been compromised by their social alliance with Big House unionism.

Constitutional unionism was estranged from the détente and incipient class re-alignment that on and off for a decade before the Agreement had been contemplated by loyalist thinkers, and began to take shape in the report of the unionist task force – as if it was affronted by their political autonomy. The unionist elite did not tolerate the possibility that the men who had lived with and by violence might have greater redemptive potential than those who had merely colluded with it, or commissioned it.[8]

Thus it was that former combatants developed the most creative unionist contribution to the peace process. Insofar as unionism assimilated their programme, it was because the unionist establishment, ultimately, had to depend on the despised 'military men' to relieve it of the burden of its own history – its appeasement of sectarian fundamentalism. Introspection was an endeavour that had not troubled unionism's elite since the 1960s. However, loyalist volunteers who had been inspired by the 'Paisleyite Movement' to take up arms, and had paid by the loss of their liberty, found themselves in prison doing something that unionism had not encouraged them to do before: think. Some of the ex-combatants *thought* their way into the peace process.

The agenda that the ex-paramilitaries and ex-prisoners formulated from their own experience therefore became the most progressive and pluralist programme within unionism. When these men insisted on participating in the talks – with Mowlam's encouragement – it was not with a view to bolstering intransigence. On the contrary, the aim was, said Davy Adams, a member of the UDP delegation (the political wing of the UDA), to contribute to 'conflict resolution', for 'the prisoners had to be part of it'. According to Adams, mainstream unionism felt no responsibility for the ex-prisoners: 'there was a load of hypocrisy – total detachment from the manifestations of the conflict and the atrocities – as if they'd been parachuted from outer space. But there wasn't a person above 18 years of age who didn't have some share in responsibility for the situation here.'

British politicians had a tendency to condemn the paramilitary organisations, and hail the constitutional parties as if they were – like the British – the centre, the plumb, of sensible politics. But unionism's vaunted moderate centre had always been characterised by excess and intransigence. Force animated every part of unionist popular culture. With or without the militias, unionism's calendar was organised around the rituals of the annual 'marching season' – the summertime capture of the streetscape by the Orange Orders: the sash-wearing faux militarism, and the bands that threw the sound of the Lambeg drums into the soundscape, were pageants of dominion. Workplaces, community halls, lodges, churches and the streets were the locales where men's power as men, and as protestants, was regularly rehearsed. The modes of assembly, secret societies and lodges had their origins as men's movements, hierarchical and sexually segregated. Violence was invoked in the songs, marches and ceremonies, as their ever-ready first or last resort. This was a context for the making of masculinity as mastery, a means of maintaining the intensely patriarchal character of unionism.

Violence has been represented as the primitive, tribal specialism of Britain's rowdy neighbour across the Irish Sea. But this is to underestimate protestant paramilitarism's strategic importance to Britain as a vector of sectarianism – in the streets, within the state and in mainstream unionist culture.[9] At exactly the time when the parallel peace processes were finding a form and gathering momentum, the British state was re-arming the auxiliary armies and sponsoring death squads. Indeed, without access to the state's arsenal and even sponsorship, the protestant paramilitaries would scarcely have been effective before and then during the armed conflict.

Collusion by the British state with protestant paramilitaries had a history as long as – nay longer than – the armed conflict itself. Violence as a transaction between men, sanctioned by states everywhere, has offered a special power to working-class and marginalised men. Violence is part of a discourse of masculinity, a way of making masculinity as mastery over women, and other men and social space. Before and during the armed conflict, working-class protestant men, as trade unionists, members of the Orange Orders or the paramilitaries, constituted the social base of unionism. Working-class protestant men had given to this conservative and parochial political culture its remarkable hegemony.

It was the militias, however, that gave a transcendent power to the most marginalised men. The 'social alliance' may have given them proximity to power, but it also gave them subordination. Militarism – unlike trade unionism or orangeism – gave them relative autonomy. By gaining access to the means of violence, marginalised masculinities acquired the means to assert themselves with and against respectable masculinities – they were simultaneously a resource and a challenge to the authority of the unionist state.[10]

A struggle for authority circulated endlessly between the paramilitaries and the patriarchs of the unionist establishment, and ambivalent allegiance swirled around the state itself. The usual alibi for the involvement of state agents in the paramilitaries – that they were used to save lives, to keep an eye and to restrain the worst excesses – is not supported by the evidence, or by the paramilitaries' own emerging versions of events. The state penetrated the paramilitaries to control them and to mobilise them. At the same time it denounced the violence and militarism upon which it depended. Donaldson's walkout was a reminder not only of that ambivalence, but of the rhetorical power of denunciation to obscure what was new: the military men's interest – above all their class interest – in the deal.

A MAN TO END IT ALL

Gusty Spence was the man who was often said to have started – and finished – it all. He was up in Castle Buildings with the loyalist negotiators right to the end. There were more than fifty of them sleeping everywhere, on chairs, tables, floors, in the corridors. 'There are those who referred to themselves as "constitutional politicians", as purer than thou, but these men knew they were risking their lives becoming part of the peace process,' commented Monica McWilliams, whose Women's Coalition worked closely with the former combatants during the talks. 'There was very little recognition of the difficulties they faced'.

Augustus Spence was born in 1933 in the Shankill, which had fielded workers and soldiers for the Ulster Volunteer Force raised in 1912 to resist Home Rule for Ireland, for the Somme in World War 1, for military service in the post-colonial British army, and for the Orange Order's citadels – where men rehearsed the rituals that made them men, and for the shipyards, where Gusty Spence himself had worked. Spence says he was 'born into an atmosphere where masculinity was everything. And men were hard then'. The armed conflict began early for Gusty Spence. As a Shankill ex-Serviceman, his skills were enlisted in the new Ulster Volunteer Force that was being formed in 1965. The UVF was part of a unionist mutiny against Prime Minister O'Neill's treachery in doing diplomacy with the south, and it included members of O'Neill's own party.[11] Spence was jailed in 1966 after being convicted of killing a catholic as part of a seditious conspiracy. His wife had known nothing about it – this was secret stuff shared between men – and after this his family managed life without him for nearly nineteen years.

Spence was moulded in the image of a military man. His home after he was released was a glinting bungalow in the Shankill, decorated with ornaments of little terrier dogs and family photographs, with an office lined with display cabinets of military insignia. His bearing, his erudition harvested from military histories, and his collection of military memorabilia, badges and livery would be familiar to anyone from his generation, or from the generation of children anywhere in Britain whose fathers had been thrown into world wars and never got over it. For working-class Northern Ireland protestants, that history was mobilised for the invention of a unionist 'tradition' that united the UVF to the martyrs of the trenches. 'If we'd lived in 1912 we'd have been on the road to the Somme … There are two things deep in our psyche, the border and the Somme when men were sacrificing gloriously, and somewhat needlessly, their lives.' Within unionism the

Somme was re-imagined as part of an inventory of debt owed by
Britain not to Irish men, but to Orange men. Sacrifice, discipline,
stamina, fatalism, all of this stirred in the alchemy of militarism,
masculinity and loyalism.

Spence's experience as a British soldier transferred to his mode of
survival in prison. 'I had 18 years and 7 months in prison so I had
plenty of time to think.' The young men who had flooded into paramilitary organisations and then poured into the jails in the 1970s had
thought they were responding to a papist republican threat: 'the
protestants couldn't understand the cry of discrimination against
catholics, but of course there was discrimination.' In prison Spence
changed his mind and came to believe that 'sometimes the threat was
manufactured by the government – we had an abusive government'.
For the loyalist volunteers pouring into the jails, it was 'gun, gun, gun':
'Our task was to wean them off it, people had to know what they were
fighting for. There was a young lad, a teenager with a school blazer,
he'd shot two people in the head. What was society going to do about
that?' Spence said of himself that when he joined the UVF in 1965 'I
didn't know if it was Easter Monday or Pancake Tuesday'. When the
civil rights movement emerged, 'protestants were told, and believed,
that it was out to overthrow Northern Ireland. A load of nonsense, of
course.' As a young man, a father, billeted in Nissen huts at Long Kesh
prison, languishing all day with nothing to do, Spence had to make
sense of the mess outside. He had to think his way into a future, and he
had to do something with the lads with whom he was now sharing his
life, for whom he was responsible. He became their mother and father,
their teacher and their commanding officer. 'So I imposed military
discipline.' Military organisation was designed to make the men fit,
thoughtful and disciplined. 'On the outside they hadn't heard people
like us, they didn't see the light in our eyes, that society could change,
they hadn't thought about society.' What these lads had learned was 'to
defend and attack, they'd learned to fulfil the traditional role of obedience to others'. 'That was the atmosphere they'd grown up in, they
were hard then.'

Spence's regime, encouraged by the prisoners' self-organisation in
the huts, promoted self-awareness, and some of them tried to take
responsibility for their *body politic*, in all senses, to do what they'd
never had to do, be carers. On the outside these men would not have
expected to take care of anyone, that was women's work. Their
personal stamina had to cope with the vulnerability of the body. They
were stripped, they endured intrusion, they were subjected to unin-
vited gaze – that was women's experience.

Through the education programmes in the prison – which had been campaigned for by both republican and loyalist prisoners – for the first time these ill-educated loyalists experienced respect from people of another culture and class, and they were exposed to teachers who included among them republicans, feminists and communists.[12] Among the loyalist ranks were men who pumped iron but rarely read a book, faithful Paisleyites and dutiful unionists, men who couldn't stop crying for their mothers, and men who fell into stupefied prison sedation. But there was also a corps of hungry cadres who were fascinated and empowered by Spence, and it was among them that he mentored a new generation of articulate and literate loyalist leaders.

One of these boys was Billy Hutchinson. If there had been no armed conflict Hutchinson would probably have become a typical, respectable protestant man in the patriarchal mould. He had been schooled in a secondary modern school for manual work, and trained with other protestant men in James Mackie's engineering factory, enthusiastic about becoming a married man, a provider, and an Orangeman. But there was civil war and he had come to believe that the civil rights movement's agenda was 'to bring down the state of Northern Ireland'. Like Gusty Spence he had believed the propaganda, but later came to believe that it was a travesty with tragic consequences. 'Most protestants believed this was a protestant state for protestant people', he said; 'they were reluctant to admit the levels of disadvantage and poverty'. Hutchinson's journey into unionist manhood had swerved into the paramilitaries in 1972, and it was in this same year that David Ervine joined the UVF. It was a year of bloodletting, and this Belfast teenager felt his decision was prompted by a visceral feeling of 'to whom I belong and to whom I do not belong'. In 1974 the UVF was engaged in a debate, 'sectarianism versus militarism'. Was the war being waged against catholics, or against republican soldiers? According to David Ervine's biographer, Henry Sinnerton, sectarianism won the argument and an intense bombing campaign was launched.[13] Young David Ervine remained in the UVF and was arrested in 1976 in a car carrying explosives and a detonator. In prison he was intense and intellectually ravenous. In the context of the learning culture, it was 'the first time we ever had an articulate conversation in our lives upon issues that were beyond football, horse racing or the weather. It was new for us. It was vibrant, it was also a learning process that said, "our society has to change".'[14]

The experience was much more eclectic than anything these young men would have expected on the outside. They had access to ideas, and they often consumed those ideas in the company of their enemy – Open

University students in the prison shared classes with republicans. Breige Gadd, Northern Ireland's reforming chief probation officer, promoted prisoners' access to education. She noticed that it was seized on by the lifers, who moved away from war and 'began to train themselves to be community resources for peace on the outside'. In prison Ervine felt that he had been 'emancipated by education'. He had discovered the power of the word, it entranced him, he acquired a reputation as a word-spinner. Sometimes he was derided – how dare a working-class man presume to take such pleasure in the *mot juste*. What he later tried to give back to his ill-educated community was the effort of eloquence – not as holy-rolling poetics, not as Paisley's voluptuous populism, but as a search for meaning, for precision, elegance and candour.

Spence and his coterie of prisoners ran their own huts, and, though they were exiled from the streets where power-sharing was being violently repudiated, they were thinking independently; they were crit-icising sectarian killings and openly contemplating pluralism and peace. Loyalist and republican prisoners were by then skilled in self-organisation. In 1974 they publicised the formation of a camp council to address their shared issues as inmates; it was announced that in the Maze and Crumlin Road jail prisoners had formed a united front. But this structure was doomed. The embryonic 'political forum' develop-ing in the camp council attracted calumny amongst unionist politicians outside. Then the prisoners heard with astonishment of the Labour government's rejection of a prisoners' welfare liaison centre in down-town Belfast, an idea that had been nurtured together with the progressive probation service. What, they wondered, could justify opposition to a service to facilitate re-settlement and re-integration? Then, in 1976, they were aghast at the abolition of Special Category status and the 'criminalisation' of the paramilitary prisoners. Special Category status, and the self-organisation it licensed, had mitigated the banal, empty, degraded routines visited upon 'ordinary criminals'. But all of that was wasted by the strategy of criminalisation introduced by Labour Home Secretary Roy Mason. Colin Crawford, who worked as a prison welfare officer at Long Kesh, argued that criminalisation led to escalation of the conflict, and in this he was cruelly vindicated by the Conservative government's deadly confrontation with republican pris-oners during the 1980-81 hunger strikes.[15] Crawford's experience told him that Special Category experience had engendered among the pris-oners 'a conflict resolution strategy'. He believed the prisoners had shown their potential to influence a peace process by creating their own. Given the importance of the prisoners to politics outside, this was important. But criminalisation squandered everything.

During the 1970s Spence had been trying to formulate a progressive unionism. In 1977, in an address to the UVF prisoners to mark 12 July, the great day in the Orange calendar, he said: 'we are living in the most socially and legalistically oppressive society in the Western Hemisphere, the manifestations of which are strewn over that society like scabs ... polarisation complete ... jails filled to overflowing and legislation that the apartheid countries would envy'. He urged the volunteers on both sides to consider a ceasefire. Some time later, two of his younger UVF comrades, Billy Hutchinson and Billy Mitchell (who had been arrested early in the conflict, and who was later to become a devout advocate of the equality agenda), wrote with aching candour that 'some of us held similar views as long ago as early 1974, but to our eternal sorrow, did not have the moral courage to pursue these policies ... Instead we espoused the policies of "populism" for fear that we would be branded as disloyal by the vast army of super-Prods who have so much to say and so little to offer.'[16] Billy Mitchell recalled plaintively the cold meetings with DUP and UUP politicians: 'we realised they didn't regard us as part of their family. All along we were poor relations ... they said you're scum, you're murdering dogs ... they use our violence, to rattle their sabres, threaten the Protestant backlash, use us as cannon fodder, then dump us.'

In Cage 21 in Long Kesh Spence made a speech describing Northern Ireland as 'a police state with the accompanying allegations of torture and degrading treatment to suspects undergoing interrogation'. 'Even yet we still have men nonsensically counselling that victory is round the corner. Victory over whom? The IRA? Or do they mean victory over the Roman Catholic community? ... We, in Northern Ireland are plagued by super-loyalists ... with their bigoted and fascist views'. Why not begin dialogue between the paramilitaries, he asked. Once he was released from prison he was soon to discover why not.

PEACE-MAKING AND INTRANSIGENCE

After his release in the mid-1980s Spence re-connected with his Shankill community and found his political home in the Progressive Unionist Party. This was a time when some loyalists and republicans were beginning to confront the impasse of permanent war, and permanent direct rule from London. But early attempts by former combatants to address the democratic deficits in the political system and the state were overwhelmed by mainstream unionism's intransigence. The PUP urged mainstream unionist leaders: 'you must assure nationalists that there will be no return to the abusive, divisive regimes of the past, which the old Stormont represented'; and this effort was ultimately to yield a direct intervention in the peace process, and the creative participation in the Agreement. But that was to take a further decade.

In 1985 Sinn Fein won 59 seats in the local elections. For the first time unionist politicians had to do business with republicans who had an electoral mandate. They were horrified. London and Dublin were alarmed. Something had to be done.

Margaret Thatcher commissioned Cabinet Secretary Robert Armstrong to embark on a secret project with Dublin. The project became the Anglo-Irish Agreement.'[17] But as soon as Dublin and London published the AIA, its historic compromise was undermined by the secrecy that had led up to it and the exile from the process of the protestant masses. In Dublin that outraged Mary Robinson, then a Senator; and in England former Labour Secretary of State Merlyn Rees commented, 'it's not good going from ignoring the minority, then ignoring the majority'.[18] However, the unionist leaders had in fact been offered the opportunity to participate and didn't take it.[19] Not-know-ingness was to be unionism's alibi thereafter.

Its paranoia vindicated, unionism again mobilised. A new network of Ulster Clubs proliferated, mass demonstrations were organised and insurgencies were murmured. The Ulster Clubs fathered the Ulster Resistance in 1986, yet another incarnation of Carson's citizen army, registering a respectable profile to the militias already active – the illegal UVF and the still-legal UDA.

It was a bad time for any former combatants promoting power-sharing. In loyalist hangars the militias waited for someone to push the button. One of the great intransigents, the fundamentalist christian cleric and Paisleyite MP the Rev William McCrea, warned that unionists 'may yet even have to fight the British to remain British'.[20] The meaning of *fight* was unambiguous: 'We will fight to the death ... this could come to hand to hand fighting in every street in Northern Ireland. We are on the verge of civil war ... the people must prepare themselves as in the days of Carson ...' David Trimble – at that time a relatively junior politician, though he had been a veteran of the 1974 unionist strike against the Sunningdale Agreement – cautioned: 'I would personally draw the line at terrorism ... but ... violence may be inescapable.' Ian Paisley's 'perilously close' connection to paramilitary violence would come and go.[21] Paisley threw himself to the brink, only to regain his regal piety and pull back. Rebellion flared and foundered. The unionist leadership commissioned a task force to think beyond 'Ulster Says No'. It could not avoid consulting paramilitaries and ex-prisoners at this point, and it could not but hear their critical re-appraisals of the unionist mission. The Task Force's report, *An End to Drift*, contemplated independence, and – worse – power-sharing;[22] and it duly faded away. The spectre now confronting the unionist elites was that some of the lower orders were indeed thinking, and they were thinking the unthinkable. In 1985 the Progressive Unionist Party published Spence's 'sharing responsibility' strategy – which carefully eschewed the inflammatory grammar of 'power-sharing'. David Ervine was also working in the PUP on the development of a progressive unionist programme. But it was struggling for audibility against the 'Ulster Says No' campaign.

Within the UDA, which was legal and larger though less politically literate than the illegal UVF, some individuals were contemplating an 'independent Ulster'. During 1986 John McMichael, the UDA's second in command, was working on a new strategy with UDA leader Andy Tyrie, who had been one of David Trimble's associates in the hard right Vanguard movement, and in the 1974 Ulster Workers Strike. The UDA leaders were also thinking the unthinkable – a devolved power-sharing executive – and their ideas were published in *Commonsense* early in 1987. The UDA had been at the heart of the campaign against the Anglo Irish Agreement, and yet even here, among its thinking leaders – admittedly few – there were attempts to find a settlement, even as it was being steered by the British army and intelligence towards a new crest of violence. Some estimates put the proportion of agents or informers in the UDA senior echelons at that time at about 50 per cent – and that combination of deep penetration and the shield of legality made the UDA a uniquely *controlled* organisation. But the UDA was nothing if not perverse – controlled and yet uncontrollable. Revisionism thrived, and manifestos were written and re-written that confronted not only the AIA impasse, but the doubtful legitimacy and future impossibility of the Northern Ireland state that 'pro-state terrorism' had been dying – and killing – to defend.

So, while in some circles there was rethinking, the political impasse was being filled by young men who, en masse, translated what they were hearing from the unionist leadership as the cry of the recruiting sergeant. They once more flooded into paramilitary organisations. One young man, who joined the UDA when he was 22 years old, said he had made his decision after 'Ian Paisley's recruitment campaign around the estates':

> I was influenced by him and what he was saying about the AIA as the foundation for a united Ireland: this was the final straw, we must fight to

the death. People fought and they landed up in prison – lots didn't really know why they'd joined.

Another young man, who joined the UDA when he was 17, recalled the thrills and the hatred:

> The adrenalin! I was 17, running about with eight or ten fellas, it was exciting for us, we were never off the news, road blocks, blocking roads, putting up posters, and they started talking about civil war. Apocalypse Now. Fight back. I didn't think it was about killing, but protecting your areas – being the police. I went to jail in 1989 for attacking the security forces. It was like a blood rush, you thought you were important, protecting your community, out every night, people looking out of their windows at you. You thought you were King Kong, indestructible.

He wasn't, of course, he was arrested and jailed.

Looking back on his school days in the 1980s, another UDA member and former prisoner, a genial, thoughtful 'big fella' who later became a community youth worker, recalled an atmosphere of intoxicating paranoia: 'we were worried about the republicans taking over Ulster, it was very much "No Surrender"! That was inhaled in the atmosphere. It was all over the country, the same generation, the same views, it was massive.' Ian Paisley seemed to be 'the only political figure around', and we thought 'this is the way, he's not going to sell us out'. It was Paisley's alliance with the respectable UUP that was irresistible:

> That created a united front, and that added to his credibility. Then I became involved in different disturbances, and once that started everybody I knocked about with was becoming involved, trying to fight against betrayal. We felt we were represented by the UDA and John McMichael, we felt he was the paramount voice for us, what I appreciated was that he referenced everything to the street.

He was jailed in the 1990s for terrorist offences.

THRILLING FORCE

During the years after the debacle of the AIA, paramilitarism came once again to belong to the 'military men', and to a cult of violence that was in tension with the Spence generation. These men were alienated from the 'discursive exchange' of politics, and from the advocates of a settlement in the political wings of the UVF and the

UDA. Two very different local commanders later exemplified this estrangement from politics: Johnny 'Mad Dog' Adair and 'King Rat' Billy Wright. Both men were accused of belonging to the criminalised culture of 'late loyalist' militarism and both were enmeshed in the security services.

Adair was a commander of the UDA's C Company in the Shankill who became an iconic figure, the antithesis of the 'learning loyalism' developed among the prisoners who returned to their communities in the mid-1980s and designed a strategy for 'progressive loyalism'. His flamboyance, and his gangsta idiosyncrasies, encouraged the representation of the Adair persona as a rogue – and therefore a rogue element – and yet Adair and his comrades were more culturally promiscuous than their critics often credited; they were loaded with popular cultures of music, militarism, masculinities, authority, the hyper-body and Britishness; the cast of players were straight and gay, they wore casual, military, gansta bling and queer chic, and they were men's men.

Adair's public life began in the early 1980s as a skinhead gangster, and as a member of the band Offensive Weapon (which borrowed from the brute noise of UK neo-nazi band Screwdriver and flirted with the neo-fascist National Front). His C Company was one of the UDA's most audacious outfits, and its life and times were broadcast in murals all over the Shankill. His comrades watched in amusement, wonderment and sometimes exasperation his ravenous consumption of women, weapons and drugs. Beginning his UDA career as a street fighter, he progressed to become bodyguard to the notorious 'Tucker' Lyttle – another British 'agent' in the UDA leadership (see pp234–5). Once Tucker's generation had been dispatched – assassinated or arrested – at the end of the 1980s, Adair and his generation took over. According to his biographers, Adair was not, like so many of the UDA cadres, a British agent. But no *formal* arrangement with high-ups was necessary. The UDA was corporately resourced by the intelligence services and the police, and Adair was among its senior cadre. His relationship to the security services and the police was intimate, if informal, a relationship of mutual surveillance. The UDA's commanders were being used, according to British officers, as 'surrogate killers'. [23] His biographers admit that RUC officers were well aware that Adair and his comrades were receiving 'a regular stream of intelligence from the security forces' on republicans.

And Adair was alluring to businessmen in suits, who openly turned up at his home to donate cash and goodwill. The UDA's notoriety as warriors who were simultaneously criminals – accessing big money through organised crime – was mitigated by a sensibility that catholics were fair game and, anyway, the state was on their side.

There was frisson in this liaison dangereuse, of course, between low life and chaps, grandees and capitalists. It reiterated the cross-class alliance between working-class protestants, capital, and the Big House; and it generated the kind of excitement at the illicit that had energised Berlin in the 1920s, Soho in the 1950s and New York in the 1970s, where the rich and powerful played with the gorgeous and the dangerous. The Shankill's modest landscape – terraces of tiny dwellings thrown up to warehouse the working class, discount stores, bookies, chip shops, bomb sites and murals glorifying armed men and martyrs – was patrolled by blokes whose cars, women, gold and guns announced both power and leisurely profligacy. Sex and violence were the armour of their reputation.

Adair and his UDA coterie were wanton, they appeared to love violence. 'I was always military', he'd boast.[24] In August 2002 he was to order that his own son be shot in the knees – a storyline worthy of *The Godfather*, according to journalist Rosie Cowan. No one in the streets doubted that Adair's C Company had done the shooting. One of his men claimed that Adair the father was a 'man of principle and dignity' who wouldn't want his family to be treated any differently from anyone else. He didn't report what the boy's mother wanted.

Adair's activities contributed to a cult of manly discipline: a relationship to men that was bonded, and yet unfeeling. The shooting revealed not only the endemic violence of his culture, but also the precariousness of its power: its maintenance, whether personal or public, required investment, work, more violence. It was never settled, it had to be defended and displayed. Clearly, the power of this patriarch was no guarantee that the son could be subdued.

Adair exemplified the template of loyalist man as a built-body, conjured from a galaxy of superheroes – from Tarzan and Terminator to Rambo and Spartacus. He had entered manhood as a squirt, a paleface who had been nowhere, done nothing. But he went on to fashion himself as a scary body. He invested hard labour in this achieved body, a mass and a surface that announced his aspirations: a man striving for supremacy and dominion in his space, not least the space of his own skin. His bulk and curves – his achievement – made him someone who had to be seen, as compelling as royalty. But his built-body also suggested work, pain, time invested in its production, all for the manufacture of a greater self, a self to be admired by an audience, to be seen (not least by himself). Adair's body represented a triumph of the will, 'mind over body'.

His operations were thrilling excursions that put Adair and his boys in front of a person's house with a gun, diving bullets into the body. The planning would generate great excitement, talk, maps, stolen cars, guns moved from dump to safe house – what has been described by Klaus Thewelweit as 'the wicked bliss of anticipation'.[25] The product would be someone else's shock, pain and blood, or a dead body. The thrill would be doused by a forensic process of denial – washing, incinerating clothes, stripping the evidence from their bodies. Then they would join their apostles and get into boozing and boasting. This was not – as is often implied by their critics – just the unfortunate side effect of the buccaneer's genetic engineering, the way these supposedly cunning but primitive men were wired. On the contrary, havoc had a purpose – control through chaos.[26] The spectacular violence, as with other militias, was functional: the UDA's lore was gendered, its ethos was physical and sensuous, and its violence celebrated 'liberation through destruction'. [27]

Adair didn't go far, he operated within a radius of a few miles in his own city. Insofar as his raids took him into foreign lands, they were only neighbourhoods nearby. Even then, they were as inaccessible to him as the Congo or Tasmania. Here was the truth of it: though this wasn't gang warfare between boys hanging around corners, this was civil war, big stuff, people killed, whole neighbourhoods traumatised by pogroms, the fact was that Adair and his men couldn't occupy that terrain by themselves, still less take it. They could not manage a trail into hostile territory, they could not interpret the terrain, they couldn't get there on their own wits and intelligence, and they couldn't survive there. They were not only intimate enemies of their neighbours, they were strangers. So, they were guided there, or taken, or invisibly chaperoned and guarded by their mentors, the security services. The frisson of risk was also, therefore, the bearer of humiliation. What appeared to be big and impregnable was also fat and subsidised by steroids – just as the contours of Northern Ireland itself, and its extravagant maintenance, depended on the subsidy of a bigger state machine.

If Adair personified the degeneracy of the urban UDA, Billy Wright embodied the UVF bible belt. His milieu was packed with notorious gunslingers, extortionists, robbers and drug dealers. His hinterland, however, was the secluded, militarised holy land of mid-Ulster, and he was a charismatic born-again Christian. He had a neat beard, cropped hair and a gold earring, and his livery was usually laundered denims that housed a lean, statuesque body – another body that demanded attention, that had to be seen. His coterie comprised spectacularly dangerous loyalist gunslingers. He would choreograph his presence as if in a cowboy ballet directed by Sergio Leone. His soubriquet, King Rat, evoked an unsavoury reign that was simultaneously regal and feral. He and his gang were involved with scores of killings, in many of which the security services were implicated. He was opposed to the ceasefire called by the Combined Loyalist Military Command (CLMC) in 1994 (see below), and campaigned against the UVF's joining it. He also criticised the UVF for inaction in the Drumcree showdown of 1995. It was widely reported, and denied, that his most audacious ambushes were chaperoned by Special Branch. One theory is that Wright was a creature of the security services, and that he regularly received security forces' files: 'some of this material was simply delivered through a pre-arranged letter box at the home of UVF sympathisers who were also members of the security forces.' [28]

In 1995 Wright and the mid-Ulster UVF provided a stalwart military presence at Drumcree after the RUC had banned Orangemen from marching down their usual July parade route through the nationalist Garvaghy Road.[29] They forced the RUC to back down and allow the jubilant Ian Paisley and David Trimble to lead the march along the road together. By 1996 the Drumcree controversy was threatening to put the UVF ceasefire in jeopardy, and Billy Hutchinson ordered that Billy Wright and his Portadown men be stood down from the UVF. On the day of the march, however, defiant King Rat Wright commissioned a tractor and digger to go to the site. Rumour raced around Drumcree about the thrilling menace that this farm machine might throw at the soldiers. The slurry-thrower could as easily become a flame-thrower. That did it, the police caved in. Observers recalled Wright's confidence as Drumcree's main man. The sea of Orange militants parted as he strode, wordless, towards the church hall, flanked by his bodyguards, and stationed himself in an upstairs room where he received deputations from constitutional politicians. David Trimble spent an hour up there. [30]

If in 1995 Billy Wright had been an unwitting king-maker – the Orangemen's triumph was vital in the election of David Trimble to the UUP leadership shortly after the march – in 1996 he now became the King. He set up his own dissident Loyalist Volunteer Force.

Journalist Paul Larkin was granted several interviews with Wright, all involving predictably elaborate arrangements and wary dialogue. He noticed an unsettling habit: Wright spoke of himself in the third person. The journalist was safe 'until Billy Wright says different ...'; and 'I will tell you what Billy Wright is happy to tell you ...' When Larkin challenged him that he did not 'live by the Ten Commandments', he became cold: 'Billy Wright is a saved soul who has strayed from the path but who will return to that path. Next question.' Larkin reckoned Wright was 'aware of himself as a concept'. The poise, the stillness, the vigilance, all signified the goals of masculinity as a martial art. Yet they also implied a longing for stoicism and wisdom. The distance between 'I' and 'Billy Wright' also seemed to measure the effort to produce the persona. The unflinching gaze, the fierce handshake, the poise, it was all work. Wright's religiosity enabled him to find the language to translate that distance into rhetoric, as if he was part of his own congregation.

Larkin interpreted the breach between the UVF and the LVF as much more than a butch power struggle. It was an ideological schism between two political cultures: between the metropolis and the countryside and its country towns; between faith-based sectarianism and a secular unionism more interested in national than religious identity; and between those for and against a settlement.

HOW ARE WE GOING TO WORK TOGETHER TO MAKE THIS A NICE WEE ISLAND?

But in spite of this new wave of violence, all over the country people were starting to witness something never seen or heard before: the political voice of unionist militarism walking away from war. While Adair and Wright were ratcheting up the violence, intense debates were raging across the airwaves; working-class protestants were becoming engaged, as never before, and for the first time they were hearing the sound of people who were – themselves.

Dawn Purvis, a young woman living in a protestant enclave in the inner city, remembers it as a life-changing moment: 'In my family we'd never listened to the news, the television was turned off or switched over'. In a household in a staunchly loyalist neighbourhood, her mother adopted a strategy of distraction. 'The news interrupted my mother's flow of things, she liked music, she'd say she didn't want to hear about bombs going off, shootings going on. The news was irritating. We were in the thick of it, but it was never talked about.'

When Purvis heard the new loyalist voices she was fascinated, a feeling that came from a sense of lack, 'our lack of a voice'. What she heard suggested a new kind of political confidence not borne by dominion:

I knew there was a will there. I was smitten by that voice. When the power had been wielded in our community it had been the voice of Paisley, but he only articulated the fears, he didn't articulate the deprivation and the bad housing. Lots of women had the feeling, 'fuck Northern Ireland, put food on my table, and if I don't have the dinner on the table tonight I'm getting another hiding, and he's fighting for his country.'

It was when she heard the men of her own generation, Ervine and Hutchinson, that things changed:

> that was when I started to watch the news. Before that the news never had any debates on social issues, just who was dead. But they were start-ing to talk about how we had to sort out the Troubles. They were ex-paramilitaries and they were saying the country needs to change. That appealed to me. They talked about 'bread and butter issues'. I remember thinking what's 'bread and butter issues'. Billy Hutchinson was being questioned on television and he was saying, 'is this going to improve the housing?' and I remember thinking 'he's good!'

Dawn Purvis had relatives who still didn't have an inside toilet in the house:

> But you didn't speak out against your Unionist government. The best version I ever heard of that was the phrase 'you'd neither in ye nor on ye but we're in power' and that's what prevailed. You didn't speak out because the people who spoke out were catholics. Unionists and loyal-ists said: we can't complain, it's our government.
>
> I knew about the Civil Rights Association in 1969, it was seen as a popish plot, a national uprising. Of course it wasn't, it was catholics and protestants initially together, it was British citizens asking for British rights. If protestants had joined the fight then we wouldn't be where we are today – it would have been a case of our own government taking notice of what I call the peasants revolt, all the working classes together.

Including women. Dawn Purvis was also struck by the confident refer-ence to those tricky words, equality and rights.

Barbara Morton was a young Shankill woman who'd usually voted UUP, but she, too, joined the PUP, because she, too, heard from its advocates something she'd never heard before, people speaking to *her* needs, not for dominion, but for a better life. During the referendum campaign she said:

> They don't want to see any more coffins up the Shankill. The 'No' people weren't the ones carrying the coffins. The PUP laid everything on the line. They said, we're ex-terrorists, we want peace, and we want some-thing *new*, to make change. Why would women like them? We always needed change. Always saying 'no', and saying 'we are the majority', was getting us nowhere fast. I'd have had that position myself: No Surrender! But the nationalists were downtrodden, I'm only starting to think that

now. Why? Well, because I went to a meeting and I heard David Ervine, I don't know why I went, but I did, and I listened to that man. He was saying that the UUP wouldn't talk to Sinn Fein, but that we'd have to, and they were probably thinking along the same lines as us: like, how are we going to work together to make this a nice wee island. I'd never thought like that before, all I'd thought was, we're the majority!

The rush of young men back into the paramilitary organisations in the mid-1980s had rehearsed men's secrecy and segregation: their mobilisation was simultaneously hidden and yet on display. There was in reality a faultline running through the very concept of community. The women who shared the space of community were not consulted when their men went to war against the AIA. This is not to say that neighbourhoods were held in a paralysed thrall to the military men. But these were societies where secrets circulated openly among the men and women's voice was muted.

'I had my suspicions,' recalled the wife of a UDA man living around Lisburn who was arrested at the end of the decade for conspiracy to murder:

> It was the kind of people coming to the house. They were all his friends. He'd been at it three or four years. Football was always the excuse. They sat round the kitchen table having football meetings, while I was upstairs bathing the babies. The radio always played, to drown out their voices. I asked him a couple of times, but the answer was always no. What would I have done if he'd said yes? I'd probably have been angry. But you have to think of his views. He was brought up in a very strict household, very christian, so strict, so hard. He had his views on the political world, I had mine. We never talked about politics.

Then her husband was arrested and charged with aiding and abetting a murder.

> We were told right away, he'd get life. It was death. I was 24 years old. I kept saying 'but you didn't need to join!' ... He thought he had to do something. I didn't ... It made me feel as if he put everybody else before me and his children.

Billy Hutchinson's constituency office in Belfast was run by an Orangewoman, Frances Dunseath, whose husband had also been a loyalist prisoner: 'I didn't have any commitments to the cause. I would probably have fully backed the UVF because they were protestants and they were defending me, but to get involved would never have entered my head.' Once a devout follower of the Rev Ian Paisley, Dunseath came to see him as 'living in a different world'. Her alienation began through her lonely life as a prisoner's wife: 'Paisley's wife didn't have to suffer the way we had to. I'm sure she didn't travel on the Loyalist bus to the prison. I lived on income support, I took three parcels a week.'

Another woman, recalling her 1970s childhood, recalled the misty silences that were imposed both by the militarisation of the neighbourhood, and by the impossibility of women's experience finding a vector:

> there was always an acceptance that there were men who carried out shootings and bombings. People knew who they were, but you didn't talk about it. We knew they were there, I wouldn't say they were protected by them, I'd say the community felt the need of them. When they started killing innocent catholics in the early 1970s it repulsed everybody. But if that had been articulated you'd have been put out of the community. At the start it was men in their 30s, then the boys joined – never the girls – you left school, met a local boy, married him, stayed at home with the kids. He'd probably join something, but you didn't.

If a woman was being battered and the neighbours saw her being thrown out of the house, 'the neighbours went behind their doors'. She remembered one woman who was burned to death after her husband set the house on fire. Everybody knew what had been going on: 'the women in the community were saying "it's *him*", while the men were telling him "sorry for your loss".' Women were excluded from violence in the streets, but not within the home. These exclusions and experiences of violence led some into women's organisations, and sometimes into wider participation in political life.

Hundreds of women's organisations in the north, from across the community divide, networked together through Women Seen and Heard, a reconciliation initiative designed not to bury their differences but to project women's agendas into the peace process. This organisation was one of the unheralded peace initiatives, that has never been accorded its weight in the work of creating a social base for the peace process, a constituency that wanted more than an end to war, and more than stability. Its aim was the reform of a conservative, patriarchal and brutalised society.

For many unionist women all this was a huge risk. Even in the context of the ceasefires, the mid-1990s were still dangerous times. In summer

1996, a time of drift in the peace process, when within loyalism the focus was on a riotous marching season, a women's centre in Belfast was regularly thrown into crisis. It was a protestant group, but it employed some catholic workers, and during the marching season the women could not guarantee that catholic workers would be safe. The ordinary traffic of everyday life became impossible. That generated a big debate within the centre: should it close during the marching season – the *men's* marching season. If 1996 was a spectacular triumph for the Orangemen and their praetorian guards, it brought spectacular humiliation to these women. The loyalist workers couldn't guarantee the safety of their own colleagues, and nor could they guarantee the normal service, or even the survival, of their community centre. This left women with a kind of ache: 'you feel powerless to sort things out. Where do you start?'

A couple of years after the ceasefires, Windsor Women's Centre in a loyalist neighbourhood in Belfast hosted a visit by Mary Robinson. Robinson had already visited nationalist neighbourhoods in the north, most famously during the West Belfast Festival (see pp41–3). Now she took the opportunity to engage with loyalist women. Though the women's centre knew she would not be welcome in their neighbourhood, they wanted her to come. She was interested in them, and they were interested in her, too. This was a big thing for them. No one – except perhaps the Queen – could better confer the legitimacy they needed. The President's visit was again obstructed. Whitehall didn't want her to go. But, as on the previous occasion, women guarded her and guided her into the community. When she arrived at the Women's Centre Robinson was confronted by a hostile demonstration outside. She got into the building, met the women and then left. She was safe. But the other women weren't. The demonstration got bigger and more frightening. That night the centre was torched. Staff and their homes were threatened. 'These people were our friends, we knew these people personally', they recalled.

But they could scarcely engage the police. After taking evidence of the threats, the police response was 'we warned you this could happen'. Women's centres around the city rallied, and volunteers came in to clear up the rubble – and users still turned up to use their services:

> There's a lot of talk about us being *with* the community. We were – with some parts of the community. When people came back there were no lights in the building and they were climbing over rubble to get their children to the creche and to their classes. We interpreted that as support. But nothing got said, because things don't get said. Because saying things could put people in danger.

CEASEFIRES

For almost a decade the violence seemed to all but overwhelm the efforts within loyalism to find a progressive settlement. After the assassination of UDA leader John McMichael in 1987, and his comrade Andy Tyrie's retreat from the UDA to safety, new activists took over their attempts to craft a political strategy. McMichael and Tyrie had been monitoring, and trying to match, Sinn Fein's extraordinary and unexpected political capital gained from the hunger strikes, followed by their entrance into political society. After his father's death, McMichael's nineteen-year-old son Gary stood as a candidate for the United Loyalist Democratic Party (ULDP) – recognised by everyone as the political wing of the UDA. Together with the party's Davy Adams (later a leading pro-Agreement campaigner), he was interested in distancing loyalism from the DUP and the UUP, and in airing the ideas from *Commonsense* within a political party. 'For years equality and civil rights was seen to be a cloak to undermine the constitution', explained Davy Adams. 'Mention equality and human rights and there was a natural aversion, not to the concept but as a disguise for something else. They thought of them as gains for nationalism; we said they're rights and liberties for everyone.' Adams's experience of living in a rural community on the edge of unionist Lisburn, one of ten children, had given him 'a firm attachment to the socio-economic realities – they'd not been addressed, the constitutional issue had been used as a smokescreen to avoid dealing with the bread and butter issues'. Adams also believed that unionism's obsessions and protestant fundamentalism obscured what he admired about Britain, its complexity as a 'multi-cultural, multi-lingual, multi-religious society.'

By the mid 1980s the PUP had also adopted a programme that promoted a new culture of rights and socialism, and before the end of the decade Ervine and the PUP were approached by the UVF to explore political room for manoeuvre. Spence was pushing hard for a cessation of violence at this time. They established a 'kitchen cabinet', an intense, small, partnership, which logged the way that political space was being expanded by Sinn Fein and by the then Secretary of State, Peter Brooke (see pp36–40). They believed that a joint initiative would provide mutual protection and mutual benefit. In the early 1990s the Combined Loyalist Military Command was born, which brought together the leaderships of the paramilitaries. Spence urged it to be bold, to show that violence was not the only modus operandi of the militias, and to show it in the most surprising way: by calling a ceasefire.

The first ceasefire lasted only six weeks, ending when new Secretary of State Sir Patrick Mayhew stopped the talks initiated by Brooke. But it was a turning point. It introduced into the loyalist mind the idea that withdrawal from war could advance their political prospects. Ervine often referred to it as 'the theory of ceasefire'. And loyalism's bunkered isolation was breached somewhat when they began to meet republican and socialist community activists north and south of the border, and when they were contacted by the ubiquitous priest of the peace process, Father Alec Reid. They became close to activists around the Workers Party, whose leftism was also markedly anti-republican. They also met Irish-American trade unionists and business people visiting Northern Ireland to check out progress on equality, and had confidantes with access to both the Irish government and Sinn Fein. These kept the CLMC alert to the Irish government's thinking and to Sinn Fein's anticipated ceasefire in 1994.

But the kitchen cabinet was sorely tested during 1993 and 1994 by gross UVF violence. And these inauspicious outbreaks were compounded by reluctance within the UVF to relinquish their ample arsenal, and by the organisation's failure to consult UVF prisoners. The UDA, with a less hierarchal formal structure, was busily visiting its own prisoners – encouraged by the NIO – to canvass and encourage their support for a ceasefire. This paid off. Even Johnny Adair, who had arrived at the prison while the CLMC was presenting its conditions for a ceasefire, was in favour. His lover at the time Jackie Robinson, remembered him complaining about the peace talks. 'He was really giving it rock on,' she told journalists. 'I says to him, "Johnny why don't you go away and why don't you sit and think. Think".' He did, and he decided "I'll go for it".' [31]

When the republican ceasefire came at the end of August 1994 it attracted a medley of triumphalism and suspicion among unionists, and the CLMC was not yet ready to respond in kind. But on 13 October 1994 the CLMC proclaimed its own ceasefire at Fernhill House – the hugely significant site where, eighty years earlier, 30,000 protestant men had mustered to fight with Sir Edward Carson. The CLMC gave to Gusty Spence the privilege of reading their text. It affirmed that the union was safe, that loyalist volunteers had not therefore died in vain, and it offered – on his insistence – 'abject and true remorse' to the loved ones of innocent victims. These loyalists were joining the world. They had toiled to bring their organisations to this point. The CLMC was also reminded, however, that though – as the proclamation declared – the power to stop making war and to make peace lay with the warriors, the unionist leadership still wasn't talking to them. And neither was the British government.

The declaration of ceasefire – which meant relinquishing the source of their relative autonomy – 'received no reciprocal gesture', said PUP councillor Plum Smith. 'Neither the DUP nor the UUP felt the need to engage with loyalism.' That was when the CLMC understood that loyalism needed to present its own political programme and representatives. [32] When talks began, the abstention of the DUP made the former combatants indispensable to the UUP, as they emerged from their claustrophobic milieux, and began to engage with nervous civil servants.

During the preparation of the Downing Street Declaration of 1993 and then the Framework documents in 1995, the Reynolds government in the Republic reached out to protestant organisations and churches to reassure them that they had nothing to fear. Though the British were not in dialogue with the parties close to the paramilitaries, the Irish government was; and, through intermediaries, the PUP fed to Reynolds's team their proposals on equal opportunities for the Downing Street Declaration and later for the Framework documents. The response of the DUP and the UUP to these initiatives was predictably negative. But the response of the parties close to the paramilitaries, the UDP and the PUP, was a less predictable yes. They went on saying yes, up to, during and after the final Agreement.

Their grip on the militias was, however, inevitably more and more precarious over time. After the Agreement it was the loyalist militias, rather the republicans, that were most reluctant to disarm. And the PUP particularly came feel that the feuding and gangsterism of the post-ceasefire militias forfeited support in the 2003 election for the smaller 'progressive' loyalist parties. Indeed the International Monitoring Commission fined the PUP following the feuding and almost bankrupted the party. But it was the fate of the Agreement itself that grieved many of its most enthusiastic advocates. 'The peace was never in question', said Plum Smith, 'but the Agreement was under threat'. The loyalist parties had made themselves indispensable to unionism;[33] but after the referendum 'pro-Agreement unionism walked away from the Agreement'.

NOTES

1. Thomas Carlyle, *The French Revolution, A History*, 1837.
2. Margaret Ward, *Unmanageable Revolutionaries: Women and Irish Nationalism*, Pluto 1995.
3. M. O'Callaghan & C. O'Donnell, 'The Northern Ireland Government, the "Paisleyite Movement" and Ulster Unionism in 1966', *Irish Political Studies*, Vol 21, No 2, 203-222, Routledge 2006.
4. O'Callaghan and O'Donnell, op cit.
5. Jonathon Bardon, 'O'Neill warned his cabinet but he was swept away', *Irish Times*, 3.1.00.

6. The documents were first reported by Justice for the Forgotten and the Pat Finucane Centre, *Irish News*, 2-4 May 2006.

7. Robert Fisk, *The Point of No Return*, Times Books 1975.

8. This is Judith Jones' insight and I'm not only grateful for it but greatly influenced by it.

9. See O'Callaghan and O'Donnell, op cit. See also Susan McKay's eloquent insights in *Northern Protestants, An Unsettled People*, Blackstaff 2000.

10. See B. Campbell, *Goliath: Britain's Dangerous Places*, Methuen 1993; R.W. Connell, *Masculinities*, op cit; and J. Messerschmidt, *Masculinities and Crime*, Rowman & Littlefield 1993.

11. Roy Garland, *Gusty Spence*, Blackstaff 2001, p54.

12. H. Sinnerton, *David Ervine – Uncharted Waters*, Brandon 2003; Garland, op cit; and C. Crawford, *Defenders or Criminals: Loyalist Prisoners and Criminalisation*, Blackstaff Press 1999.

13. Sinnerton, op cit, p37.

14. Ibid.

15. Colin Crawford, op cit.

16. Garland, op cit, pp216-217.

17. Margaret Thatcher, *The Downing Street Years*, HarperCollins 1993, p 402.

18. Brendan O'Leary and John McGarry, *The Politics of Antagonism*, Athlone Press 1996, p240.

19. O'Leary and McGarry, op cit, p 240.

20. F. Cochrane, *Unionist Politics and the Politics of Unionism Since the Anglo-Irish Agreement*, Cork University Press 1996, p142.

21. E. Moloney & A. Pollack, *Paisley*, Poolbeg 1986, p438.

22. Cochrane, op cit, p230.

23. T.P. Coogan, *The Troubles: Ireland's Ordeal and the Search for Peace, 1966-1996*, Arrow 1996, p310.

24. David Lister and Hugh Jordan, *Mad Dog, the Rise and Fall of Johnny Adair and his C Company*, Mainstream 2003, p113.

25. K. Theweleit, *Male Fantasies*, Vol 1, Polity Press 1995, p182.

26. Messerschmidt, op cit; Campbell, op cit.

27. Theweleit, *Male Fantasies*, Vol 2, p201.

28. P. Larkin, *A Very British Jihad*, Beyond the Pale 2004, p233.

29. For more on Drumcree, and the involvement of Rosemary Nelson, see pp250–2.

30. Peter Taylor, *Loyalists*, Bloomsbury 1999, p241.

31. Lister and Jordan, op cit, p233.

32. Aaron Edwards and Stephen Bloomer, 'The Political Strategy of Progressive Loyalism Since 1994', *Conflict Transformation Papers – No 8*, LINC Resource Centre 2004.

33. Ibid.

7. The Republicans come in from the cold

BODY POLITICS

In the British imagination, the prisoner was a proxy for the intolerable mystique of the republican movement, and more generally the Irish as a people: the prisoner represented everything – their stamina and their suffering, their bodies, their poetry, their pleasures, and, of course, their resistance. At the same time envied and untouchable, the Irish foxed Britain: it did not understand what it was that the Irish wanted so much, what they felt they had lost. It could or would not reason why republicans thought that rights were worth everything. But these were the people with whom eventually the British would have to do business.

No one in these islands was more marginalised than Irish women in general and catholics in the north until the electrifying convulsions of the civil rights movement. It was one of those historic moments when the denigrated re-define themselves, and the mighty deploy any available legal and illegal violence against them. Force subsequently came to acquire a quasi-sacred status for republicanism, not from a love of it – though no doubt the elixir of violence in a macho culture should never be underestimated – but because resistance met overwhelming force in the north and modern republicanism never forgave itself for its unreadiness, for its failure to protect catholic communities from the shock of the pogroms in the early 1970s. Violence emptied the space of politics, terrified the citizens and instantly created a generation of political prisoners. In no time there were a thousand of them. They were ordinary, they were everywhere, there was scarcely a working-class neighbourhood without them; but they were ordinary people who, as well as the capacity for making a useful life, discovered a talent for resistance.

Republican prisoners transformed the iconography of the body in men's politics, none more than the grainy smiling portrait of the emaciated Bobby Sands – Che Guevara without the cigar, and without victory. They deployed bodies that were humiliated and vulnerable as weapons, transforming their incarceration into an arena, where the distance between their own helpless skin and the hard concrete of their cells disappeared into surfaces covered in shit: if their bodies were despised, they would disperse the disgust.

When the Labour government abolished political status in 1976, the prisoners converted their category into another sphere of struggle. They refused to submit, wear prison uniform, clean out their cells; they wore nothing, they flung their slops as missiles, and when the windows were barricaded they splattered their slurry everywhere. When they were allowed out of their cells they wore only a blanket. They stank, their cells stank, the prison stank. The women prisoners in Armagh organised their own 'dirty protest', too, in 1980, and smeared their menstrual blood on the walls.

They infused the atmosphere with the scent of waste, wasted time, wasted bodies, wasted spaces. They were giving back to their hosts the contempt in which they were held. By covering their space in shit they inverted the representation of the Irish as shit. They languished naked all day, exposing themselves to their guards as the 'fearful bodies' the guards believed them to be.[1]

They could live with the worst of themselves; and this was a way of saying that, whatever anyone thought of them, they were more than the worst of themselves. They would not become the disappeared ones. They smuggled their news out on scraps of paper hidden under foreskins, under tongues, up their rectums – the most demonised of men telling their story through the most denigrated orifice. They told any amount of stories. During the interminable lightless nights they shouted to each other the stories of books they'd read, they talked and talked, filling the space with the sound of themselves. They created *presence*. It was ghostly, faded and filthy, and it was eerily invincible. There were at any one time more than three hundred men involved in the dirty protest, and their presence, their bodies, their stories, their smell, defined the atmosphere of the prison. So, in their tomb they were cultural revolutionaries. They'd 'seized the means of cultural expression'.[2] These people could survive, day in day out, like soldiers in seeping trenches, sharing their arid bunkers with other beings, creepy crawlies, maggots, who wandered in and out of their mushy warmth. The prisoners' bodies were the only hospitable surface in the place.

The man the prisoners called Sagairt Mor, the forthright Cardinal O'Fiaich, who was an unusually faithful member of the catholic hierarchy, visited Long Kesh in 1978 and said that what he'd seen reminded him of 'the spectacle of hundreds of homeless people living in sewer pipes in the slums of Calcutta'. Tim Pat Coogan, a chronicler as well as a participant in those times, visited the prisoners and recorded his encounter with men who were naked save for their blanket, who 'stood silently, fear hardening into defiance'.[3] Coogan was haunted by the encounter. It was the most shocking experience of his life, he said – until he visited the women locked up in Armagh.

Abolition of political status was expected to produce resistance, perhaps a fight to the death. In January 1976, the NIO decided that force-feeding would not be applied and, therefore, 'this may well result in prisoners being allowed to die'. Another report received by the MoD urged the government not to be squeamish, 'we should not be unduly sensitive in our treatment'. [4]

Abolition was accompanied by the construction of the H-Blocks, the most modern, high tech, high security compound in Europe, jails within jails, a confusion of identical walls and shapes, or 'steriles' and 'inertias', built to maximise immobilisation, surrounded by a moat, concrete walls, fences, razor wire. The entire complex was topped by control towers. Seamus Sweeney, in his discussion of 'British Army Gothic', the militarised landscape of Northern Ireland, rates the Maze as 'British Army Gothic Triumphant'.[5]

By the end of 1970s the dirty protest was in difficulty, confronted by a new and implacable enemy – Margaret Thatcher. The 1980s began with a new tactic, hunger strikes. This had a long tradition, used by powerless people across England's empire.

Now it released the republicans from political quarantine. The prisoners, the most sequestered people, lived a paradox: they were confined to the most private life, but in a thoroughly public place, under perpetual scrutiny. Their narrative walked through walls. Their campaign created a crisis for the governments in Dublin and London. It alarmed the Pope, presidents and politicians in the US and Europe. Margaret Thatcher was unmoved and within Parliament she was comforted by a cross-party alliance, led by Labour's veteran leader of the left Michael Foot and the liberal leader David Steel. Their complicity was an index of Parliament's alienation from the Irish.

If the campaign had a moment of good fortune it was an inspired idea that Bobby Sands should stand as the H Blocks candidate in the April 1981 Parliamentary by-election in Fermanagh. Sands won the election by 30,492 votes to the Unionist candidate's 29,046. The prisoners' campaign had got the republicans into politics.

PRISON POLITICS

The struggle in the prisons may have seemed to yield little movement, but it was, nonetheless, a life and death struggle. Internment dominated the prison politics of the early 1970s, but it was political status that dominated the late 1970s and 1980s. An entire community of men found themselves in a situation for which their experience and history *as men* left them unprepared: nakedness, the prying eyes and fingers of people wielding power, the potency of their gaze, the penetration of every orifice. Out of that vulnerability they had to find some strength. Brendan McFarlane (known as Bik) co-ordinated the 1981 hunger strike. He recalled:

> You could find yourself brought into an area, stripped, 12 other men making fun of you, holding you down, probing you, say in an anal search, you were totally vulnerable.

Unionist men wielded absolute personal dominion:

> It didn't matter how strong you were, you couldn't physically resist. You could only steel your resolve mentally, and this was an essential part of the struggle – if they succeed you lose, you lose everything. Some of the screws appeared to enjoy it – the vast majority were from loyalist or unionist backgrounds, and we were republicans who they were intent on destroying. They were there to break us. Some of them took to it with relish.

McFarlane's correspondence with Sinn Fein President Gerry Adams, transmitted on smuggled cigarette papers, is one of the important social documents of the armed conflict. So, too, is the account of it by David Beresford in *Ten Men Dead*, perhaps one of the most poignant texts of the conflict, where McFarlane is described as 'a surprisingly gentlemanly character'. McFarlane had been in the last year of his studies at seminary when the conflict exploded. He denies any priestliness, however, in his brisk account. 'I was studying at the seminary in the 1960s, came out in mid 1970, that was the end of that.' Religion, he says, was not what animated his position: 'My area, Ardoyne, was coming under attack. What animated me was the defence of my area against attacks by the RUC.' He was arrested for the horrific and bloody attack on the Bayardo Bar in Shankill Road, which killed five people. He had wanted to join the hunger strike, but he didn't, because his record would have been a 'public relations disaster'.

Despite their isolation:

Whenever anyone was brutalised we would publicise it, we'd use legal battles. This was important because before that, in the 1970s, the republican movement was on the streets, primarily a military machine for attacking the British state. The republican movement was focused nearly exclusively on the IRA. Sinn Fein was generally treated as the poor relation of the republican movement, almost a dirty word.

The prisoners wanted to be present in the political sphere, which was not the main focus of republicans. McFarlane argues that this concentration on the military had been made in reaction to the shift to the political during the civil rights movement, which had left republicans unable to defend catholic communities from violence:

> That was blamed on the move towards political struggle, attempting to reform Stormont. So it was a black and white analysis. It was very difficult to develop a political struggle. But it was necessary. You can militarily bang away and achieve nothing. There needs to be action in the community. But that wasn't developing until – for me – the hunger strikes and Bobby Sands' election victory.

McFarlane believed that, 'from the blanket protest to the hunger strikes … the foundations were laid upon which republican politics were built – that was completely and utterly the direct result'.

When the hunger strikers ended the 271 days of their collective fast in October 1981, they knew they were not defeated: they were embarking on a new phase – the resumption of their priorities, education and escape. 'What we needed to do was to effect a proper regime conducive to developing the republican family in the prison, to develop our politics and our culture.' McFarlane was unusual. He was already educated person.

His comrade Gerry Kelly was unusual, too, he'd had a job. These men nonetheless exemplified the prisoners' journey. During Kelly's sentence his education took him to places he would never otherwise have ventured intellectually. He read Adam Smith and Karl Marx, Frantz Fanon and James Connolly, and he read the feminist novelists and polemicists Marilyn French and Marge Piercy. Years later Kelly rated Piercy's *Woman on the Edge of Time,* a novel of pain and futuristic transcendence, as one of the best books he'd ever read. The young men in prison assimilated more feminist politics in the education they received inside than their contemporaries did on the outside.

THE BEAUTIFUL GENERATION

During the election campaign following the Agreement children would stop Gerry Kelly in the street in his North Belfast constituency, the site of the greatest number of deaths during the conflict. 'Are you Gerry Kelly?' they would ask. 'Yes,' he'd reply. They are ecstatic and stand, staring. The tall man holds out his hands and shakes their thrusting paws. 'Hello Mr Kelly', they say, before rushing down the street to tell everyone about their famous friend. What made Kelly a celebrity in his community was what made him notorious in other circles – and what made him a necessary face in negotiations. Peter Taylor reckoned that Downing Street had no doubt that when it was talking with Kelly and McGuinness it was talking to the Provisionals' Army Council; and that Number 10 believed that 'there was no point in talking to anyone else'.

Gerry Kelly was one of the Old Bailey bombers – together with the sisters Marian and Dolours Price and Hugh Feeney. This gang of four were all young and bonnie, and had they been born in Liverpool or London they would have belonged to the beautiful generation, wearing long hair, loons, zapata moustaches, Biba frocks. But they were born in a bad place.

Their allure came from gender, two boys and the soldierly radiance of the Price sisters. But the sisters retained an implacable commitment to a united Ireland above all else, and Dolours Price would not forgive Kelly his later support for Sinn Fein's journey into the peace process and the Agreement. 'I respected and admired the boy I went to jail with', she said thirty years later. 'I'm baffled, he was a great lad, and I could never have foreseen an outcome such as him as an upholder of British rule'.[6]

Kelly remained devilishly handsome. 'No man deserves to be so good looking', declared an American diplomat. Rumours of romance swirled around the man when he was released from prison, but they also swelled his enemies' fantasies: the Rev Ian Paisley claimed that MI5 had reported to the NIO secret rendezvous between Kelly and Martha Pope, chief of staff to George Mitchell. Pope successfully sued. Not only was she not having an affair, she'd never even met the man.

Gerry Kelly was to catholic popular culture what John Mills or Steve McQueen were to British and American popular culture – the great escaper. In each decade of the conflict he made a spectacular exit. In 1972 he escaped from Dublin's fortress, Mountjoy. He was one of the 38 men (including McFarlane) who escaped from the H Blocks in 1983. And in 1998 he escaped in handcuffs from an RUC jeep after being arrested during a sit-down protest against the Orange Order's annual Tour of the North. (Kelly had been present at the sit-down as the elected representative, but that hadn't stopped him being thrown into a jeep and handcuffed. He got out and ran to a house where a friend cut the cuffs with a grinder. Then he went back.)

Kelly was also to become emblematic of republicanism's transition from war to politics. In their incarnation as ex-prisoners, Kelly and McFarlane spread into republicanism's community activism – a belated engagement in a form of politics that had been, until the 1980s, almost exclusively sustained by women. (This was an ancient division of labour – men did war, women largely did the community's politics.) A human rights advocate who knew the republicans well reckoned that their enemies never understood what motivated the ex-prisoners: 'their passion was that they really loved their community. With their communities they are completely at one. The Adams generation shared an ethos. It took different expressions, but to them that commitment was what you do – or die, or kill.' Their enemies were missing the point to argue that Sinn Fein was only the IRA in civvies, that they were all warriors, or rather murderers. Militarism may have given them the gleam of certainty, and their discipline. But it was not the fact that the prisoners had been deadly in the past that made them dangerous now. It had not been their action, but the nigh-impossibility of political action, that had taken them to prison. Now, however much constitutional unionism might huff and puff, there was no escaping the ex-prisoners in the peace process – by engaging in non-violent politics they had decided to be dangerous differently.

DEATH TO LIFE – CREATING THE NEW PARADIGM

The hunger strikes might have given global resonance to republicans, but they did not resolve their internal, institutional exile. They were still displaced persons. They were not without resources, of course: they could bomb, they could defend, they could organise. But the military campaign had been conducted at the expense of the political. If politics is the art of peaceful conflict, they had few places in which to acquire its arts.

Institutionally, they were hated. They had no champions, no institutional existence; and that meant, in a sense, they were nowhere. By contrast the equality movement, which did not engage in armed struggle, regarded the project as the means of radical intervention in the society – *any* society. Republicanism did not yet have a strategy for the transformation of the society. *The enemies of both never understood this distinction.* After the hunger strikes, engagement, rather than abstention, was vital and that was now the republicans' radical turn.

The secret manoeuvres that brought Sinn Fein out from the cold have been chronicled with verve by Adams himself, and by Tim Pat Coogan. And there are many other indispensable accounts – including those by Eamonn Mallie and David McKittrick, Brendan O'Leary and Ed Moloney's surprisingly bitter tale. The secrets of the process were not really revealed until the time of the Agreement, but there were glimmers of what was happening during the 1990s – usually through leaks disclosing the supposed scandal of contact with the demons. Sinn Fein was still banned from the airwaves, after all, and they still lived in an exclusion zone. A medley of Irish voices created the historic détente – priests, nationalists on both sides of the border, diplomats from Dublin to Washington, all were involved in the creation of a conversation (it could hardly be called a coalition, and sometimes not even a consensus). This conversation was absolutely new. It created a new Ireland paradigm, it changed everything.

It began with confidential conversations between old friends – Gerry Adams and two priests, Des Wilson and Alec Reid. Reid's Redemptorist community gave him relative autonomy from the church hierarchy and a mandate to facilitate dialogue in the service of peace. Sinn Fein's continuing commitment to the armed struggle was understood, but the project was to work out what conflict resolution might mean. Republicans, Adams told the church, had 'as much right to peace as anyone'. He told Fr Reid he'd do dialogue with anyone, and the priest – known as the Sagart – gave himself to improvising diplomacy, discovering routes, bridges, spaces, identifying emissaries and alliances. The republicans were still excluded from official dialogue, and the Brighton bombing had sealed their exile. Thatcher had seen the Dublin-London dialogue as a way of completing their exclusion. But Fr Reid saw in dialogue another life.

So did John Hume. What those involved in the dialogue sought was some declaration of intent by the British, a statement of neutrality on Northern Ireland's status, and the option of Irish self-determination based on the views of the majority. Hume held to this tenaciously. He could be scathing about Sinn Fein, seeing them as the IRA's subalterns; 'one of these days Sinn Fein will disappear up their own contradictions', he complained. But when Reid invited Hume to talk to Sinn Fein in 1986 he readily agreed. That began a historic dialogue that came to be known as the Hume-Adams initiative in deference to Hume. For his part, Adams admired Hume's readiness to break through the cordon sanitaire.

Adams's coterie knew from the beginning that he was involved in the dialogue. Although the talks were secret, they were sanctioned by

Sinn Fein's Ard Chohairle (party conference). Adams and his colleagues – most importantly Mitchell McLaughlin – were becoming engaged in the business of building a mass party. (McLaughlin was never an IRA man, always a Sinn Feiner; he was credited with its metamorphosis from neglected rump to mass party.)

Though the aftermath of the AIA had been bloody, in 1987 Sinn Fein's peace prospectus finally took shape. Their *Scenario for Peace* proposed an all-Ireland constitutional conference, with the participation of civil society; and it invited loyalists to throw in their lot with the rest of the Irish people. As if to pre-empt opposition to a catholic constitution, it recognised social realities: for example it acknowledged that there would need to be provisions for family planning and the right to civil divorce. The prospectus was both grandiose, and underdeveloped. But it was a beginning.

If Sinn Fein had to mount a great case to persuade the Army Council, the former prisoners, as a community, were uniquely important to the party's political trajectory. They had not created republicanism's practice of politics: they'd been absent, they'd been *away*, and their absence had relieved them of the stress of everyday life and the burden of inventing politics for inhospitable institutions. They'd often gone into prison as brave ingénues, but many had returned to their neighbourhoods empowered and educated; they'd often gone away as teenagers, and were now re-entering a universe that was transformed by new relationships and political possibilities, largely excavated by the women they'd left.

Thousands of other former prisoners gave to Sinn Fein's embryonic political culture the blessing of an awesome reputation. They needed a political life no less than they needed a 'normal' life. Prisoners who had been committed to war now found themselves busy at advice centres, navigating the benefit system, housing politics, motorway campaigns, 'dealing with issues we'd never been able to deal with'. There were former prisoners in every aspect of the struggle, and in every aspect of this society, said Kelly.

In their transition from the military to the political, the former prisoners believed that they understood *before* the British that there had to be a settlement at the level of politics, 'the British had to scramble to deal with it as a political problem'. Their dialogue with their communities implied a more complex republican conversation than the dominant narrative representing Adams as dragging the military men reluctantly towards non-violence. The military men weren't only the IRA or members of the Army Council; they were also those being released from prison. And though the former prisoners may have been shunned by the constitutional parties – may have been unemployable – they didn't need to apologise to their communities. For them the prisoners' suffering and passion contributed to their social capital.

For Bik McFarlane, the prospect of political – rather than military – activism was a gift. He believed that republicanism did not lose by not being militarily engaged. 'I don't feel I lost anything – people like me, and others working in the communities, have had the opportunity to gain from political progress. It's a political struggle, not a military struggle.' These were men who'd been prepared to kill and die for their people. The beginning of the peace process, amplified by a transformative agenda, encouraged them to believe that they now need do neither. 'I'm glad I survived', says Kelly. Politics had released another kind of engagement within their society, 'pushing hope back into it'.

The two nationalist parties met in 1988 – they lived in the same neighbourhoods, they knew each other's faces, and yet they were unknown to each other. Unionism was outraged, but they kept talking for the next six months. Sinn Fein, primarily working-class, surprised the SDLP with its papers and research and energy for refining documents and ideas; the SDLP, more middle-class, surprised Sinn Fein with its lack of follow-up. The talks were tough. Sometimes very rough. But they kept talking, and Adams reassured republicans habituated to the mantra 'our selves alone' that there could be life after dialogue, and that 'dialogue between consenting adults may be good for each other'.

This was the beginning of the end of Sinn Fein's isolation, and the beginning of the long march to a constitutional settlement. Reid enlisted his old friend Tim Pat Coogan, and Cardinal Thomas O'Fiach, Bishop of Armagh, to make contact with the Dublin government. Taoiseach Charles Haughey's adviser Martin Mansergh now began his role as an enduring and stringent participant in the process. In 1991 he distilled Hume's conversations with Sinn Fein, and he and Sean O'hUiggin (and, later, the Irish ambassador in Washington) artfully finessed the texts that, with creative ambiguities – some would say contradictions – later emerged as the Agreement.

SURVIVING THE PICADORS

While Peter Brooke was Secretary of State he re-instated secret contacts between MI5 and republican intermediaries, and between a British government representative and Martin McGuinness and Gerry Kelly. The republicans insisted on a signed document confirming that the contacts had been sanctioned at 'the top'. And they kept records, which were vital, as it turned out. On the eve of publication of the

Downing Street Declaration (see p46), mutiny within the Establishment produced a crisis, and the British then denied that there had been communication. However, they soon had to confess. Sinn Fein scoured its archives and found the records. 'I think they just thought we didn't keep records,' said Gerry Kelly. 'They'd probably have been right ten years before. These people have run colonies for hundreds of years. They think "we are the British government, you must believe us". They came out with lies and they expected them to be swallowed.' But they weren't. After the British admitted the contact, the government tried to re-interpret its origins, and Brooke's successor Mayhew presented to the House of Commons Library a chronicle that implied that the British had merely responded to an IRA request for help. But the Sinn Fein records revealed that the British had initiated the process, that the MI5 link had secured agreement on the timing of a ceasefire and talks with Sinn Fein and the British government, only to have the timetable crashed by the Cabinet. The British records were created as if to pre-empt posterity's verdict and to provide cover for the government in the event of disclosure. [7]

Patrick Mayhew was no Peter Brooke. His priority was to defeat the seemingly indefatigable enemy, and in the wake of the 1994 ceasefire disarmament became a proxy for defeat of the demons.

Kelly learned that British politicians were briefing journalists about him, suggesting something sinister. 'They put nonsense out about me in the talks in 1994, that I never said anything. What's that got to do with them?' It was, of course, a signifier of his reputation as a warrior; a status that was mobilised in British rumours in order to overshadow the importance both of reputation – heroism as a resource – and of the soldiers' transition from waging war to making peace. The story of this generation of former protagonists was also a story of what makes men change. It was not a narrative of defeat.

If it was important to the peace process to deny the IRA membership of Adams and McGuiness, it was equally important to assert, by Gerry Kelly's presence, the Army Council's endorsement. Kelly knew the symbolism of his participation: 'I can say I *was* in the IRA. The difference between me and people who have not been in jail is that people know my background – there is respect for that here, this is a highly politicised community'. Just as the British government had its mandate 'Sinn Fein had a mandate in the worst of circumstances. Very few have the mandate we have.'

The intelligence man who had participated in the secret contacts between the British and the republicans, Michael Oatley, later wrote a chagrined critique: the Conservative government's behaviour had been 'an example of picadorism at its most provocative'. It had put the pro-peace elements of republicanism under pressure, and then when the republicans overcame that problem the government 'found a new excuse to avoid the pursuit of peace – the de-commissioning impasse'.[8]

Disarmament was not written into the 1998 Agreement, and when it was invoked again and again, to stall republicans' inclusion in the new executive, Oatley took the remarkable step of intervening in the public debate: 'de-commissioning is presented as the central issue in the peace process. It is not,' he wrote. The IRA's volunteers 'are not sheep'. 'All of them joined to pursue an armed campaign for agreed objectives, which have now been modified. Discipline in the face of such changes has been remarkable.' But once more 'the picadors' were having an effect.

Picadorism rose again in 2002, when a so-called republican spy ring was 'unmasked' by the PSNI at Stormont. Kelly reckoned that had the police stormed Westminster and brought down its elected parliament 'it would have been a world-wide crisis'. But this was Belfast. He was in the office when jeeps began to line the avenue leading to the assembly building and police swarmed up the steps. 'We had what was supposed to be a parliament. The police were doing what you only see in dictatorships, taking over the building. A political decision made by a cop brought down an elected assembly.' He rushed to the entrance. 'I went up to the television crews outside and I said "come in". The cops tried to stop me, I said: "*I* am an elected representative to this building, *you* get out."' Bairbre de Brun, Sinn Fein's health minister, and Kelly watched as the police and the press poured into the building and left with three Sinn Fein staff under arrest and two computer disks. The disks were handed back to Sinn Fein a couple of days later but the three men were held until the end of 2004 when suddenly the prosecution was abandoned, and the men were released. One of them, Denis Donaldson, soon afterwards admitted that he had been a British agent within Sinn Fein for more than two decades. His function had been to report to MI5 and Special Branch.

Special Branch chief Bill Lowry had organised that raid. 'It was a scam and a fiction', said Donaldson. There never was a spy ring at Stormont. The exposure of Donaldson shocked republicans to the core. But if it was expected to have a ruinous effect on their reputation it also released the conclusion that the British had orchestrated a coup. 'The only certainty in the Stormontgate affair is that the only spy working at Stormont was a British one.'[9] It was believed that the decisive moment in the collapse of the prosecution was when it asked for a public immunity certificate and, unusually, it was denied.

'From that moment the prosecution case was dead in the water.'[10] When the Assembly and the executive were restored in 2007 loyalist ex-combatants and former prisoners watched their mandate shrivel, but the republican volunteers who had been part of the transition into the political arena witnessed Sinn Fein establish its democratic hegemony within nationalism. Of the 27 republicans elected to the Assembly in 2007 12 were former prisoners. Picadorism may still have been loitering the security state, but Gerry Kelly was appointed minister of justice.

NOTES

1. Iris Marion Young, 1990, op cit, p11.
2. Ibid.
3. Coogan, op cit, p267.
4. 'Whitehall's Secret Plan to let the IRA hunger strikers die', *The Times*, 4.1.05.
5. Seamus Sweeney, 'The Maze', *nthposition* online magazine 2003.
6. Dolours Price, in *The Blanket*, 17.7.04.
7. Sir Patrick Mayhew's version and Sinn Fein's version of the narratives can be compared in the House of Commons Library. Sinn Fein's chronicle is fuller and offers a compelling alternative narrative, later confirmed by one of the trusted go-betweens, Dennis Bradley.
8. Michael Oatley, 'Forget the Weapons and start to Trust Sinn Fein', *Sunday Times*, 31.10.99.
9. Colm Heatley and Paul T. Colgan, 'Questions left unanswered after "outing" of British Spy', *Sunday Business Post*, 18.12.05.
10. Ibid.

PART III

SPACE AND SECTARIANISM

8. The blockade of Holy Cross

Nothing like it had ever happened before. The route to school of little catholic girls was blockaded by unionist men, often hiding their faces behind Rangers Football Club scarves or baseball caps pulled low over their eyes. Between the blockade and the girls stood a barricade of riot police in their Darth Vader livery, but the RUC were inexplicably facing the girls rather than their unionist assailants, who were throwing improvised missiles over the heads of the unseeing police: paint balloons, dog shit, hot tea, urine, and even a pipe bomb. The blockaders held up pornography at the passing girls and proclaimed their priest a paedophile. Twice a day in July 2001 – three years after the Good Friday Agreement – and again when school resumed in September, the children did what Holy Cross children had always done: walked a few hundred yards along Ardoyne Road in North Belfast to and from their school gates. But in the new millennium that meant passing the imaginary boundary between catholic Ardoyne and protestant Upper Ardoyne: this neighbourhood was one of the most spatially polarised in the city. The demographic drama of the conflict had left the catholic school marooned in an almost exclusively protestant enclave.

The blockade of Holy Cross was broadcast across the world to dumbfounded television audiences. What on earth was it all about? To some it seemed to confirm every prejudice about the conflict, an unfathomable and parochial encounter between thick loyalists and intransigent republicans. But we shall see that Holy Cross was neither atavistic nor unfathomable: the events were complicated, for sure, and their interlocutors often seemed to claim a parochial privilege of translation: you could only understand if you understood; or they were diagnosed as suffering from political melancholia. But they were not a mystery, nor were they inarticulate. They were contemporary and clear. They mesmerised and shamed the society, and they spoke for themselves about the modus operandi of sectarianism and the role of the state in the new times. This chapter is concerned with what was being enunciated.

Behind the blockade were institutions that behaved with decorous inertia. Apart from the daily mass mobilisation of the police, the scaffolding of Northern Ireland's institutions remained unshaken by the atrocity of Holy Cross. That inertia was not nothing, however: it was an achievement. It required thought and effort to do nothing to stop the picketing of the children. The institutions, in effect, decided to be untouched by the Agreement during the opportunity offered by Holy Cross. There was little sense that they were mandated by the Agreement and now the Northern Ireland Act to do something different: to affirm 'the right to freedom from sectarian harassment' wherever it showed itself on their property, in public spaces managed by public authorities. This assumption that the Agreement should have implications for such events might be regarded as fanciful, as beyond the reasonable remit of the law. The institutions that might have intervened were compromised by the 'common sense' of the conflict, and perhaps by the notion of the street as public yet private, or rather as a voluntary space unavailable for cultural regulation. But the traffic of everyday life is, of course, no less regulated by history, power and law than public companies, courts, driving, sex or sewage. Street life appears in common sense to be a domain of spontaneity, but it is ordered, disciplined by manners and solidarities, property and propriety. In Northern Ireland streetscapes had become intensely sectarianised; they were not without thrill-seeking or 'local colour', but they were the antithesis of cosmopolitanism. However, the segregation was not a consumer choice, it was a political project. This was one of the most aberrant episodes of that history, and it could therefore have been the subject of intervention in the spirit of the Agreement. The reaction of the public authorities – from the police to the departments managing highways, housing, street lighting, crossings, schools and public safety – was revelatory about their interpretation of the warrant of the Agreement and the statutory duty to pro-actively promote good community relations. Section 75 of the Northern Ireland Act in its entirety (equality and good relations) was expected to extend to all public authorities in all their activities, to invite something new. Instead by both omission and commission the responses of the authorities reinstated the sovereignty of particular institutions, ideologies and interests. The busy networks of civil society seemed becalmed, too. Not one organisation turned out to walk with the children, not one brought its physical presence to bear upon the blockade to get out of the children's way.

The blockade came to be represented as culturally working-class: it was visceral, a desperate measure, the work of the 'disaffected', to be understood not as a way of addressing the world, but as its opposite – as exasperation. But, on the contrary, the excess at Holy Cross was an idiom of political expression. In its excess it was simultaneously exceptional and yet exemplary. Violence, hyper-vulgarity, the sexualisation of sectarianism, militarism, recklessness, causing havoc – all were *resources* of loyalist masculinism, deploying a local, low-tech strategy to shock and take space. Significantly, it was affirmed by women. And it achieved crucial products: the men's control by means of chaos, and through that, the transformation of disordered masculinity into masculinity as dominion. The chaos and menace of the blockade, and the long-term reluctance to 'be reasonable', frustrated the protesters' champions, but it was productive: protestant masculinity was exonerated within its own constituency, and that was all, historically, that had ever really mattered. And it was vindicated: it was impenetrable. It appeared to be beyond the reach of reason and institutional restraint.

Respectable unionists were quick to distance themselves from the violence and vulgarity, whilst lending legitimacy to the sense of grievance; other critics read into the shell-suited, baseball-capped, football-scarved barbarism an absence of sense. All of this missed the protesters' fastidious pleasure in their own livery and patois. Class snobbery obscured the men's resources in the performance of their power over the girls and their mothers. Apparently unpredictable and wanton, the protesters' excess was also mobilised against the ordered, law-abiding, official masculinity embodied by the police. There was an implicit contract between protesters and police, expressed through their negotiations during the blockade. The RUC appeared as the *servant* of the protest, and therefore the *master* of the pupils, parents and priests. So, in one of the most extravagant public order crises of the post-Agreement era, lawless loyalists and law-enforcing police converged in the control of catholic girls' freedom of movement. The girls were also a proxy for an attack on their parents, their mothers – 'fenian whores' – and their fathers – 'republican bastards'. Gendered prejudice infused the perception of the children: the girls' fortitude in 'walking the walk' defied the demand for their submission as good catholic girls. That their mothers allowed it and accompanied them became the source of double contempt. Their endorsement of their girls' resilience was interpreted as feckless, or worse, political. Sexist sectarianism invoked the despised body of catholic femininity, and against that the defiance of the girls and mothers appeared subliminally as transgressive. Having positioned themselves as protectors of the civil rights of the unionist protesters, the police constituted the girls' unreasonable vulnerability as the problem. This was explicit in the RUC's strategic calculations. The police interpreted the determination of pupils and parents to 'walk the walk' as equivalent to the protest, as if the blockade were a parade and the walk to school a demonstration. There was no strategy to implement the primacy of the children's rights and needs as children. Policing, therefore, worked to contain – just about – the protest and to control the pupils and parents. So fragile was the perception of children's rights, so overwhelming the claims of protestant men, particularly when they were backed up by paramilitary men, that this representation of rights became hegemonic. The blockade split the Human Rights Commission. One tendency – dominant – worked with a human rights agenda that sought a holy grail of 'balance'. It read Holy Cross as the troubling tension between two sets of rights – the protesters versus the parents and children. Another, minority, tendency sought a strategic approach deriving from the 'paramountcy principle' in the Children Act, which requires the courts to act on the best interests of the child; they interpreted Holy Cross as the oppression of the girls by an illegitimate blockade.

The new democratic duties and opportunities offered by the Agreement were not ignited by Holy Cross. There was no debate within the Assembly of the specific rights of these pupils; there was no inter-departmental plan to end or re-locate the protest, and there was no attempt, either by the British Secretary of State or the Stormont Assembly's First Minister, to run the hazard of taking themselves to the road and using their public authority and personal presence to call a halt.

Although the blockade enjoyed no legitimacy, the police behaved as if they were afraid of the UDA, the shadowy presence behind it. They treated it as if it were a mangy, hungry lion likely to kill if provoked. Political society tilted towards an explanation of, and appeasement of, the unionist protesters. But there was no equivalent attempt within the establishment to embrace the parents, the pupils or their priests. When the Queen sojourned in Hillsborough Castle during the blockade, the protesters' pastor, Rev Norman Hamilton, an anti-ecumenical presbyterian, was invited to her lunch table. Father Aidan Troy, who faithfully escorted the pupils and parents daily, was not invited. When Archbishop Desmond Tutu, the most celebrated protestant on the planet, agreed to show his solidarity with the girls of Holy Cross, church leaders made clear to him their distaste.

Of course, polite society condemned the blockade. But it did not extend solidarity to the girls. It was as if to empathise with these girls would be too gruelling – would have shown just how little, and how much, was needed to sort the place out.

As time went on, then, the victims metamorphosed into perpetrators: those girls, and their mothers, they just would not give in! And those protesters, it was said, they may have been horrible, but they were incoherent and incontinent because they were losing everything. The world just did not appreciate how difficult it was to be a protestant in post-Agreement Northern Ireland. So, Holy Cross became the subject of a pathological kind of projection: the burden of responsibility for a resolution rested not with the instigators, the protesters, or the police or politicians, but with the parents and pupils. And just as the burden of responsibility fell to them, so did the burden of blame.

LIVING AT THE INTERFACE

Part of the context for the blockade was the vicious loyalist feuds that flared between 2000 and 2005. The most fevered episodes tended to follow historic initiatives by the IRA. In the summer of 2000 international inspectors appointed to supervise IRA disarmament arrived in Northern Ireland for the first time to oversee a large stock of weapons being safely – unusably – bunkered. Over the next few months there were several deaths, and hundreds of loyalists were forced out of their homes by other loyalists. In the summer of 2005 the IRA completed the process and announced that it had ceased all activity; volunteers would seek their objectives by exclusively peaceful means. That summer the Orange Order, the UDA and the UVF, and hundreds of young men, took to the streets, organising lethal rioting against the police. In one incident, according to the Chief Constable, about a hundred masked men attacked officers in Ardoyne Road – as it happens, the route to the Holy Cross school. Loyalism and unionism were reacting to losing their enemy. This was their crisis. They were losing the raison d'etre for the militarism and emergency powers upon which the state had been founded. The loss of an enemy was putting new and different pressures on their territorialism.

The Holy Cross events began during the 2001 summer marching season – a season of traditional ill will and celebration of ancient conquests. The dramatic shifts in the demographics of Belfast had changed the context for the parades. Here in North Belfast – the most dangerous locale of the conflict – boundaries had shifted treacherously. Holy Cross School was located in an interface area, in Glenbryn, in Upper Ardoyne.

Ardoyne had been one of the most fearfully incendiary neighbour-hoods in 1969, the first year of the conflict. According to the Scarman report into the 'civil disturbances', protestant activity in Ardoyne during the summer of '69 may with some justice be described as an invasion.[1] The residents of Ardoyne therefore determined that they had no alternative but to police their own neighbourhood. But after the British Army was sent in, the IRA – small and taken by surprise by the ferocity of the attacks on catholics [2] – resolved to remove anything resembling a weapon from the community. Ardoyne then turned to the protection of the Provisional IRA. Ardoyne had experienced the summer of 1969 as a frightened catholic and 'nationalist' community; what emerged out of this was a politicised people, and the beginnings of 'republican' Ardoyne'. [3]

Loyalist Upper Ardoyne, in contrast to neighbouring nationalist Ardoyne (where the schoolgirls of Holy Cross lived), was in decline – its population was about 3000 in the early 1970s but was half that in the early 1990s. In the same period Ardoyne had grown from 4500 to 6400. Between the two was a mighty wall. Like all the twenty interface areas in the city, it was a magnet for unceasing attrition – the geographer Peter Shirlow calculates that around 70 per cent of deaths from politi-cally-motivated violence have occurred with 500 metres of an interface.[4] These were places of constant anxiety – 60 per cent of the population were estimated to be suffering from some level of post-traumatic stress – where people's journeys across their landscape were elaborate, long and vigilant. In larger Ardoyne there was no leisure centre, but only 18 per cent would use the nearest leisure centre (in Upper Ardoyne). In Upper Ardoyne, only 20 per cent would use the nearest shops (in Ardoyne).[5]

Despite the aggravation of interface life, many houses in Upper Ardoyne, like Ardoyne, wore the evidence of optimistic home-making: wishing wells and wheelbarrows, and gnomes and flower-baskets full of fuchsias and pansies in the front gardens of the terraced streets. Upper Ardoyne was represented by a Unionist MP, the adroit Paisleyite Nigel Dodds, and by unionist city councillors and Assembly Members. Like several North Belfast protestant communities, Glenbryn was aging and shrinking because of the determined drift out of Belfast into expanding protestant suburbs and small towns. The protestant view was that catholics were set to take over *their* territory; the catholic perception was that their communities were not allowed to spread into empty spaces beyond their own enclaves. Jim Potts, one of the Glenbryn leaders, confirmed the protesters' quest for control of what they regarded as besieged terrain, *their* protestant property.

Though Holy Cross had been built in what had once been a mixed area, it was now perceived as protestant: 'Catholics have to accept that there are lines and boundaries, you can't just keep claiming protestant homes because you are over-populating. That was what the protest was really about.'

Adjacent Ardoyne was relatively overcrowded and young and locked in – housing pressure from the Ardoyne would, in any other locale, have been accommodated in adjacent Glenbryn. There were empty properties and empty land. But, as one public planner put it, 'the protestants feel the nationalists want their land. Nationalists see vacant land and vacant houses. But it would be crazy to build houses in a protestant area when it is declining, and if nationalists moved in there would be World War III'. The conundrum for the planners was that £8 million had been earmarked for regeneration in Upper Ardoyne but there were doubts about whether it would be effective. The big issue was whether people would move back even after all the investment: did protestants want to live there? Millions might be wasted on what might prove an unsustainable community. This was reinterpreted by protestants as collusion in 'a plot to de-populate'. The area was subject to flight blight, and a protracted process of degradation. The fortifications, walls and fences that towered between modest terraces produced neither safety nor sustainability.

For Glenbryn residents and their representatives violence was part of a response to what they perceived as a pogrom, a sectarian mission to clear them out of their territory. Andy Cooper, one of the Glenbryn spokespeople during the blockade, believed that there was a pattern of 'sporadic incidents to make this community move away'. The city was being stolen from them. It was, he said, 'ethnic cleansing by stealth'. Jim Potts regarded the incident that triggered the blockade as a deliberate tactic, 'orchestrated to make people feel terror and move out'.

Both sides of the interface felt victimised by attacks. And the police refused to shed any light by sharing with the public statistical analysis of the sources of the incidents, arguing that 'it is an interface area, it is all sectarian'. Asked who was doing what, their response was 'We don't get into that, it's not for us to break it down'. How then could they manage the incidents – and intervene against sectarianism – if they were determined to not know? 'The score is this', replied the irascible spokeperson: 'the police are not involved in blaming one side or the other. We are simply there to keep the peace.'

And yet there had been intelligence that a deadly campaign was being planned for the neighbourhood by loyalist paramilitaries. Assistant Chief Constable Alan McQuillan and his colleague Chief

Superintendent Roger Maxwell had become alarmed during the June Orange parades. Maxwell stated later, in evidence to a judicial review: 'In particular we were concerned at the activities of Loyalist paramilitaries and the UDA and how they might attempt to exploit community tensions to murder Roman Catholics or police officers'. According to Maxwell, the police were learning from Special Branch intelligence that 'loyalists in the Glenbryn area were in possession of blast bombs that they intended to use under cover of darkness. It was their intention to engineer a confrontation with nationalists in which police would intervene. They would then throw the blast bombs over the police lines into the nationalist crowd.' Police penetration of the UDA was thoroughgoing, and they had evidence leading them to believe that the UDA was planning to provoke community conflict in order to provide legitimacy for the murder of catholics and police officers. Holy Cross was to be that community conflict. However, these police intimations of a loyalist offensive seemed to be mobilised not to confront loyalists but to control catholics. This intelligence was invoked in the review not to attribute blame but to give the police an alibi for the mode of policing they adopted.

On 19 June young loyalists, said to be UDA men, were leaning a ladder up against lampposts along the Ardoyne Road and hoisting their union flags. What happened then – which was the trigger for the events that followed – is as contested as everything that followed. There are three different versions of events even within the loyalist community. The dominant one is that offered by Jim Potts. According to his story, a car carrying three or four men passed the flag men and knocked them over. The men in the car then produced cudgels and attacked the flag men. Fighting then erupted and cars suddenly appeared, as if from nowhere, bearing their comrades. 'It couldn't have happened unless it was planned'. Pott was not present, but this version of events became the conventional wisdom that circulated around the city's shops, bars, taxis and kitchens. A woman who was there that day said a car 'rammed into the ladder, knocking one man off'. The driver got hold of something, menaced the flagpole man, and drove off up to Holy Cross School. 'That's why it kicked off.' Suddenly there were men with hurley sticks.

A third, different, version was offered by eyewitness Gail Blundell. She was a vigorous community activist, active in the credit union, and the keeper of an incident book. She had been chatting with a friend while the loyalist men 'were putting up flags, as they do'. Then she noticed 'a car slowing down and as it drew up to where the boys were, they said "orange bastards" and they were laughing'. The car did not knock the men or the ladder down, she insisted, it drove on up the road. Though her eyewitness account differed from the hegemonic version, she was outraged by the behaviour of the men in the car and became a strong supporter of the blockade. She watched the men get down from the ladder and chase the car, throwing a flagpole and the ladder 'at the back window of the car'. The car screeched to a halt and she then saw the two men inside – one of them wearing a Celtic top – get out and grab a screwdriver and hammer from the car: 'and they started attacking the young lads. The guy who put the ladder through the car window was fighting hand to hand. All hell broke loose'.

Children coming out of school were panic-stricken: 'The patrol-woman was screaming "somebody help me get these kids back into the school"'. Once the police arrived Blundell was keen to report to an officer that she'd seen a driver whose very *presence* was a provocation – a man wearing that Celtic football team top. She offered herself as a witness to his reaction to the attack on his car, which she described as an attempted stabbing. The police officer 'got his notebook out, took the registration number ... walked across the road to the other officers and ignored me. I've heard people say this before, but I still find it very hard to believe of somebody who's supposed to be there to protect my community.' The perception was that protestant territory had been violated and the police offered no protection.

According to ACC Alan McQuillan, the police arrived at Holy Cross and were 'attacked by a large crowd of loyalists, some of whom were carrying iron bars'. And they later found evidence of the manu-facture of paint bombs, acid bombs and pipe bombs outside a house on the loyalist side. The RUC's response was to block the road. As one Holy Cross parent described it: 'Kids were running back and men were running amok. But you couldn't get past. The police prevented any contact with our children. The children were running, panicking. We had to watch children crying and wetting themselves.'

Linda Bowes worked as a legal secretary. Her mother worked at the school as a cleaner, and often waited up at the gates to collect her granddaughter. On the day the drama began her mother had tele-phoned: 'she said I'd better get up there, it was bedlam, but on no account to use Ardoyne Road.' Bowes sped up towards the school, and saw parents already there, barricaded inside the school gate, watched by a crowd of protesters. 'The police were treating the parents as a mob. People were saying "I don't know if my child is up here, let me up the road" and the answer was always "no"'.

By the end of that day, when ACC McQuillan collated the events at Holy Cross and intelligence coming to him, he concluded: 'There was a serious threat to life and public order in North Belfast and much of the street violence was being orchestrated by the UDA. I was aware that the organisation had access to a range of firearms and other weapons, including pipe bombs, and intended to use these against the police and nationalists.' He believed that Holy Cross was the site of a 'specific threat of this type'. This version of events implies a degree of planning that directly contradicts the account of the origin of the conflict offered by the protesters.

On the day after these incidents, Isabel Grann went up to the school with other mothers, escorted by one police car, past residents in their hundreds, silent: 'When we walked back down the road through them people started shouting: "you'll never walk that road again!"'. The blockade had begun.

For the rest of the week the police, protesters, parents and political leaders were in seemingly permanent meetings. On 20 June PUP Assembly Member Billy Hutchinson, in an attempt at mediation, helped set up a meeting which was also attended by his fellow North Belfast Assembly Member Gerry Kelly of Sinn Fein. Jim Potts put a proposal to the parents: they could henceforth walk up one side of the Ardoyne Road on their way to school while the loyalist protesters watched them from the other side. This offer was rejected.

The police, however, decided that the pupils and parents should follow the route that had been demanded by the protesters. They believed that 'loyalist paramilitaries were prepared and ready to use firearms and pipe bombs against them ... and to spread these attacks and disputes to other roman catholic schools in other areas.'

On the third day the RUC told the parents that their protective screens didn't work and they could no longer guarantee their safety on the way to school. Isabel Grann told the RUC: 'from when I was growing up, the protestants walked Ardoyne Road for the marches, and *we* were barricaded'. She then walked away in disgust.

POLICE: TO PROTECT, OR NOT TO PROTECT

Right from the outset the protestant protesters demanded that catholic parents and children should no longer use Ardoyne Road as a route to school, and should confine their approach to Crumlin Road – a longer, busier, nastier road, through a sports field and a boys' school. This was Proposal One. Their other proposals concerned conflict resolution. 'There wasn't a problem with the others', said Philomena Flood. But the protesters took rejection of the Proposal One as an assumption that there was no room for negotiation on anything. This became a discursive theme of Holy Cross: the refusal to surrender their freedom of movement was fundamental to both sides. The parents also felt that they were perceived solely as a shadow of demonised republicanism, and their ordinary responsibilities and rights as parents had become invisible. A parent taking children to school was seen as a sinister activity if the parent was a 'known republican'.

The excitable complaint that 'known republicans' and former prisoners were among the parents found its *cause celèbre* in Gerry Kelly, an Assembly Member and former bomber. But, as Kelly pointed out, Ardoyne – like Glenbryn – was inevitably home to former combatants and political prisoners. There were up to 30,000 ex-prisoners in a population of 1.5 million, and they lived in every working-class neighbourhood. In fact Kelly was never likely to be the representative of parents in their Right to Education campaign, because he would then become a prime UDA target, and his presence among the children could make them targets too. He took a decision that a unionist politician would not have to make; although he was their elected representative in the Assembly, in this dispute the Ardoyne parents represented themselves. Their safety depended upon it.

The protesters were a miscellany of unionists – Paisleyites, progressive unionists and paramilitaries. Nothing unusual. Their protest was lived as the thrilling experience of a formerly becalmed community that was suddenly engaged, political, galvanised. They felt that they were having, if not influence, then power.

Holy Cross school closed early that term: the police could not protect the community of cleaners, janitors, teachers, parents, pupils, priests. On 25 June ACC McQuillan told them that, had those under threat been adults, 'I might have been disposed to push back the protesters'. But as they were children, it was all too much. Their vulnerability apparently diminished rather than enhanced their entitlement to protection. Talks facilitated by the Mediation Network went on through the summer. Gerry Kelly and Billy Hutchinson, both ex-prisoners, both tenacious politicians, and with contacts among combatants, were in regular informal contact throughout. Hutchinson was a rare voice in the unionist firmament, an articulate socialist. He urged the loyalist community to get itself organised, create a committee, make a case, negotiate: make a game plan, he said, to end it. But the UDA, who were a presence – 'a couple of dozen men' confided one of the organisers – had no stake in sorting out the crisis, and nor did the other unionist politicians. Thus Hutchinson's initial problem was not the republicans, but – as a former UVF man – the UDA.

Towards the end of the summer, the parents and the protesters came close to agreement on a set of principles that included mutual commitment to security for both communities. But restoration of the children's usual access to their school was still not an option and the negotiations came to an end.

The prospect of the beginning of the school term and a new blockade so alarmed the NIO that it facilitated a secret meeting between parents and protesters. The protesters repeated their agenda of 'wider issues', and the parents their 'one issue'. Jim Potts thought his 'compromise' – 'We'll not protest if you use Crumlin Road' – was reasonable. He saw any police guarantee of the children's safe passage as removing the protesters' 'right to negotiate'. Gail Blundell felt betrayed: 'We're having all these emotions building up, then your police force is telling you that you have your rights taken off you. It was just pure frustration. We already felt our right to life taken away. Then, to have the police say they were going to push these children up that road! Where were our rights? Where were our children's rights?' The NIO's attempt at mediation failed. One of the Glenbryn organisers conceded that though the parents might have 'the moral high ground, we have the tactical high ground, we can keep this going indefinitely'.

At the end of the August, the security personnel at the highest levels in the Northern Ireland Office and the RUC reviewed the impending crisis. Bizarrely, they interpreted it not as a security crisis but as a community relations problem. ACC Alan McQuillan and senior colleagues agreed to facilitate both the children's right to go their own route and the protesters' right to peaceful protest – even though it was sectarian and police intelligence indicated that paramilitaries would be active. McQuillan later explained that the police aim was balancing the rights of all those involved.

This balance was to be achieved by allowing protesters to have proximity to the children and parents, who were to be contained and separated from the protesters by protective Perspex screens. But on the first day of term: 'even with large numbers of police and army resources it proved impossible to put those screens in place', said the police commander. In any case, it was also admitted that the screens were unsafe: 'small missiles could easily penetrate' and the screens 'would then shatter'. It seemed that nothing would stop the protesters, who could merely 'retreat to the gardens lining the road, where they might have got even closer to the parents and children and represented a greater risk.'

The police strategy succeeded only in engineering proximity between pupils, parents and protesters. On the first day of school children and their parents were squeezed onto the footpath while protesters spat and shouted at them, while whistles – and a claxon wired up to one of the houses – blared out.

THE NEW MAN

During the summer the gloomy Holy Cross monastery at the top of Crumlin Road – Victorian gothic outside, polished wood inside – had acquired a new superior, Father Aidan Troy. This was likely to be his last posting. He was in his 50s and had been ordained a Passionist priest in 1970.[6] Father Troy's work had taken him to Africa, the Far East and the United States, where, in San Francisco, he had witnessed the devastation of AIDS. He trained there as a tutor and school counsellor, working in particular on child abuse. When he returned to Ireland in 1988: 'I was surprised to find that my offers to speak on child abuse in church circles met with some blank stares or suggestions that this did not exist in Ireland.' Finally, after a stint at the Vatican, he found himself in a place that was defined by historic religious wars, and yet where many felt that 'the role of the church is to keep hands clean and not become involved in events happening around them. There are people who lived in the North for 35 years and could well have lived on another continent.'

Father Troy's duties included being Chair of Governors of the school. He could never discern what they had already done about the crisis, but he resolved that they had a duty to safeguard the children and the school. On the first day of term he got up very early and checked out the road just after 6.30 am. Already 'it was like going on the set of a Vietnam war film'. Fr Troy and his colleague Fr Gary Donegan decided to walk up to the school with the children. Up the road the protesters' big banner, 'Walk of Shame', was waiting for pupils and parents. As they trekked slowly up the road, Lisa Ervine recalled that residents were screaming 'how could you do this to your children? I wouldn't inflict this that on my children'. Her response was to wonder how they could do what they were doing to *any* children. Her own daughter was determined to go to school up that road. 'We, and our kids, were learning a very big lesson in life: you don't give in to bullies'. 'What people missed in all this', she added, 'was how important the school was – this was a catholic school that its very own pupils were prepared to fight for'. As the walkers approached the school missiles started raining down. 'To my dying day I'll never forget the sheer force of what you can only call raw hatred', said Troy. Bottles began cascading upon the children and parents, and protesters ambushed the police and the pupils from all sides. Women fell to the ground covered in blood and people were running in all directions. Fr Gary Donegan recalled the impact on the four-year-olds approaching their first day at school: 'they saw their mothers shaking and in tears, they heard nothing but vulgar and foul language, and saw abuse hurled at other children.' That was their introduction to the public world.

Brendan Mailey was with his daughter. 'They were calling kids abortions,' he said. 'On that first day my wee girl was practically terrorised. She wouldn't go near the place after, we kept her off school for three weeks.' She refused to return. Mailey was also terrorised. The media broadcast the image of this big, red-haired man, his eyes and his arms wide as he sheltered little girls under his arms and rushed them through the storm.

But the parents would not countenance sneaking their children to school via the awkward round-about route. From this he learned a lesson: 'I'll never tell my daughter that she's not good enough to go through the front door', one of the parents told him. 'People say "how could they!", but who created the protest? Not the parents,' said Troy. 'Are we saying to children "this society is so broken down that you can't go to school?".' Troy had assumed that the abuse and aggression directed at the children would lead to a review of the police tactics, but it did not. He came to believe that equal weight, if not preferential treatment, was being given to the rights of the loyalists. A clue was the continued orientation of the police towards the children, as if the protesters needed protection from the girls.

Police warnings that lives could be at stake were now supported by specific death threats against three Ardoyne parents issued by the Red Hand Defenders. According to Troy, the police asked him 'do you want to tell them or shall we?'. They never said "we're going to search till we find the snipers".' Brendan Mailey was one of these. Philomena Flood, another, was forced to leave her home and go into hiding.

On the third day of term, a pipe bomb was thrown into the crowd. Jim Potts said he was 'surprised' by the bomb, and it had not been 'helpful'. The UDA people who had been involved from the beginning 'were asked not to come back. By and large it was accepted that the bombing was a mistake'. Billy Hutchinson said it was more than a mistake: 'I am ashamed to be called a loyalist after seeing those girls attacked'. After this, Secretary of State John Reid cut short his holiday and returned to Belfast, holding meetings with RUC Chief Constable Ronnie Flanagan and Security Minister Jane Kennedy. On 7 September Reid and the Office of the First Minister and Deputy First Minister issued a statement calling for dialogue to address the issues of both sides. But they still did not ask for the removal or re-location of the protest away from the children. This call for dialogue continued the assumption that it was its absence that was causing the problem, rather than an irreconcilable struggle over space and power.

At a community meeting that night others spoke up, including UDP spokesperson John White, also a former prisoner. White mediated with the UDA and urged the protesters to behave themselves, to be 'peaceful and dignified'. The politicians closest to the paramilitaries understood that the bomb had been a disaster. But the Paisleyite MP Nigel Dodds, unmoved, resumed the argument: the pupils and parents should travel the alternative route: 'that would allow a breathing space in the community'. Unionism began to re-group and redistribute blame away from the protesters towards the parents. This was their pathological projection of culpability.

Brendan Mailey appealed to church leaders to show solidarity and walk the walk with the children. They didn't. Unison regional secretary Patricia McKeown in a radio broadcast denounced the protest. 'Schools are sacred', she said. Fr Troy met Nigel Dodds, Billy Hutchinson, and other loyalist leaders – 'everybody was saying how awful it was'. But still, 'this was seen as a legitimate dispute between two equal parties: scumbags of republicans, ex-prisoners and criminals, against respectable, god-fearing people'. Even the nationalist newspaper the *Irish News* on 6 September urged pupils and parents to offer something: agree to take the alternative route. This gave to the pupils and parents the burden of resolving the conflict, and the burden of blame. That pathological projection had now become hegemonic.

BALANCE OF POWER

The bomb on 5 September had altered the balance of power among the unionist protesters. After the bomb the UDA had lost credibility. Nigel Dodds, however, while sharing the view that the blockade was 'a terrible tragedy', continued to endorse the rage that people in Glenbryn felt about everything. People 'felt totally isolated, under threat, and that nobody was doing anything about it. I think it got to such a point that they didn't care any more.' He explained the absence of a strategy among the protesters as deriving from 'a great lack of political capacity'. Protestants, he mused, were 'more fragmented, individualists doing their own thing'. This notion of a dissenting protestantism was the 'common sense' hypothesis offered to explain the difficulty of engaging the protesters in a recognisable political process. Presbyterian leader John Dunlop argued that protestants 'lacked self-confidence'. Although unionism had dominated the state since its formation, he saw protestants as disempowered by democracy. They had 'very few political skills because they worked through representative democracy. If they had problems they would go to their local councillor or MP and expect them to make representations through state agencies'. Billy Hutchinson offered another account: clientism, political dependency, had been encouraged by big house unionism.

The Rev Dunlop also believed that the protestant protesters were faced by a formidable enemy, a catholic community which had 'two parties and one church'. Catholics had 'a long history of fighting as communities, not individuals'. They were much more effective, he said, 'at downloading all sorts of funds'. When he considered who was powerful, and powerless, he was clear: catholics had power, because they had 'cohesive self-confidence'. The Ardoyne, agreed a senior public planner, was more 'monolithic'. Nigel Dodds believed that 'the nationalist side are much better at community infrastructure than unionist areas where there wasn't an ability to get things done'.[7]

With the UDA in the background, the blockade acquired a habit and routine of its own. No discourse, no law, no institution seemed to know how to stop it. Nothing illustrated the society's difficulty more than the role of Human Rights Commission chief Brice Dickson. Professor Dickson contacted the RUC to ensure that the protesters' rights to protest would be safeguarded. Had the RUC carried out a full human rights audit, he asked. Yes, replied ACC Alan McQuillan, 'our operation was designed to balance all the conflicting rights'.

During October, Assembly Members in North Belfast and a senior civil servant, Derek Wheeler, accelerated already-earmarked regeneration and security investment. For weeks the elected representatives tried to sell the deal to the protesters. They failed. Fr Troy became so troubled by the daily routine, framed by the police timetable and their tunnel, that it began to haunt his sleep. One night in October he woke in the small hours. He told himself this had to stop. 'Supposing we were to say: "we've had enough, it's over"?' Every day the choreography was rehearsed, parents and children assembled, the RUC opened their barrier. 'We'd walk through, escorted by police with shields etc. Then we'd walk back. We'd almost slipped into a ritualised thing.' The ritual would be repeated at home time. For the rest of the day the barrier was left open. What if they just walked when and how they wanted, he wondered. What did the protest mean if the road was open 23 hours a day, and closed only when the girls went to school? He put his proposal to the police. The police said no.

HUMAN RIGHTS, CHILDREN'S RIGHTS AND THE STATE

Around this time the human rights community in Northern Ireland began to find a voice, appalled by the sectarianism, sexism and violence of the protest and shocked by the bungling of Human Rights Commission chief Brice Dickson. He had visited the road, then contacted the RUC to ensure that the protesters' rights to protest would be safeguarded.

When the Committee on the Administration of Justice accepted parents' invitation to meet, they were unequivocal: the state had not exercised its responsibility to protect the children's rights. It advised the Northern Ireland government, the Chief Constable and the Human Rights Commission that the state had not based its action on its international and domestic obligations. The UN Convention on the rights of the child specified not only that a child must attract 'special safeguards and care', but, under Article 3, that public and private authorities had, in *all* their actions, to make 'the best interests of the child ... a primary consideration'. And the Children's (NI) Order 1995 specified that the child's best interests should be *'the'* paramount consideration in all matters coming before the courts. HRC Chief Commissioner Brice Dickson parried that the matter was not before the courts. Oh, but it should be, and it soon would be, replied CAJ.

In October several HRC commissioners 'walked the walk' and visited the school, and persuaded the HRC to call for an end of the blockade. However, the battle within the HRC was not over yet. The solicitors Madden and Finucane asked the HRC to support a case on behalf of a mother, a prominent parent who had been forced to flee her home. She was suing the Chief Constable and the Secretary of State. The HRC's casework committee – which had complete autonomy on cases – decided to support her. But Chief Commissioner Dickson disagreed. The casework committee sought the views of other commissioners and found enough support to go ahead.

The commissioners then met with the Chief Constable to discuss Holy Cross, and, according to their minutes, he admitted that the RUC had not factored in the 'best interest of the child'. Nor had the police invoked video resources to make arrests. (Flanagan disputed this version of the meeting.) The commissioners voiced the same criticism – and got the same admission – when they met the British minister responsible for security, Jane Kennedy, on 31 October.

Then suddenly, during the half-term break, police strategy changed. This coincided with the demise of the RUC and its reincarnation as the Police Service of Northern Ireland. The police now had to be *seen* to be different. When school resumed the RUC's riot gear had been shed. The tunnel of glinting helmets and faceless men was gone, replaced by a line of men wearing luminous tabards. Darth Vader seemed to have been re-born as a traffic cop.

Even the Office of the First Minister, hitherto primly disengaged, finally got involved. Then, at the end of the month, the protesters reluctantly agreed to accept a regeneration and security package – broadly similar to the one they'd rejected many weeks before, and the blockade was called off. Father Troy said he 'never knew why it was called off – because we never knew why it was started in the first place.' Jim Potts said he had 'no regrets': after all, it had harvested big money.

NOTES

1. Lord Scarman, *Violence and Civil Disturbances in Northern Ireland in 1969*, Report of the Tribunal of Inquiry, Cmd 565, HMSO 1972.
2. Ibid.
3. Ardoyne Commemoration Project, *Ardoyne: the Untold Truth*, Belfast 2002.
4. P. Shirlow, 'Who Fears to Speak: Fear, Mobility and Ethno-Centrism in the Two Ardoynes', *Global Review of Ethnopolitics*, Vol 3, No 1, September 2003.
5. Ibid.
6. Passionists are not tied to a diocese. They take a vow of poverty, chastity and obedience, and to keep alive the memory of the passion of Jesus. They were founded in 1720 to make the link between the crucified Jesus and crucified people anywhere in the world.
7. Such arguments were taken up by John Spellar in 2004 when he set up the Protestant Working Class Task Force, on the grounds that protestant community organisation was weak and therefore needed greater assistance; see 96–9.

9. Girls and men, innocence and violence

What was it about catholic girls that encouraged the protesters to risk public calumny? It was as if populist revolts against political correctness had obscured the specifically sexualised sectarianism of the protest. The protesters were represented as people of few words, whose primitive vocabulary vindicated an Orwellian caricature of the working class as a caste doomed to unthinking toil.

So the sexism of their sectarianism went unregistered, as if sexism – like swearing or smoking – was proof merely of limited intelligence, nothing that could be deemed strategic. The sexism of the sectarianism was normalised through the filter of class.

But the proximity of the protesters to the girls was not unintended. Jim Potts admitted that to remove the protest elsewhere 'would not have had the effect'. What effect? It gave to the men the experience of dominion. Had the children been boys, had their parents been fathers, had their teachers been men, it is unlikely that the pacific temper of that walk back and forth to school could have been so sustained, and so unsettling. Protestantism, like Catholicism, participated in what R.W. Connell has described as the cultural disarmament of women.[1] Both imagined masculinity through rituals of regulation of the female body.

The combustion that produced the blockade was, as one of the loyalist mothers had put it, '*men* fighting hand to hand'. The history invoked to explain the unionists' exasperation, and to legitimate their blockade, was their experience of interface attrition by other men and boys. What appeared to be an argument between men about men was being waged over the bodies of girls, their mothers and their teachers. This trinity were perceived as an affront – they were relatively autonomous, beyond reach, quietly and mysteriously invincible. They foxed both the protesters and the police.

The catholic girls attracted an intensely gendered aversion. There was an expectation that they must be mastered, if not by their mothers,

who in turn must be mastered by other men, then by a public community of men who were extremely vexed by their stamina and their
unthinkable self-determination. Chief Constable Ronnie Flanagan is
said to have confided to human rights commissioners that *he* would
not have allowed a child to go past that protest. President of the
Methodist Church Harold Good also reproached the parents: on being
asked what he would do if a child herself insisted, he answered, 'I'd not
give the child a choice'.

The coalition of impenetrable femininity symbolised a crisis for
patriarchal authority. It had to minimise any conception of the girls'
autonomy. Nowhere in the debate about the blockade was the girls'
intelligence and resilience allowed a hearing. The mothers insisted that
their daughters' school had raised their awareness of bullying and
encouraged the girls not to tolerate it. That emboldened the mothers,
who felt obliged to extend that ethic from the school to social space –
though not without a great deal of thought, thoughts that weren't credited by their critics. As Linda Bowes recalled: 'from the day it started
it was like dealing with a death in the family, and for three months we
were in a constant state of shock'. When girls wanted to defy the blockade, and yet were very upset by it, their parents told them the blockade
was not the children's fault – and, added Linda Bowes, 'at the end of
the day it wasn't *our* fault'. The Holy Cross staff's fidelity to the girls
went beyond the limits of mere professionalism 'The teachers never
said to us "why are you doing this?", said Louise Grann. Their priority was the children. 'They said, "we'll not let anything happen to you
in here"'. And they didn't.

The girls were undoubtedly political agents: they were taking a
stand. But their stamina and grace were traduced by polite society. The
hegemonic consensus was that they could not, themselves, exercise
choice. How could little girls possibly consent, complained their
critics, especially little girls who belonged to a culture deemed by
protestants to be dominated by monoliths. 'Common sense', derived
from traditional expectations that girls should be protected from the
world and, above all, saved from men was amplified by legal definitions
of children's age of *criminal* responsibility. The girls' agency was
unthinkable. All they could be was 'innocent'. That meant they could
not, should not, be consulted, and, even if they were, their *feminine*
rationality could not be relied upon.[2] The girls were denied recognition
as members of the public.

The register of the girls' agency was both their suffering and their
choice. Their suffering was mobilised not to understand the impact on
their sensibilities, but to malign the motives of their parents. One of the

HRC commissioners who 'walked the walk' believed that the failure to make paramount the best interests of the child, and to put them at the 'centre of the exercise of public order', not only scared the children but stopped them doing what they do: 'it stopped them smiling on their way to school'.

The Holy Cross girls embodied not only the assertiveness of the supposedly dependent, but the jewel of *interdependence*, the social relationships within which children, like adults, thrived and discovered their subjectivity. What was utterly unseen and unheard in the political debate was what had made their journey bearable, worth it – the relationship between the children, their parents and their teachers that was defined by empathy, reassurance, and commitment.

So, the children were both dependent and assertive. The discipline of the girls, their mothers and the staff at the school defied the fantasies and expectations that flooded the road. They could be patrolled, abused, frightened, but they were managed neither by republicanism and the church, nor by the loyalist protesters or the police; they did not lose their dignity and they would not be stopped. Their self-possession was their great transgression.

The public highway, garrisoned by hundreds of riot police and patrolled by the state, was universally deemed to be dangerous, while the school, protected only by the staff and the parents, was a place of safety. The blame nailed on those journeys up and down the road ignored the industrious and affectionate serenity of life inside the only place around Ardoyne at that time that was truly besieged, the girls' school.

Having defined the protest as a contest between men, it was assumed that anything could be said. And it was. The men, and women, too, waited and watched as the girls assembled and then began their slow walk past, bare knees between socks and grey skirts, faces in fright. The children could not stare back at these people, who hated them but couldn't resist staring at them.

For a few moments in every day the men gave themselves permission to stare and to talk dirty to the little girls, to project on to them the most despised and desired object – the whore. The excited sexual ambivalence around the reputation of the whore swirled around the ears of little girls, many if not most of whom had no idea what it meant. But if the word itself had no resonance, the violence projected from the men's bodies, whether rioting or shouting, announced their 'will to power'.[3] The girls understood what that meant. They lived in a violent universe. Their imaginary road maps around their neighbourhood were tactical, designed to avoid ever-present danger. The punishing ritual of the protest relied upon the knowledge harboured in all oppressed communities that violence is always incipient, 'always at the horizon of social imagination'.[4]

The idiom of sexual contempt was undoubtedly referenced to a core complaint of the protesters: catholic breeding. Their fear and loathing was reported, apparently uncritically, by *Guardian* journalist Maggie O'Kane (8.9.01): shrinking Glenbryn was surrounded by baby-booming 'hardline Catholic Ardoyne', where Fr Troy had baptised sixteen children in the previous month. '"Why should we be pushed out to take care of their breeding?" fumed Kate Riley, whose husband had been a victim of the Troubles two decades earlier. "It's fuck all to do with the school. They want our houses"'. Glenbryn presented itself as a reluctant neighbour to an incubator that, like Nicholas Ridley's *Alien*, threatened to harvest yet more catholics in its midst. Here were catholic mothers, parading up and down a protestant street with their daughters, who would themselves, no doubt, be breeding in no time, spewing babies into their terraced streets.

The violence of the blockade was so strange that it appeared to friends and foes alike as an enigma. In part that derived from a traditional representation of violence as a kind of masculine incompetence. But violence is part of the repertoire of domination; 'authorised by an ideology of supremacy' ... 'and though not all men use violence, and many men repudiate it, and are also victimised by it, violence is a way of *making masculinity*'.[5]

Mainstream unionism measured itself against the coarseness; it reserved for itself a reputation for respectability. Still, it assumed the power of interpretation, it claimed to decipher primitive runes, insisting on the violence as a vocabulary of despair, the language of people without words. The protesters were infantilised, described routinely by elected representatives of unionism as if they were political ingénues, who deserved to be chided but cared for, guided, patrolled – in a word represented – by their political patriarchs.

Nigel Dodds articulated the consensus shared across the protestant political establishment: the violence expressed 'a feeling that they're under siege, targeted for removal by nationalists and republicans who have their eyes on their territory'. Dodds was clear: 'there are elements of the Republican movement who see it as part of their long-term strategy to have protestants removed from parts of North Belfast'. He described Glenbryn as a community that felt 'totally isolated'; 'they were left leaderless, nobody fighting for them'.

But this approach obscures the political division of labour in

Northern Ireland between the British state, unionism and its paramilitary auxiliaries. The UDA had for some time been intimidating loyalists out of Shankill, and had spent the summer orchestrating summer conflagrations – from Orange parades to the Holy Cross blockade. Neither the politicians nor the paramilitaries had any lack of capacity. But it was vital to unionists that evidence of paramilitary sponsorship of the blockade should be muted. Their conventional wisdom that republicanism was the deadly enemy of peaceful politics was being jeopardised by a bout of warlordism between protestant paramilitaries, and proliferating conflicts over parading.

The televisual magnetism of the blockade focused the collective mind on intolerable evidence about an aspect of the much vaunted protestant culture. The wanton violence was at first a source of embarrassment to unionism, but this was later superseded by the irate complaint that the protesters were victims of a snooty media that was leading them on to disgrace themselves. 'I'd have to say, I was appalled by the role of the media,' complained Harold Good. 'It became like a soap opera, setting up a stage for people who had come to confirm the stereotype.'

MELANCHOLIA AND DISENGAGEMENT

The theory that an irresponsible and cynical media had worked as virtual agents provocateurs, using stagecraft to encourage, nay incite, hapless protesters, vindicated the unionist establishment's preferred version of events: that these protestants were wounded souls. They did not know how the world worked, they were political ingénues.

The blockade could be read another way, however: as the confident performance of protestant bigotry in all its sexist, sectarian audacity. What was seen was what the protesters wanted to be seen. They meant it. They enjoyed it. When they gathered to greet their enemy they were not the dregs of a dying political planet, they were not alone. The blockade became, for a listless community, the intoxicating pleasure of participation, congregation, potency, anticipation and aggression without risk. They were not endangered: the policing safeguarded them, it gave them their place. The blockade became part of the rhythm of the day, the crowd was keen and awake, and aroused, savouring the wicked bliss of anticipation as it waited for the ensemble down the road to begin its exquisitely fearful journey to school. Within minutes the protesters would be face to face with the target and the proximity that allowed raucous intrusion into the girls' silent, quarantined enclosure. That, momentarily, provided their meaning.

The blockade did not need to speak sense, its purpose was to produce the protesters as force, as the frontier. Though condemned for ruining the reputation of respectable unionism, it was also re-interpreted by unionist apologists as not power but powerlessness, as loss of identity.

This was a further misreading of the purpose of violence and its history in the formation of the Stormont state. But it was also a mis-interpretation of the relationship between violence and grief. The difficulty of the protesters was not just the discomfort of life at the interface – something they shared, after all, with the catholics on the other side. Their tragedy was their nostalgic attachments, which exceeded their contemporary investment in new opportunities. In that sense, interface attrition renewed their mourning. Their pessimism and grief were attached to *history*, a melancholic attachment that 'super-seded their desire to recover from it'.[6] Eulogising the mean streets of protestant community, and indulging in sectarian sentimentality about their culture, allowed them to defer any critique of a project that had given them so little.

It was both deference and melancholy that produced the disen-gagement from political processes that so exasperated some of their representatives. Billy Hutchinson complained publicly that efforts to enlist Glenbryn residents as participants usually met with inertia, an effect of Big House Unionism's encouragement of dependence. But melancholia is more than the manifestation of loss: it is a 'tena-cious self-absorption' that sanctions withdrawal from the world. If melancholia motivated the protesters, it also relieved them of responsibility.

Violence was itself a form of engagement: anything justified their protest against everything. An engagement with political processes, or even catholic neighbours, however, would be more risky. It would involve a different approach to selfhood, to rights, distribution and power.

Having repeatedly repudiated the discourse of rights as a 'provo agenda', when it did appropriate it unionism conceived of rights as the distribution of property and power, not as relationships and processes – as in the Agreement. This was a 'distributive paradigm' that focused on possession – in their case of space, omnipotence and now of the loss of it. Such a paradigm 'tends to preclude thinking about what people are doing, according to what institutionalised rules, how their doings and havings are structured by institutionalised relations'.[7] Iris Marion Young, in her discussion on justice and rights, offers a critique of this approach: 'Rights are not fruitfully conceived as possessions. Rights are relationships, not things: they are institutionally defined rules specifying what people can do in relation to each other.'

Her approach envisages negotiation, contestation and participation in a political realm, and for working-class protestants that confronted them with the consequences of their class compromise, at the expense of catholics: working-class protestants had been constituted as simultaneously privileged and marginalised. Only a re-alignment of their group interests within the political realm of the new state offered them the opportunity to address that dilemma.

Meanwhile power could certainly be exercised in violence and spatial dominion. But marginalisation could only find resolution in political processes that were full of risk – the effort of self-awareness, the hazard of empathy.[8] Their neediness required participation in the political process, but that, it seemed, in Glenbryn in 2001, was a risk too far. It was a little, local manifestation of unionism's larger difficulty with the new political dispensation. Participation in a process of political negotiation would have involved, in Young's terms, 'doing rather than having'. It would have meant engaging with 'enemies', the challenge of assimilating and responding to the presence of the scorned Other, navigating institutions, calling powers to account and themselves becoming accountable, finding mandates and modifying them through the practice of politics itself – risks, therefore, everywhere. That, not loss or republican guns, was unionism's political crisis. And for marginalised people politics risks exposure, without guarantees of respect and reciprocity.[9]

The Assembly was at work and Northern Ireland was at the beginning of an experiment in pluralism. But the blockade offered a way out of the effort of creating a culture defined, at the very least, by good manners, and for avoiding the ordinary political etiquette that permits, as Young puts it, 'pity, comparison, parody and proximity'.

The protesters ended the blockade with the promise of regeneration already allocated and bigger and better walls. That was the achievement of their pleasurable, pitiless blockade of catholic girls.

NOTES

1. R.W. Connell, op cit; see also Messerschmidt, op cit.
2. For watershed explorations of rationality, morality and citizenship this text relies on C. Pateman, *The Disorder of Women*, Polity, Oxford 1980; and C. Gilligan, *In a Different Voice*, Harvard University Press 1982.
3. Iris Marion Young, 1990, op cit.
4. Ibid.
5. B Campbell, 1993, op cit.

6. Walter Benjamin, 'The Work of Art in the Age of Mechanical Reproduction', 1937.

7. Young, 1990, op cit, pp24-25.

8. S. Felman & D. Laub, *Testimony: Crises of Witnessing in Literature, Psychoanalysis and History*, Routledge 1997.

9. Young, 2000, op cit.

PART IV

POLICE AND STATE

10. What's missing

Journeying through the Agreement's proposals for the 'new beginning', the reader discovers something stark: policing, security, and the post-conflict emergence from a state of emergency fade away from the Agreement; it isn't there. The negotiators had decided to not make decisions. The Agreement proclaims the necessary transition from emergency powers to the peaceful rule of law, but it offers not so much a plan as an inference, a note – an aide memoir to the British and Irish governments. Actually, the Agreement's references to policing and security are consigned to annexes. Everything else in the document was detailed – the participants had conferred, haggled, compromised and finally agreed to detailed duties, arrangements and schedules. Above all they had been present, participating in word-by-word, line-by-line textual struggle; their presence and the deal's proximity to the place – it wasn't Oslo, or Camp David – was utterly productive. The outcome was the words on the page which they had helped to write. This offered serious promise for a new regime of respect for human rights. Christine Bell's classic text on peace treaties tells us that equality and human rights regimes introduced by peace treaties have their best chance in societies where 'civic society was involved in the peace process, and where civic society was given a structural place in the negotiations and/or the deal'.[1] Civic society's presence in the Agreement was palpable. But policing and justice was not given a structural place in the deal. They were politically homeless.

There were several issues that the negotiators expected to become a 'moment of truth' – the border, transnational jurisdiction and north-south institutions, themes that had dominated talks about talks about talks since the Anglo Irish Agreement. These would require everyone to be innovative. But everyone knew there would be compromises on these issues. Equality was no less contested, but here too agreement had been reached, and indeed the alliance of interests – so polarised on other issues – actually extended the Agreement's egalitarianism during the talks.

But policing and justice rallied no coalition, no consensus. Why? If a rainbow coalition could be built around equality, including erstwhile mortal enemies, why not around policing, security and justice? Their institutions, despite three decades of international exposure and scandal, had remained impervious to accountability and representivity, they were armoured by special powers and special courts, withdrawn from scrutiny, from censure and change. That had produced an extraordinary and permanent exception to Britain's ancient principles of justice. Was that enough to barricade them, though?

This section explores the implications of the structural problem for the deal represented by the security and justice system, and suggests that the coalition-building that might have overcome sectarianism was politically disabled for a number of reasons.

Firstly, policing had been enmeshed from the beginning in the founding project of the state: its duty was 'policing the enemy', republicanism; and it was later enmeshed in the violent response to the civil rights movement. The duty of the police force was to keep the unionist state secure, and this was expressed rhetorically in the enduring narrative that the conflict was a problem of security rather than of politics.

Secondly – and related to this – there was a unionist, loyalist and armed police confederacy, both before and after the creation of the state, and this relationship was compounded in the early 1970s by the British Army's intervention in the crisis created by the Stormont state's response to the civil rights movement, and by its role in the state thereafter. Though initially detached from this confederacy, during the armed conflict the British state became the central, guiding hand; its penetration of the paramilitary organisations was so ubiquitous that the British security state emerges as a hydra: it is everywhere. This confederacy bent the law in the service of 'order'; it secretly sanctioned the killing of citizens; and in one of its final strategic manifestations it conspired to assassinate political figures.

Thirdly, though it was an organ of the state, the whole ethos of the police was partisanly unionist. In no other workplace had sectarianism flourished so vigorously as in the RUC and in the special constabularies. Policing had remained inhospitable to catholics/nationalists, with grave consequences for legitimacy of the police, security services and the state itself.

The security state's ubiquitous penetration of the paramilitaries helps to explain the impossibility of a policing and justice coalition to match the Equality Coalition. Working-class unionism found an interest in equality, and, through community activism and the parties closest to the paramilitaries, was able to affiliate to the Equality Coalition. But working-class loyalist militarism, as militarism, gave loyalists a sense of power; it operated with relative autonomy, circulating between non-state and state forms, operating in and for and against the state. It can be seen as a form of class militarism, most potently organised during the 1970s and 1980s against Westminster's promotion of power-sharing. (The loyalist militias' power as a partner of the state was in fact contingent and contradictory – although they may have felt like equals in this partnership, they were dependents; they had been stewarded by the state, and they had relied on its intelligence, its arms, targets and territory.)

The codicil of this conspiracy was that the paramilitaries shared the state's secrets. *They were the state's secret.* And the need to protect this secret became a major obstacle for the reform of policing. Ranged against this secrecy were the forces campaigning to reveal the shameful secrets of the security state, and to introduce democratic policing into Northern Ireland. Typically, the patterns of exposure in the context explored in this book – the quest for a non-violent solution to the crisis of the state that emerges in the 1980s – were haphazard and accidental. They emerged from reckless boasting, self-defence by combatants, campaigns by human rights movements and desperate relatives seeking justice for lost loved ones, and from retired police officers' imperative to tell the truth. These amounted to only a handful of sources, and their disclosures were strongly denied. Although some of the worst scandals have now been brought into the light, the state is still continuing its efforts at concealment.

Inevitably, policing and justice, violence and security were central to the narrative of Northern Ireland, and also, therefore, of the key protagonist – the British state. But unlike in South Africa, for example, where violence was constituted as a determining feature of the national narrative by the Truth and Reconciliation Commission, the convergent interests of the state and the paramilitary organisations served to disable any equivalent transformative project in Northern Ireland. Thus, in spite of the policing reforms, ten years after the Agreement the PSNI remained 78 per cent protestant, still reluctant to confront itself.

WHY

There were intimations in the first few months of 1998 that pointed to the negotiators' difficulty. Mo Mowlam had made it clear that reform of the police was imperative. But warning shots were being fired by

unionist paramilitaries, who launched a climactic spree of violence as
the settlement loomed. The main perpetrators were the Ulster Defence
Association – a network that had been heavily penetrated by RUC
Special Branch and Army intelligence for many years. This organisation
was not alone, but it was the favoured killing partner in collusion
between the state, the security services and loyalist paramilitaries.

Although the New Labour government was not responsible for this
history of collusion, it did now have a unique opportunity to expose its
corruption and criminality, and to address the political implications.
This could have embedded the British government's ability to institute
radical – rather than rhetorical – reform. However it was implacably
reluctant to do so.

Just as the negotiators were going into the final phase of talks at the
beginning of April 1998, the government was given a timely reminder
about the importance of these issues – by none other than the United
Nations. On 1 April UN Special Rapporteur Param Cumaraswamy
delivered his report on allegations of collusion between state forces and
paramilitaries in Northern Ireland. Cumaraswamy had publicly challenged the Chief Constable for interfering in his report on collusion; he
also found the allegations of collusion in the case of the murder of
solicitor Pat Finucane compelling; and he recommended a public
inquiry. No issue could be more important to the administration of
justice and democracy, he reminded the government, than lawyers'
independence and freedom from threat.

But even this rebuke failed to move the new tenants in Downing
Street. New Labour's great mandate after the 1997 general election
masked its insecurity; this was not a government to take on the security services. After the experience of the 1970s, when Harold Wilson's
government had been the victim of destabilising sabotage by the
elements of the intelligence services, no conceivable Labour government was likely to enthusiastically contemplate confronting the
security establishment. So powerful were the fortifications, and so
shaming the secrets interred in Northern Ireland, that the government
recoiled from risking the exposure of past scandal in the service of the
future reform. And there was no alternative social base within
Northern Ireland itself, no cross-party alliance that would champion
change. Britain's counter insurgency strategy was not capable of
winning the war, but, in some fundamental ways, it was successful in
compromising the paramilitary organisations and their political parties
and their capacity for coalition building. These parties all supported
root and branch reform of policing – that was not at issue – but their
capacity to script a human rights programme in the Agreement was

demobilised, both by the fortifications of the state within them, and by the paramilitary organisations' own participation in human rights abuses.

Despite a series of reincarnations during the period since partition, policing and security services had remained steadfastly unreconstructed throughout the history of Northern Ireland. They were always around 90 per cent unionist, protestant and male. More than any other institutions, the police and security services' alienation from the nationalist minority, and the aggression of their methods, had forfeited the state's legitimacy. The security services regarded nationalism and republicanism as the enemy.[2] There was no sense in which they could be seen as impartial keepers of the peace, or as neutral. This was a key reason for the ungovernability of that small place. Fionnuala Ni Aolain argues that Britain's resort to lethal force and special powers had bent the law out of shape; it had transformed the emergency, and the extraordinary, into the ordinary. It was just as Frank Kitson (later General Sir Frank Kitson), one of Britain's most influential ideologues of colonial 'counter-insurgency', had argued in the earliest days of the conflict: counter-insurgency rendered law not a principle or a standard, but as 'just another weapon in the Government's arsenal'. [3]

The state's counter-insurgency repertoire in Northern Ireland had included ambush and assassination, and a secret weapon, death squads fielded by the protestant paramilitary organisations. This assassination strategy had enabled the state to denounce sectarian violence while orchestrating it – choreographing, by proxy, spectacular sectarian murders. Meanwhile the security services were in a more or less permanent cruise to recruit spies and killers in the most stressed-out neighbourhoods, both nationalist and unionist. Political activism had been criminalised from the moment of internment in 1971, and community crime was used as a reservoir for recruitment. All of these manoeuvres participated in a racist representation of the men of Ireland as brawling, bigoted, low life celts who just couldn't get along together. But the state itself accelerated the incendiary polarisation of the landscape: its violent riposte to the civil rights movement and its deployment of the loyalist militias spread fearful segregation. The state was engaged in a form of low-intensity militarisation of everyday life, which cooked community anxiety and insecurity and crime.

Fear had a centrifugal effect on Northern Ireland's social space – a landscape that was already spatially segregated became more so. People were forced out of neighbourhoods, they scattered and clustered for safety. Segregation worked as sanctuary, but it also worked as a space of surveillance for the security forces. The communities of

the disadvantaged were those that were most harassed and disabled, by
posses of angry young men making careers in crime; and, at the same
time, they were those most dependent on other men – the combatants
– to preserve public order. Criminality was a resource for the state;
community crime provided a stable source of conscripts from among
vulnerable young men who were at odds with both the authority of the
state and the authority of their own community leaderships.

FROM ROUGH JUSTICE TO RESTORATIVE JUSTICE

In the three decades since the Cameron report, British security services
had refused to acknowledge that their loss of legitimacy was *their*
crisis, which demanded that *they* change. During the period leading up
to the Agreement, debates about policing, in this society emerging
from dictatorial dominion into a modern democracy, were already
circulating in some of the least protected communities, in evolving
conversations between former combatants and community and scholar
activists. They envisaged a settlement that offered a once-in-a-lifetime
opportunity to achieve acceptable policing for all, and an approach to
justice that transcended the limits of the crime and punishment paradigm. The conflict had created the political necessity for stressed
neighbourhoods in general, and nationalist neighbourhoods in particular, to develop self-help and community justice systems. But these
debates and initiatives had not succeeded in becoming part of the
Agreement. Instead, an independent commission, chaired by the
former Conservative MP Chris Patten, was set up by the Secretary of
State to consider policing.

The deferral of the debate about policing and justice did not necessarily default these debates. But it made them more difficult. It allowed
the RUC to re-group, and it indulged the RUC's refusal to undertake
the work of renewal itself. And the continuing focus on paramilitarism
– rather than policing – as the problem enabled the NIO, the police,
and the so-called constitutional parties to oppose the integration of
community restorative justice into a new template of policing as both
a state and community practice. The deferral, in other words, re-
assigned the difficulty: instead of the problem being the RUC, it was
presented as a problem of political polarisation, paramilitarism, and of
the impossibility of consensus.

The demand for reform came not only from nationalism and republicanism, and from human rights organisations, but also from those
communities most at risk of harm and loss. They all had something to
offer.[4] And what was on offer was more than a critique: they had also
consulted other experiences of conflict, and other sources of expertise

to improvise their practical alternatives and amendments to both para-military and state systems of justice. But if police reform was deemed too difficult for the peace process then how could the citizens offer their critique and their contribution? How could they define the debate? What context could allow their innovations to be considered? How could citizens consent to be policed? And how was citizens' withdrawal of their consent to be interpreted? And finally, how could the citizens give their consent, if their refusal to consent was given no meaning, no respect? [5] This was of the greatest importance in the peace process and the legitimacy of the new state. In this field, there had been no parallel peace process – no convergence of interests to overcome the resistance of Britain as an unaccountable stakeholder, and to cohere an alternative model of policing and security within the deal. The Agreement, and the referendum to endorse or reject it, was the only opportunity the citizens ever had, or would have, to consent, or with-hold their consent, to the jurisdiction of the police over their persons and communities and to contribute their own innovations to public peace.

The stories that follow cover the consequences of deferring the debate about policing. They go to the heart of the connections between the police, the state and the loyalist paramilitaries, and they show how these connections linked them into intransigence, undermined the authority of Mo Mowlam and allowed her successor to minimise implementation of the reforms proposed by the Patten commission.

NOTES

1. Christine Bell, op cit.
2. Lord Cameron, *Disturbances in Northern Ireland*, HMSO 1969; Hunt Report, *Report of the Advisory Committee on the Police in Northern Ireland*, HMSO 1969; Scarman, 1972, op cit.
3. Frank Kitson, *Low Intensity Operations: Subversion, Counter-Insurgency, Peacekeeping*, Faber 1971.
4. Kieran McEvoy and Harry Mika, 'Restorative Justice and the Critique of Informalism in Northern Ireland', *British Journal of Criminology*, Vol 42, No 3, Summer 2002.
5. Carole Pateman, op cit, p13.

11. Policing and truth telling

THE PATTEN COMMISSION

Christopher Patten sat at a long table with other members of his commission in the first of the meetings that would take the commissioners to every corner of Northern Ireland at the end of the year of the Agreement. There would be more than thirty of these encounters, but none had quite frisson of this visit to a West Belfast college. He had been invited by a crowd of community groups in working-class West Belfast. His hosts were the men and women he would have been warned about by the securocrats when he did time as one of Margaret Thatcher's ministers in Northern Ireland during the 1980s.

The task of Patten's Independent Commission on Policing was to do what the Agreement had not been allowed to do: describe representative, reformed policing. The British government announced his appointment without bothering to consult its new partners in the Republic – the etiquette of co-operation between the two states did not yet come easily to the British in Ireland. In some ways Patten was an appealing appointee: as a former conservative minister, on the 'wet' wing of the Conservative Party, and as a Roman Catholic, he seemed to embody satisfying compromises. Patten's allure for the Secretary of State was also that he had a reputation for being his own man, he had not been afraid of Margaret Thatcher, and he had not been afraid of China when he negotiated Hong Kong's re-unification with the colossus.

But his manners at this meeting were tense, he seemed aloof, even afraid. These were republicans and nationalists who, despite the state's best efforts, had not been pacified. Patten seemed unable to read this congregation. They had so much to tell him, but they were left with an uncanny sense that he knew everything about them and nothing. The suspicion was confirmed at the beginning when he addressed one of their revered advocates, Father Des Wilson. Wilson was a genially implacable community priest, whose reputation was 'the people's priest'. Everybody knew him as Father *Des*, but Patten breached political decorum by calling him Father Dennis Wilson. Poor Patten, he didn't know that this was not a mark of respect, but a *faux pas*, a misreading of the tone of the relationship between Father Des and the community, which was more than solidarity, it was a bond of love.

Father Des honoured the condemned communities of the North thus: 'think of a constant creation of alternative education, alternative welfare, alternative theatre, broadcasting, theological and political discussion, public inquiries and much else. They also created at various times alternative police and alternative armies. The authorities who had power over them in the past were and are still engaged in an equally constant struggle to regain control of them ...' Wilson had arrived in Belfast in 1966 – the year that the newly reformed UVF had begun its resistance to any rapprochement with catholics. 'People like me had to battle our way from a conservative background to realise what was going on.' He was stunned by the impoverishment of his congregation. From the late 1970s, he encouraged the community to bear witness, to hold its own public inquiries, and in the early 1980s he worked with the Redemptorist priest, Father Alec Reid, to initiate a peace process with republicans (see p139), when the government 'saw it as a defeat to be talking at all'. Wilson attributed the initiative to Reid's awesome tenacity. 'He then took off in a miraculous direction. He had immense patience. I admired that, because I have none!' Clearly, Father Des was aligned. And he went to that meeting with a caution about consensus: the people should have the right to withdraw their consent and to 'exclude the police on their own authority, because things have been so abusive here'.

Patten could not resist expressing his impatience. He wanted a portrait of a police service that these people could tolerate. But the meeting would not oblige. It wanted something more complicated. He wanted something from them, but they wanted something from him, too. They had 'never been able to get close enough to people like this before', recalled the priest. They wanted to tell their story.

To Patten's credit, he was at least there. But he seemed like a judge in civvies. Couldn't they get on with it, couldn't they offer him something 'positive' to work with, he pressed them. But they wanted to say what they wanted to say, not what he needed to hear. Gerry McConville, director of Falls Community Council, explained that people wanted Patten to know that their experience of the RUC 'was not just a bad experience of policing, they wanted to explain the historical context, that it was set up to control people, not to make them safe.'

Patten hurried the business to a close, and tried to reassure them that he was serious. After all, he added, trudging around public halls in the run up to Christmas was not exactly what a chap would want to be doing. People were not reassured. It wasn't a trudge to them, it was life. He didn't behave like a patrician old colonial, he didn't lord it over them, but he seemed shut; he offered no flicker that he understood that he, like them, was participating in a historic process. The tetchiness of the occasion rendered it banal. 'Damn it,' muttered Father Des. 'His government had been responsible for what had been going on, but here he was, sitting in judgement. I got the impression that he thought his business was to make *adjustments* – it wasn't a discussion about how you'd change the attitude of the police from being the political police, intent on controlling the people, to a service that was there to protect the people and their property.'

This meeting was just the beginning, a foretaste of the unruly intensity to come. Nothing like it had happened before – the state dispatching important personages around the nooks and crannies of the place to give people a hearing about a sanctified service, the police.

Nobody with power had bothered to trail to places where the police themselves would not venture without flak jackets. That gesture endowed the Patten Commission with a bigness that grew less from the experience of it than the expectations of it. It was not long before their journey was designated a quasi truth and reconciliation process, a modest British surrogate for the mighty catharsis in South Africa, where 'truth for amnesty' had been offered as part of the society's reckoning with apartheid.

Nationalists had been waiting a long time for this opportunity. 'The hurt was inside, and it was dying to come out,' said Father Des. People had emerged from the violent decades wounded, their memories wary. 'It was a terrible time, there was a cultivated forgetfulness. It didn't do to have too much knowledge about anything; it did us an awful mischief afterwards.' His sighs evoked the fright of the times.

Policing was about freedom of movement, whether – literally – you could cross your own street. And it was about freedom of thought, whether what you had in your head would put you and yours in danger.

Many of the consultations took place in divided townships and re-enacted the difficulty of speaking, and of listening. There were occasions when listening to 'the other' seemed too difficult, too much like sympathy. Enniskillen exemplified the drama of hostile hearing. It had hit the global headlines on Remembrance Day in 1987, when the IRA tried to bomb a British Army colour party but instead killed 11 people and injured more than 60 others, many of them children, none of them soldiers. People of catholic origin make up 60 per cent of the population in the town and the villages around it. Shortly before

Christmas, hundreds of people turned up at a hotel ballroom. The hall was silent while a woman described the shooting of her father, a policeman. 'You people think you have a monopoly on suffering,' she said quietly, pointing her words at the nationalists. She was followed by a man who tried to talk about the origins of the state. 'We don't need a history lesson,' someone heckled. He pressed on: 'nationalists were trapped ...' He couldn't get to the end of his sentences before he was interrupted. 'No change ... no surrender ...!' He tried again, 'Need I mention collusion with paramilitaries ...' No he need not. 'You're in the wrong meeting ...'

The meeting rocked between the RUC's defenders and its critics. Groans greeted the story of Jim Murphy, a catholic petrol station owner shot at close range in April 1974 and dumped by the roadside. 'I'm sorry for bothering you,' said the narrator. Murphy's murder was remembered by everyone – he was the 1000th person to be killed in the conflict. The RUC didn't try to find witnesses for three days. 'They either condoned what happened to him or murdered him', the panel was told.

A woman described her experience of an arrest by the RUC followed by incarceration in a psychiatric hospital. People laughed. Another woman said this reminded her of an incident when she was away nursing in England. A patient had recognised her accent and told her he'd just returned from a tour of duty in Northern Ireland. 'He'd heard shocking reports about the RUC interrogating people ... "as an Englishman", he said, "it was a shocking state of affairs"'. More roaring from the unionist men. 'Are you on your own ...' they mocked.

A young man tried to raise the tone and remind the company that the Good Friday Agreement was 'a singular moment of hope, of previously unimaginable equality'. The hall was quiet until he ventured, 'the RUC are totally out of control, they've grown too used to absolute power ...' Then there was a wave of vociferous yawning. The RUC 'has taken very badly to being reformed ... it must be representative, just as the executive must be ...' he urged, and the yawns turned to derision.

A businessman insisted that the RUC had served the community well, under great difficulties. 'They might have been running close to the edges of the law, that was hardly surprising,' he said. He was heard in silence. A man in a blazer agreed, 'Accompanying me tonight is a man whose wife has had three brothers in the RUC killed.' With this benediction, he too, was heard in silence.

Finally, Patten addressed the crowded hall. He challenged those who suspected that the panel had already made up its mind, and rehearsed his seasonal gripe. 'We would not be holding two or three meetings a day, that would be a pretty curious way to prepare for the nativity.' At least, he added, 'people have sat in the same room and heard each other'. I glanced through my notes. Had we heard the same sounds? Had everybody been *heard*? Patten was right, they had all been in the same room, but if people had indeed been heard, they'd been heard differently.

GLORIOUS ' WE'

Down in the flourishing harbour town of Kilkeel in County Down, nesting between the Irish Sea and the Mountains of Mourne, most people work in farming or fishing. Northern Ireland's largest fleet operates from Kilkeel, a town where 60 per cent are of protestant descent and where the streets had often been bedecked in loyalist bunting.

The meeting with Patten's commission took place in a cinema one December afternoon. An RUC man recalled the assaults on his comrades, and concluded, 'We don't need a review, the RUC is acceptable to the vast majority of decent nationalists.' The purpose of the Patten commission, he said, 'is to make the RUC unrecognisable'. The nationalists in the hall would have agreed, that was exactly what they wanted. But that would mean 'spitting in the faces of those who have protected us'. An RUC man added, 'it would be an insult to me and others if the RUC were to be disbanded or changed in any way'.

Then a woman said that she would have been a police officer had she lived anywhere else in the world. 'But I joined the NHS rather than join the police.' As a child she'd been warned by police officers, 'your father is a dead man, the next time you'll see him he'll be in a box ...' She'd nursed a child brought into hospital after being hit by a plastic bullet in the chest. The child had died.

Another nurse, a republican, recalled a shooting near her vicinity, an RUC man had been killed and two other men lay bleeding. 'As a nurse, I went over to see what could be done.' She knelt beside one of the men and held his hand in hers until help arrived from the barracks. 'An officer said, brusquely, "he's dead, what's the use?". I said, "he's still alive!" But he didn't want to see that a republican, a catholic, could be human.' Then a young Paisleyite DUP activist proclaimed pride in bigotry, 'it is a badge of honour, taking a stand against Rome.' The people who spread anti-RUC propaganda 'are the same as people who make bombs in their kitchens', he said. Many defenders of the RUC offered personal experiences of relatives killed in the line of duty. Everybody knew somebody who had been hurt or killed, attacked by citizens in their own town; everyone had an experience of menace in their midst. They all knew that reform was on the agenda, but only the unionists – perhaps uniquely in the world – insisted that their police force was beyond reform. The question of what kind of police service Northern Ireland should have in the future, was, for them, a question not worth asking.

By the time the commission reached Crossmaglen Patten had relaxed. On the extreme edge of the union, Crossmaglen is a town with an awesome reputation as an impregnable republican redoubt. Crossmaglen's meeting with the panel took place during a December afternoon in a community hall on the pretty, spare, town square. Patten may have been in the middle of what was often described as 'bandit country', but he had lost the brittle impatience of that early encounter in West Belfast. 'It's not my meeting, it's not our meeting, it's your meeting,' he told them. Crossmaglen was a township of fewer than 2000 people, and according to the 2001 census 99 per cent of its population were of catholic origin. Two miles from the border – believed to have grown from a crossroads and a shebeen – in County Armagh, it was perhaps the most militarised patch of Europe. A military observation tower leaned over their town, and Gazelle helicopters droned above them, equipped with cameras and zoom microphones that enabled the army to monitor all population movement below. Soldiers had to be airlifted out, and even the Army's refuse bags had to be flown off the base. 'If you crash your car,' warned one of my companions, 'and you phone the RUC, the Army would have to check the area for booby traps.'

During the meeting a man explained that his submission was 'personal'. He described his arrest in 1993, and his removal in handcuffs, by helicopter, and then by convoy to the barracks where he was interviewed. He had made no response to any questions, he said, and during part of the process had sat with RUC officers in silence. An officer began writing on sheets of paper. 'I could read it upside down,' he explained. They were interview notes. 'He filled out three pages of fictitious questions and answers.' The same thing happened later that day. 'My arrest was only one of many in the spring of 1993 – there were 30 in South Armagh, as many again in Fermanagh and Tyrone'. All border counties. Why this wave of arrests, he asked: 'it was clear – because the Chief Constable had called publicly for changes in the law in relation to the rights of persons, in particular the right to silence.' The man asked the commission directly to investigate the arrests that took place at that time. But that was not what the commission had been set up to do.

An elderly woman in a bright red coat began her testimony. 'I was born in 1922, the year my country was partitioned.' When she was 17 years old she applied to join the police. 'I had the height', she explained. 'My school was sufficient to disqualify me.' She continued to pay attention to the profile of the police, and when the Westminster government commissioned the Hunt report in August 1969 she bought a copy and read it. Hunt recommended the de-militarisation of the RUC and recruitment according to the proportions of ethnic and political communities. Neither happened. 'I could not possibly trust the RUC, they were a bigoted group of people,' she said.

A nurse described raids on her family home, the arrests of her relatives, body-searches, derogatory remarks about their bodies, and threats to her livelihood: she worked in the City Hospital in Belfast. 'They were unhappy that I worked in a loyalist hospital, and they said if I continued to work in a loyalist hospital I'd be murdered. They openly attested to collusion between loyalist paramilitaries and the RUC.' She had been left wondering 'what if you die when you put the key in the ignition?' But she needed that job: 'I needed the hours to complete my degree. After that I changed, I became paranoid, I wouldn't allow my off-duty activities to be known, I travelled in different cars. I was isolated from people. My crime? I was a catholic from a republican area working in a loyalist stronghold. They didn't want someone like me nursing their families.' She stopped speaking, bowed her head, stared at the floor, and sat down.

A man at the back introduced himself as Tom Caraher. Everybody knew what that name meant: Silverbridge bar. 'I'm here to speak of six young people on 22 November 1998 at two minutes past six.' Marines and RUC officers, swearing 'there are old scores to settle in South Armagh and settle them we will', had launched an attack. He reminded the panel of the death of Fergal Caraher, who was killed in 1990, and his brother Michael who was wounded, when Royal Marines fired shots into their car. There was an outcry, an inquiry and a trial of two Marines. The lawyer defending the marines was Peter Smith QC, a member of the Patten commission. He was, of course, only doing his job. But his presence was difficult for Tom Caraher. It was, too, for Margaret Caraher. She'd met him before. 'The last occasion I was in the same room was when he defended two soldiers accused of murdering my husband.'

But she wanted to share her opinion of the RUC. 'My earliest recollection, at the age of four, was of a gun pointing at me.' And then on 30 December 1990 the Army killed her young husband. 'It was the RUC's job to inform me. They've never yet. They treated me neither with consideration nor respect. The police force of my childhood nightmares was charged with investigating the murder of my husband.' Addressing the panel, 'as a woman,' she added, 'I'd be aware of domestic violence and abuse. Yet who does a woman turn to – certainly not the RUC.'

The Caraher case could not have been more salient to the Patten Commission's project. The case concerned more than killing. It resulted in an indictment of an entire community. The case had been decided by Lord Hutton (whose inquiry into the David Kelly death during the tumult over the Iraq war cemented his reputation for loyalty to the state). Although the Marines did not appear to Hutton to have been persuasive, in his view the prosecution witnesses' refusal to co-operate with the RUC had rendered them unreliable.[1] In case Patten's International Commission needed reminding, the panel was reminded that RUC officers were flown in and out by helicopter. 'They are not regarded as part of this community.'

Mothers described the terrorising of their children. One recalled her three-year-old daughter being ordered during an RUC raid to put up her hands or she'd be shot. 'That left her very nervous.' Several elected councillors described death threats from police and army officers. One of them explained that: 'more than half the complaints I receive, and the facilities I offer, are about the police. We've never had a proper police service in South Armagh.' Here there was a consensus: all they wanted was 'a proper police service'.

DEFENCE AND ATTACK

The sectarian order had created protestants' dominion over catholics, and the form of the transition produced many of these protestants still as a group with a stake in defence, as the enemies of change, pluralism and accountability. Nationalists and republicans needed change. They alone, it seemed in these meetings, advocated reform and representivity. Protestants addressed the meetings in mournful lament for the old order, disengaged from any debate about a future police service, and rejecting proposals that would seem commonplace anywhere else in the islands – for a representative, devolved, de-militarised, civilianised and feminised police service.

Such themes exercised a good portion of the submissions to the commission, including a radical reform programme proposed by the PUP, but they were not what the defenders were interested in. There were only two things they wanted to talk about, and they were both the IRA. It was IRA intimidation that stopped catholics joining the RUC, they said, and it was the IRA that went around killing protestant policemen. They bristled with affronted dignity, as if they'd never get over it. Intimidation by republicans, they said, had produced the RUC as a protestant force – it was a republican creation.

But this intimidation thesis was belied by the scholars whose research was available to the commission. The investigation of RUC recruitment practices, delving into the detail of applications and appointments, told a different story. When the RUC was created after partition unionism had favoured a quota of 20 per cent catholics – to guarantee that catholic communities could be patrolled and policed. The catholic presence had begun at 21 per cent. But it swiftly dipped, and dropped to 10 per cent by 1966. During the next thirty years the RUC's exponential growth created a great opportunity for greater catholic recruitment – police numbers multiplied by three times. However, during this period the proportion of catholic police officers actually declined, by another 2.5 per cent.

If there had been republican intimidation during the conflict, then it was modest by comparison with the unionist intimidation before and after. The proportion of catholic applicants hired was lower than the proportion of protestant applicants; and of the catholics who made it, according to *Inside the RUC* by John Brewer and Kathleen Magee, many hailed from outside Northern Ireland or felt themselves to be alienated from mainstream catholic sentiments about the police – often, indeed, they identified powerfully with protestant scorn for catholics. So, even the minimal presence was a kind of anti-presence; it gave catholic endorsement to protestant hegemony in the police. But the evidence was irrelevant, it did not impinge on the unionists' dirge, that reform would dishonour the dead.

Undoubtedly, RUC officers – particularly those close to the border – had been targeted as an explicit republican strategy. But the martyrdom discourse exposed a faultline in Northern Ireland's sense of itself as a people. Appeals to the glorious dead usually invoke a national grief – the memorials and monuments erected everywhere after the twentieth century's world wars are cherished by a national 'we' and ennobled by a just cause. But there was no 'we' in Northern Ireland. The dominant imperative since its inception was to define itself as us and them, by Britishness against Irishness, and by protestantism against catholicism;[2] antipathy and insecurity, more than belonging, were 'defining tenets of the new state'.

The RUC's dead had died for what, for whom? The answer had become almost unutterable. They had died not for 'the people' nor for 'the nation' – because, of course, both of those concepts were contested. Northern Ireland was not a sustainable 'people' and it was not a 'nation'. They died for a state, they said. They died for the law.

But their martyrdom was compromised by their own ambivalence towards their state, to a British state by which they felt unloved and even betrayed.

The RUC was the emblem of a cause so bereft of legitimacy that, though its advocates loved it, it was a love that could not speak its name. These martyrs had been dying not for the people, the nation, the state or the law: they had been dying for dominion.

A TRUTH COMMISSION?

The commissioners listened. They were inscrutable. And yet, almost despite itself, the commission soon came to be designated a quasi truth commission.

South Africa's Truth and Reconciliation Commission was a great, national tribunal that hoped to open the archives on apartheid. It was hoped that amnesty for truth would elicit the perpetrators' candour, that their confessions would vindicate the victims. And even though the amnesty meant 'sacrificing justice for truth', that was felt to be a forfeit worth yielding. This was one of the historic compromises that enabled South Africa to release itself from apartheid – white perpetrators and their black lieutenants would be called to account, if not brought to justice. It was hoped that truth telling itself would be transformative, that it would produce a new national narrative. The South African TRC was not an inquiry into the injustices of the old state, and the many means by which it conquered millions of black people; its remit was violence against the person by all of the combatants during the apartheid era. This was a crisis for the liberation movements: how would their violence be above scrutiny? It wasn't. The truth commission adopted distinctions between just and unjust causes, and between just and unjust means. This obliged the liberation movements to submit to truth-telling, but it also recognised that there was no equivalence between the apartheid state and its challengers. Although the amnesty was not universal – there were about 7000 applications, many of which were rejected – and there were prosecutions, the limits of justice were built into the TRC.

The TRC attracted a great debate about its triumphs and failures. It had been criticised for its emotionality, the evidence of feeling, tears, anguish, forgiving and unforgiving. Emotionality, in the white western mind, was anti-rationality. But Archbishop Desmond Tutu's management of the process infused it with feeling. He deployed his authority as an Archbishop, as a veteran of the anti-apartheid movement, and as a man, in the service of ravishing, disciplined emotionality. He was the antithesis of President Nelson Mandela's cool. Former South African

President De Klerk also criticised the TRC for moving beyond 'individual acts'. But the enemies of apartheid criticised it for its focus on atrocity rather than the daily violations of dispossession – pass laws, lack of access to water, fuel, and to citizenship.

The TRC also raised the spectre of non-specific culpability: all whites had not committed atrocities against black people, some whites had died resisting apartheid, but white society was the beneficiary, everyone was implicated, everyone had to take responsibility. But whites in general were not called to account. Nevertheless, Antje Krog, the Afrikaner poet who broadcast regular reports from the commission, recalled her white relatives' sense that they were being witch-hunted: though they lost nothing but their power over blacks – and that, it seems, was everything – they felt bored, harassed and accused by the reporting of the truth commission.[3] This showed the contribution of such a commission to the symbolic destruction of former dominance – and that such symbolic giving up of power is always resisted.

Did emotional effort, self-awareness, amount to justice? Did appearance before a tribunal imply remorse? Did it even imply a gesture of respect for those who had been so denigrated? Responsibility, if not justice, implied *individual* work by both blacks and whites to address their existence in *institutionalised* apartheid. The TRC had tried to do that. It was, if nothing else, a torrid and contested catharsis. The commission itself was engaged in the process, it was not impartial, it was positioned, a contributor to the new society. Its mission was to memorialise: to keep apartheid alive as history after its institutional death. The TRC's creativity, its limits and its crises were all aired, the entire society was engaged by it, even when it was utterly alienated from it. No one could avoid the argument, just as no one could avoid the TRC's contribution to the dynamic between narration and nation-building. The process may have had its problems, but, if nothing else, it allowed the society to conduct a massive debate.

So, was the Patten Commission a truth and reconciliation commission? Any such reputation emerged not because of the commission itself, but because the participants who turned up at its consultations transformed them – they didn't just come with brochures and manifestos for a new police service, they came to share their experiences of the police. But it was never the Patten Commission's intention to follow South Africa's lead. And, just as Northern Ireland lacked a de Klerk – the man who asked to be relieved of the burden of history – so it lacked Tutu's emotional eloquence. The commission was a series of events, it was not a process. Indeed the commission's brief was the antithesis of a truth and reconciliation commission. It was not the custodian of testimony, it was not concerned with the clamour of contested truths, and it was not equipped to evaluate and adjudicate. It was not equipped to show emotional engagement; it did not manoeuvre between just and unjust causes, just and unjust means; it was not a process of reconciliation through truth telling. It was not an attempt to come to terms with the state's role – through its mastery of policing and security – as a contributor to the conflict. It was not, then, concerned with narration as nation-building. Why not?

Professor Fionnuala Ni Aolain insists that 'part of the narrative of any internal conflict is a disclosure of the state's role in facilitating, combating and managing conflict'. The transition from armed conflict, therefore, must be concerned with the state's use of lethal force, and there, in the use of the law to mandate lethal force, the meaning of the conflict is found; and it is there, too, that 'the past demands definition'.[4]

In Northern Ireland the state refused to submit its own past to that demand for definition. The commissioners performed as if they were *the bench*, as the judiciary, receivers of submissions that would activate no disturbance – no nerves, no grief, no tears. During the commission's journey around the thirty or so destinations, the panel performed like wood, bolt upright, unyielding, apparently unaffected, as if to bend, or split, or creak would put them at risk of connection; as if they'd break with grief or shock. Only at the end of the meetings, when the formal business was over and people would venture towards them, did the commissioners relax, meet their gaze, lend an ear, touch an arm, shake a hand and look as if they were really listening.

No, the policing commission was an anti-truth commission – it was constructed to pre-empt a national journey of self-discovery. That is not to say that it inhibited testimony, it did not. But the testimonies were enunciated into assemblies that were more or less rancorous or empathic, they were received by the panel as if it were an empty space.

This is not to suggest that the commission was the enemy of reform, nor that it was unaffected. On the contrary, its commitment was palpable. But its commitment was ultimately expressed not as a critique of the conflict, not as a redress, but rather as reform in the manner of best practice derived from police services all over the world – a discourse of *modernisation*, as if the RUC was just old fashioned, bereft of consensus, facing the same challenges to mono-culturalism that were confronting police services all over the world. The commission was not an exemplar of the effort of hearing, of the hazardous work of witnessing in Northern Ireland, a place where the difficulty of bearing witness meaningfully – so that the society would be obliged to listen – was confirmed before its very ears during its consultations.

The commission was, of course, a participant, but it participated in the idea of impartiality. It did not intervene, chide the hecklers, challenge the conventional wisdoms that were belied by forensic research, acknowledge griefs or affirm testimonies that threatened the sovereign narratives about the conflict.

NOTES

1. Fionnuala Ni Aolain, *The Politics of Force, Conflict Management and State Violence in Northern Ireland*, Blackstaff Press 2000, p119.
2. J.D. Brewer & G.I. Higgins, 'Understanding anti-Catholicism in Northern Ireland', *Sociology*, Vol 33, No 2, 1999, 235-255.
3. A. Krog, *Country of My Skull*, Jonathan Cape 1999.
4. F. Ni Aolain, op cit.

12. Punishment beatings, violence and restorative justice

THE LONE RANGER

In the summer of 1999 another flank of unionist rebellion was opened up, which was to have a major influence on the debates on policing. The target was the Secretary of State, whose commitment to the peace process had made her unpopular with unionists reluctant to give up power. David Trimble didn't talk to Her Majesty's person in Northern Ireland – and this snub was tolerated by Her Majesty's government. Mo Mowlam was under grave pressure within Northern Ireland, and her tenure as Secretary of State was at risk. She was being undermined by Downing Street and the prime minister's main man, Peter Mandelson, who wanted her job. Instead of lending his authority to Mowlam, the prime minister was allowing unionist sexism and sectarianism to enfeeble her position, and thereby to service Mandelson's ambitions. The assault on Mowlam was a proxy for resistance to the peace process itself – to its complications and its promise of new times.

During 1999 a lone ranger appeared on the political horizon, and ambushed the Secretary of State – just as policing and justice were about to emerge from their contracted-out consultancies to restart the debates deferred by the Agreement. This 'man in the mask' was Vincent McKenna, and he succeeded in bringing punishment beatings – and thereby the violence of republicans – into the spotlight, just at the time when the police were about to be put under public scrutiny. His intervention deflected the public gaze away from the police and on to the paramilitaries, and added grave embarrassments to an already besieged Secretary of State.

The continuing resort by nationalist communities to paramilitaries to manage their unmanageables, the bad lads who were making their lives a misery, was by then just about the only community manifestation of the republicans' military machine. This was largely a symptom of the lack of any other legitimate or effective form of policing, and was a practice that also occurred within unionist communities. However,

McKenna put on a publicity stunt that was perfectly timed for those seeking to divert attention away from policing reform. He organised the presentation before the world's media of two brothers who were on the run from IRA community justice – two palefaces, with cropped hair, aimless eyes and bewildered incoherence. The boys performed perfectly. They were ingénues, boys from nowhere who'd been nowhere. But they were also lads that had exhausted and terrified their community, and were embroiled in the criminal justice system. Because of this they had come to the attention of the IRA, who had passed on a warning to a community priest that they should keep away (for more on community justice see pp197–201).

On the face of it McKenna was an unlikely champion of anyone's human rights. He claimed to have been in the IRA, and to have been among the bombers. Yes, he admitted, he'd been horrible, a hard drinker and a nasty husband. But now he'd reformed, re-married and become a good father; he had found faith and he was making amends. And he was irresistible to unionism on both sides of the Irish Sea. His allure was the story he told about himself – his claim to have once been an IRA fighter. In spring 1999 he had launched his Human Rights Bureau, and in the summer he produced a torrent of statistics purporting to shame the IRA. In the autumn he went on to bless the campaign to 'save the RUC'.

This poised young troubadour was fit, he was pious – a born-again Christian who did martial arts. He was perfect – a human rights advocate and former republican who was offering himself as an advocate for the RUC on the eve of its greatest political challenge. 'Mo Must Go' became his mantra.

In September McKenna consummated his first PR *coup de theatre* with another. An arresting image appeared in the national and international news media of a packed assembly in the Ulster Hall, a nineteenth-century concert hall and Belfast landmark. The crowd had risen to its feet, applauding one man, seated and statuesque – Vincent McKenna. The meeting was a rally for the RUC on the eve of the policing report, organised by Friends of the Union. It was not so much what he said as his persona that aroused the standing ovation. There was no greater affirmation than one from a former enemy. McKenna gave the unionists permission to not participate in change, to keep on saying no.

McKenna's story had always been punctuated by controversy, but something about him was irresistible: he gave counsel to the Unionist leadership, and to the Tory leadership in London. Both David Trimble and William Hague took their statistics and their cue from McKenna during the year of Mo Mowlam's calvary. So, what was going on? Who was Vincent McKenna? Of all the charismatic movers and shakers who animated Northern Ireland's civil society, why did this man uniquely attract such attention? and what kind of human rights organisation had he founded? His background was a mystery: most of his claims about his own former activities, including his membership of the IRA (which the IRA denied) were not substantiated by any evidence. A further irony of his amazing profile was that during his campaign to champion the police he was himself under police investigation for alleged child abuse (in November 2000 he was in fact convicted of sexual abuse of his daughter and sentenced to a prison term, see below).

McKenna's debut on the public stage had been in 1998, when the press reported a survey he had conducted on the Ormeau Road in Belfast, where he had apparently found 100 per cent tolerance among nationalists for Orange parades. This was inconceivable – it totally reversed a 1996 survey by the corporate colossus, Coopers Lybrand, which recorded that 95 per cent of nationalists wanted the Orange Order parade re-routed away from their community. McKenna's survey attracted a torrent of complaints from residents and was suspected by his supervising professor to be a fiction; it was regarded by most serious researchers as completely spurious. But authenticity and accuracy were not important – McKenna got noticed: the newspapers gave him spreads of celebrity-style attention. He was the right kind of republican – an ex-republican. After this fiasco – which nonetheless had given him cachet – McKenna threw himself into the victims' group Families Against Intimidation and Terror (FAIT), a government-funded organisation that campaigned against the IRA. McKenna arrived at FAIT basking in the Ormeau Road story; his presence there was at first magnetic, his colleagues marvelling at his charisma. But his subsequent career in FAIT was characterised by havoc and internal strife. For example McKenna told stories about receiving letter bombs, and claimed to have discovered letters from the director purporting to defend a sex offender, but the RUC concluded that these were hoaxes. And a story damaging to FAIT was published in the republican press alleging that the organisation was a beneficiary of the exiled Martin McGartland, a former British agent. *An Phoblacht* had a copy of the cheque in question – and a quote from McKenna.

Eventually McKenna left FAIT, and at end of April 1999 he set up the Human Rights Bureau, a one-person office supported by money from a rich American. A year or so later he was being described as 'Ulster's most seasoned human rights campaigner'. He became a celebrity. Newspapers chronicled his brutalised boyhood, and his hyped up IRA career – one that his old acquaintances didn't recognise.

The bureau's publications, largely based on RUC statistics on paramilitary punishment beatings, became much quoted. In January 1999 McKenna and David Trimble appeared together at a press conference, claiming that there had been an upsurge in punishment beatings, and that 11 prisoners on Christmas leave had been involved. David Trimble then appeared on the BBC's *Question Time* and repeated the claim. But he had not taken the precaution of checking the information with the RUC or the prison service, and the day after his television appearance he was forced to retract after they told him that all the Maze prisoners had in fact abided by the conditions of their release.

But the stories about punishment beatings were irresistible. They were used to support claims that the IRA had broken the ceasefire and, therefore, that Sinn Fein should be expelled from the Assembly. McKenna was a weapon against Mowlam. Two deaths provided a further occasion to once more proclaim that the ceasefire wasn't holding, and to wound Mowlam's credibility. (Charlie Bennett and Andrew Kearney were both said to have been killed by the IRA. Charlie Bennett was believed to be an informer for the security forces, and Andrew Kearney was alleged to be a drug dealer.) McKenna added fuel to the fireball by releasing part of a tape-recorded conversation with an NIO spokesperson, who, on being challenged to comment on 'the murder and mutilation of our people for political considerations', answered: 'the Secretary of State has to decide whether an incident is an internal housekeeping matter to the terrorist organisation or an attack on the entire community...' This was taken as evidence of Mowlam's indifference to terrorist attacks.

No one really believed that the republicans' declared end to military operations was anything but serious, but this was damaging to the Secretary of State, and the punishment beatings were used by those who were against the Agreement as a way of discrediting the nationalists. The IRA became the butt of a jibe, 'when is a ceasefire not a ceasefire?'[1]

But the scenario was in reality much more complicated. If punishment beatings were a breach of the ceasefires, then all the paramilitary organisations were implicated (though they were represented years later by Wilford and Wilson as a peculiarly republican modus operandi and a form of tyrannical community control; according to them, the streets were controlled by 'totalitarian' Sinn Fein and the 'ethnic protagonists'[2]). In fact, by 1999 this was less a republican than a loyalist modus operandi – during that year 40 per cent of paramilitary punishment attacks were republican and 60 per cent loyalist. There had been a shift in the republican approach to community safety – a rethink that had also extended to some loyalist paramilitary organisations – that had implications for all neighbourhoods where the RUC was not welcome. This was something that McKenna's story obscured. The community policing of neighbourhoods where the RUC had no legitimacy was a newsworthy story, but to cover it would have required curiosity about the paramilitaries as participants in change, rather than as the problem.

Mo Mowlam had to respond to the stories of the paramilitaries' rough justice. She could not condone them, but nor could she deny that the ceasefire was holding. She therefore chided the republicans: they were sailing close to the wind. But the stories wounded her, as did the comment on 'housekeeping'. Her constancy in sticking with the peace process, her pragmatic avoidance of options without exit clauses, was interpreted as capricious, a code for fickle femininity. Trimble's biographer Dean Godson later reckoned that Trimble had 'missed a trick' here – that the episode 'personalised things and pitted him against the most popular politician in the country ... all because of his emotional aversion to Mowlam, which hindered rational calculation on his part'. But though Trimble may have misjudged the situation, it was Mowlam who took the punishment. It was a de-stabilising period, and people were beginning to wonder whether she was being set up for a fall.

During the summer the vigilante presented himself as a victim. He was receiving letter bombs, death threats, and he'd even been shot at: McKenna invited the news media to his home to show a bullet hole through his sitting-room window. Something sinister was going on. But what was it? When asked about the investigation of these alleged attacks on McKenna, the RUC was surprisingly candid: these were 'elaborate hoaxes' and there was no investigation. The message was clear. The source of the allegations was also the suspect. He was doing this stuff to himself.

That threw some of his messengers into a quandary – but despite all the evidence, some journalists – notably the *Guardian*'s John Mullin and the *Observer*'s Henry McDonald – remained faithful, and went on quoting him as if he was wronged, a smeared but stalwart human rights advocate. In fact, Vincent McKenna was an impostor. People whose lives had been touched by him were incandescent – they suspected he was spinning his stories to silence other stories. From republicans who had done time with McKenna, to his children and his family in Monaghan, from his own colleagues to human rights campaigners with a long track record, from journalists with a forensic commitment to detail to officials in the Garda and the RUC and social services – all had sceptical or scary stories to tell about Vincent McKenna. The new impresario of human rights had abused the human rights of his own daughter. He had hurt and humiliated his former wife. In 1999 he was already the subject of a searching police investigation and in 2000 his daughter Sorcha, the main witness in his trial on 31 counts of sexually abusing her, waived her right to anonymity. She wanted people to know what this human rights advocate was really like. That was the end of the 'reformed terrorist's' usefulness – but by then the damage had been done. The Prime Minister had pulled out the most popular Secretary of State for Northern Ireland ever.

McKenna offered me and other journalists an enriched account of his 1999 arrest for child abuse in the Irish Republic (where his children were living). His theory about the arrest was that there was 'some kind of wheeling and dealing going on'. The arrest was not about the alleged abuse, but was because of 'other intelligence issues' – the police were interested in his political connections. He was being offered up in a trade-off between security services over a cache of Browning machine guns recently uncovered by police in the republic. It was all a smear, he said. This story was risible but it 'had legs'.

Two journalists in the Irish press, Darach McDonald and Anne Cadwallader, challenged his confections. An IRA source told McDonald, 'If anybody thinks we'd hand over a spent bullet, never mind perfectly good carbines, to set up Vincey McKenna they're even crazier than he is.' When I published the first interview with his daughter in a British newspaper, the *Independent on Sunday*, stories followed that were a reminder of his importance to anti-Agreement sceptics. John Mullin exemplified the approach in October 1999.[3] McKenna was a victim, whose alternatives were to 'stay and risk assassination or quit, forced out by what he claims is a republican smear campaign'. Affirming his importance to Agreement sceptics, Mullin noted that David Trimble 'regularly quotes McKenna's statistics', though he did admit that doubters included the NIO (which would, of course, have had access to police and social services intelligence). 'There is little doubt that many supporters of the ailing Good Friday Agreement would rather conveniently ignore his arguments'. Mullin offered startling 'evidence' – a purported memorandum from a police inspector, published on 'the internet', that implied that McKenna had been set up on the day of his arrest. Actually the 'memorandum' had been posted a day earlier on the World Socialist Web Site, a partisan site that supported McKenna.[4] And McKenna still had enough credit as 'a former Provo' for Henry McDonald to run a story in the *Observer* in 2000 that offered a novel line on a conspiracy against McKenna – collusion between Irish intelligence and the IRA.[5] The source for this was Vincent McKenna.

McKenna the person was important only to himself, and to the children and the women whose lives he dominated so malevolently. But McKenna the persona was treasure – he had briefed the leaders of unionist parties on both sides of the Irish Sea; he had attracted international attention; he had been a guided missile directed against the Secretary of State. He had headlined paramilitarism as Northern Ireland's problem at the moment when its mind was turning towards policing. Of course he was an impostor, but his utility for the enemies of the Agreement was indicative of a corrupting malice in unionist culture: a greedy enthusiasm for any old thing that might hurt its enemy. One interpretation of McKenna's embrace of the RUC was that it gave him cover. Another was that he was a British agent. One of Belfast's most scrupulous observers reckoned this was unlikely. McKenna seemed weird rather than a mainstream agent, 'you'd brief an agent better than that'. But his importance was that at a vital moment in the peace process 'he becomes of use'. There were two views in the Establishment, this writer added. 'One of them, in the security establishment, is very anti-Agreement. Punishment beatings became a hammer to smash the peace process and he was a willing hammer. Whatever he was, he was used big time.'

COMMUNITY JUSTICE: STICK YOUR FINGER IN THE HOLE AND FEEL THE GORE

A big idea that got little or no airing during that formative year – eclipsed by the lone ranger's crusade – had been developed after the ceasefires by republican and loyalist former prisoners. Their hope was to bring to exasperated neighbourhoods enduring the savagery of paramilitary punishments an alternative: non-violent community justice, disciplined by international human rights standards. 'We were saying to communities that it just wasn't on to shoot people', explained Jim Auld, a founder of a republican initiative, Community Restorative Justice in Ireland (CRJI). 'We would say to people, ok, you can call for someone's legs to be shot. But what if you had to stick a finger in the hole and feel the gore? What if you had to feel the bone crunching? We would say to the people in the community, is this what you want?'

Paramilitarism was not only implicated in violent punishment, it was also participating in the production of non-violence in everyday life. This was the story that didn't get told. Northern Ireland – like South Africa and the other societies emerging from tyranny and civil war – was discovering a new paradigm: post-conflict societies are violent. Violence is the landscape in which they live, it is a terrain where there are few discernable borders between legal and legitimate, political and criminal violence. Northern Ireland discovered, like South Africa, that violence proliferated with 'peace' and democracy. 'There is no such thing as post-conflict society', argues Graeme Simpson, director of South Africa's Centre for the Study of Violence and Reconciliation.[6] Even South Africa's 'miraculous' new constitution did not, could not, of itself generate a culture of rights.

In the absence of public confidence in the state's justice system, bequeathed from before, community justice can be both 'benevolent and extremely sinister'. The affluent buy safety through the private security industry; the poor turn to 'people's courts' or rough justice. The Centre for the Study of Violence and Reconciliation argues that peace agreements are no protection against the tendency for tyranny and civil war to militarise everyday life, to create 'insecurity, fear and the culture of impunity for perpetrators'. [7] During apartheid, the Centre argues, young men made their masculinity 'largely premised on their direct involvement in violence'. After apartheid, the society reeled ambivalently around the politics of gender and violence. [8] States of emergency sponsor states of crime: security services co-opt more or less organised crime; they work with warlords; they blackmail criminals to spy on their communities; militias become mafias, marginalised young men assert their mastery by seizing the public space they share with their community; if nothing else is available, lads take control by causing chaos. Community crime always erodes the sustainability of a place, it always challenges the statutory services; and in the context of civil conflict it generates crisis, because the security services either avoid it or exploit it. Northern Ireland exemplified this paradigm.

Before the Agreement, Jim Auld and his comrades were addressing community meetings about the nature of community justice. His stoical, serene presence encouraged an atmosphere of calm and contemplation amidst wrathful hurt; a sense that he had asked himself the questions he asked of his audience, that he had imagined himself on the journey he was inviting them to undertake.

After the ceasefires, republican combatants themselves were recoiling from the brutalism of breaking skin and bones, of improvising weapons to inflict the damage, firing bullets into knees, ankles, elbows, wrists. Just as the criminal justice system over the water was discovering that its courts and its prisons were not necessarily deterrents to young offenders – trial and prison were just another arena in which to perform personal heroism or martyrdom – so it was in post-ceasefire Northern Ireland, where mutilation could be worn as a medal, poor boys' bling.

Paramilitaries were no less involved in community discipline after the ceasefires than before. The ceasefires did not produce peace in everyday life, they ended a specific form of violence. Their repertoire of physical pain attracted opprobrium as political gangsterism; it was rarely understood as another variant of the retribution fantasies frequently invoked in popular culture against 'yobs' or 'paedophiles' or 'drug dealers'. Paramilitary punishments drew criticism as coarse 'mob rule'. It was routinely denied that the paramilitaries were responding to popular demand, or that they were operating in a crisis of policing.

The critique of the punishments as a breach of the ceasefires was a deliberate blurring of the nuanced formula of the ceasefire as the 'cessation of military operations': the distinction between 'military' and 'policing' activity was understood in the communities and in the institutions, including the police. It was also understood by the Secretary of State. But this nuanced distinction had been twisted in an attempt to undermine both the republicans and Mo Mowlam.

Yet paramilitarism described policing in all its formations in Northern Ireland. The RUC was a paramilitary force. Among republicans there was a scalding memory of catholic communities' defencelessness during the first year of the conflict. Republican paramilitaries believed that they would not be forgiven by their constituencies, nor would they forgive themselves, if they abandoned public safety before their public gave consent to a new police service. The IRA was regarded as the people's protection. Loyalist neighbourhoods, too, regarded paramilitarism as a noble part of their history, as part of their social structure, as their defence against republicans and against the state's class contempt.

Northern Ireland shared with other societies emerging from armed conflict or tyranny the legacy of violence as a way of working. The problem was not the lack of authority, but its proliferation. Pat Conway, one of the authors of non-violent restorative justice in Northern Ireland, challenged the theory of lack: 'people talk about a policing vacuum, but there are police everywhere, we've got the security forces, the RUC, and community policing through paramilitarism. This is a society stuffed full of authority figures.' Sinn Fein's Gerry Kelly believed that after the ceasefires a generation of young men who had not participated in the conflict began to see the paramilitaries 'as part of established authority, and therefore as people to be challenged'. That made it imperative that the paramilitaries be released from the work of policing the communities. The practitioners of virtuous harm knew it didn't work anyway; it didn't deter the most vexing and determined offenders. It was simultaneously a manifestation of power and of weakness, and it demanded something monstrous of men.

Punishment beatings as a form of law enforcement had attracted criticism from international human rights organisations. But a human rights discourse that was concerned only with the relation between states and citizens had also been criticised by women for its failure to address personal oppression between citizens, which was intensified by the militarisation of everyday life. The organisation that had been closest to the consequences of punishment beatings for the victims, the Northern Ireland Association for the Care and Resettlement of Offenders (NIACRO), founded a crisis service in 1990 for people and their relatives under paramilitary threat. Every year until the ceasefires NIACRO handled about 200 cases. Though McKenna's one-person bureau insisted that the beatings were nothing to do with the conflict, it was NIACRO's view that 'punishment beatings, shootings and exilings occur as a consequence of 30 years of conflict and the lack of acceptable and consensual policing'.

In the aftermath of the ceasefires, the expectation, and the early evidence, of a decline in punishment beatings was swiftly confounded by a sharp rise. Referrals to NIACRO rose to 224 in 1995, to 646 in 1998 and to 906 by 2001. During the years 1995-97, according to RUC figures, the number of shootings dropped hugely, but assaults peaked to 291 per year, compared to 53 at the beginning of the decade. And the use of less lethal weapons intensified the proximity between the beater and the beaten: bodies were brought horribly close as the blows found their victim. This was not what the warriors thought they had signed up to. But, as with other societies emerging from violent conflict, from Africa to the Middle East and the Balkans, peace had not brought security, or order. Confronted by the exponential rise in community crime and punishments, in 1996 NIACRO invited ex-prisoners active in community work to research alternatives to violence.

Among the loyalists, Tom Winstone, a former UVF lifer, set up the Greater Shankill Alternatives programme, working with young offenders. 'Initially the majority of our referrals – about 45 a year – came from the paramilitaries', explained Shankill project worker Debbie Waters. 'We would not be here if it weren't for the paramilitaries. Once they referred someone to us they were out of the equation. They knew they had no further role to play. Nothing.' The republicans approached Kieran McEvoy, a criminologist and human rights scholar at Queens University, and other human rights activists, to help develop ideas about 'informal justice'. The group included people who ran the IRA's 'civil administration', the unit concerned with intra-community conflict. Together they organised seminars, training, and a germinal discussion document on community restorative justice, which they distributed throughout the republican movement and also to the British and Irish governments. Together with NIACRO, the republicans launched several community restorative justice schemes as an alternative both to the brutalism of paramilitary punishments and the deficits of the state's justice system. [9] The regime is described as an attempt to be restorative to victims, to perpetrators, and to communities, to provide an opportunity for victims to be heard about the consequences of harm, and what needs to be done to heal. [10] The Northern Ireland projects involved intensive programmes that encouraged people to look at their lives, the harm they caused, to acknowledge and atone.

Between them, it is estimated that these schemes worked with thousands of people. At the beginning of the millennium, the republican network CRJI was dealing with almost 2000 cases a year. Beyond those cases, they campaigned for cultural change: promoting the restorative ethic in neighbourhoods demanding retribution. So, during the 1999 calumny about punishment beatings, there was already a vigorous cohort of advocates with something important to say about what justice might mean to victims and perpetrators. They were pioneers and potential partners in policing. But they were rendered inaudible. One of McKenna's triumphs was to help to quell a big idea, to rehearse the old polarisation rather than to recognise demonised former prisoners and combatants as humane innovators among the people and places that were regarded as rubbish. That story would have presented the damned as people whose own capacity for change offered itself as a resource to their ruined society, to change itself.

POLITICAL VETTING

Former prisoners in Northern Ireland were routinely barred from paid work, though many constituted corps of active citizenship. But the experiences that gave them credentials in their communities were also used to condemn them and deny them resources. Since 1985 community organisations had been the subject of secretive political vetting, under principles introduced by then Home Secretary Douglas Hurd. Any organisations suspected of having close links to paramilitaries were deprived of access to public funding. In working-class areas, particularly in Belfast and Derry, that might mean anyone doing anything. The Hurd Principles became associated with a particularly anti-republican orientation: the first victim was a creche organised at Conway Mill, a regenerated industrial complex off the

Falls Road housing community groups and workshops – and Sinn
Fein.[11]

Thus the state funded the anti-republican Families Against
Intimidation and Terrorism, but not Relatives for Justice, the families
of people killed or injured by the state, and not community justice
schemes supporting people at risk of violence from paramilitaries. The
state also blocked their access to the very considerable European Peace
and Reconciliation funds. According to Kieran McEvoy and Harry
Mika, the explicit engagement of former prisoners, and the genesis in
paramilitarism, as well as leading to a loss of funds through political
vetting, also contributed to the scrutiny to which CRJ schemes were
subjected by their academic monitors – and by the mass media.[12]

In the summer of 1999, the furore over punishment beatings masked
a sly manoeuvre by the NIO to restore police control over community
justice.[13] This was exactly what the pioneers had feared. [14] However,
some statutory agencies had developed 'innovative and pragmatic tech-
niques', that balanced 'their statutory responsibilities with the
sensitivities of the communities in which they work'; this was exactly
the sort of intelligent ambivalence that Lord Scarman had called for in
his 1981 report on the Brixton riots. But now that the violent political
conflict appeared to be over this sensitivity and pragmatism was in
jeopardy. The NIO issued a protocol insisting that only those working
'in full co-operation with the police'[15] would get support. That meant
only *police* restorative justice schemes, of which there were only two:
between 1999 and 2001 they had worked with fewer than 100 cases,
mostly 'first time shoplifters who had taken goods under the value of
£15'.[16]

Furthermore, the police schemes did not engage people whose
offending brought them into dangerous conflict with their own
communities. They were not community schemes. But these were the
schemes upon which the NIO smiled and to which funds flowed – not
the community initiatives that had been handling over 90 per cent of all
restorative justice cases. McEvoy and Mika discerned an obsessive
demand 'to control the uncontrollable', and to reassert the centrality of
the state.[17]

The NIO's decision pre-empted both Patten and the Criminal
Justice Review that was meeting during 1999. Later, the Patten report
accorded a place to independent service providers, whilst the Criminal
Justice Review, made up largely of civil servants reviewing their own
systems, supported the NIO. A critical member of the review
commented that the police had 'not come to terms with the fact that the
war was over'. 'The police had no recognition of the fact that if you are

an anti-terrorist force you cannot walk into a community and be its friend. The frame of mind was that they were at war with the IRA, and they could not forgive anyone for not letting them win that war.'

The CRJI's Jim Auld argued that the police wanted to 'make us be their conduit into the nationalist community'. This would not be tolerated. 'We will not be used by perpetrators to get them out of a hole, and we will not be used by the NIO to get them out of a hole either.'

AFFIRMATION

In spite of a lack of official recognition, the republican and loyalist projects were commended by the Justice Oversight Commissioner, Lord Clyde, for 'valuable and effective work' that was motivated by the desire to make 'a positive and peaceful contribution to the welfare of the communities which they serve'. Lord Clyde added a decorous slight to the NIO by commenting that, if the community schemes had not existed, 'it might be difficult as matters stand to provide a similar service. Indeed the void might have undesirable consequences'.[18]

Lord Clyde's enthusiasm, and his invitation to the NIO to get a move on, did not go unnoticed by the Independent Monitoring Commission, the body set up to monitor the transition 'to a peaceful society and stable and inclusive devolved government'. The IMC was set up in 2004 by the Dublin and London governments, a product of the Joint Declaration in 2003, when the British government finally seem to register the irreducible importance of de-militarisation and policing reform to nationalists. The IMC took itself to the community schemes to see for itself what was happening. It was impressed, and commended the community projects for their local roots, their work as advocates with the statutory agencies for people at risk of punishment, and finally for their success. [19]

At the end of 2005, isolated but with its sanctimony intact, the NIO unveiled its restorative justice criteria: only those schemes taking their referrals from the police were legitimate. This was 'not negotiable'.

JUSTICE FOR WOMEN

The restorative justice movement was among the most practised in the arts of peacemaking within neighbourhoods. But the state's recidivism left it seeking legitimacy precisely at a time when it needed to be challenged from within the community itself. Community restorative justice didn't do domestic and sexual violence. Women and children living with domestic and sexual violence were not entitled to restoration, rehabilitation and, therefore, the community's respect. Men being victimised and wounded in public places by men were deemed worthy of human rights; women and children being violated by men in their own homes were not. They were denied a service, and their interests and insights were edited out of the transformative agenda. The collective cultures that sponsored violence were not the concern of IMC or the other official bodies such as the Patten commission – or the restorative justice movement.

Yet, as South Africa had revealed, this was the key to understanding the prevalence of violence and its mutations from war and peace. Antje Krog's lyrical chronicle of the truth commission, *Country of My Skull* – unashamedly positioned and poetic reportage – revealed the ghastly idiosyncrasies of violence endured by women in their homes and in their prison cells and police stations, and the intractable shame that attached itself to victims. The women didn't come to the commission – it had to go out to find them, it had to create the conditions in which the unspeakable could be spoken. [20]

The eminent Harvard clinician Dr Judith Lewis Herman designates domestic and sexual violence as 'crimes of domination'. Violence towards women belongs to a repertoire of historically sanctioned strategies of domination and conquest. Not all men do it, many men fear and abhor it, but the men who abuse and kill women are conventional, typical of men in general, across all classes and creeds.[21] Masculinised ideologies and institutions everywhere utilise violence as a political and personal resource to effect their will. Men use rape as a weapon of war; sexual violence is a means of intimate torture and terrorism. Wars have spawned an archive of evidence about men's violence against women and each other that then ruins the peace. South Africa is the tragic paradigm. The place the world loved for black people's gracious liberation of their country from the one of the cruellest regimes on earth is now tormented by men's violence.

South African analysts of violence and trauma repudiate the notion that the collapse of apartheid led to the collapse of authority. They see instead an apartheid state that 'demonstrated for decades its legitimation of violence as a means of maintaining political power'.[22] So, violence became 'socially sanctioned'. Apartheid was not only racist; it mobilised traditional patriarchal authority to do its dirty work. Domestic violence is deemed 'an excellent barometer of the social and political dislocation of a society in transition'.[23] To exempt personal and domestic violence from the analysis of political violence 'would be to deny the fundamental nature of power relationships'.

But in Northern Ireland that is what happened. The restorative justice movement did not address men's violence against women, or the logic of violence in masculine cultures; the Patten commission's priority was policing, not the creation of a peaceful society. And the IMC's stewardship of 'peaceful' transition did not engage women's experience, it did not investigate the personal and political function of violence; its sights were set on the paramilitaries. The Victims Commission, too, was preoccupied with the victims of 'events' not the violence of everyday life.

If the Victims Commission was concerned with victims of paramilitary violence, and IMC's priority was the risk *of* paramilitary activity, community restorative justice addressed risk *from* paramilitary activity. So, women living in neighbourhoods where the police were not welcome were left to manage personal tyranny – that was too difficult, too dangerous, too unpredictable to warrant intervention or interest. They were witnesses to their own defeat, their humiliation sealed by what amounted to a vow of silence in the community.

The problem of male violence against women is not restricted to Northern Ireland of course. During the three decades from the mid-1970s, when there was a revolution in how the meaning and motives of men's violence were understood, more women were reporting 'crimes of domination' across the United Kingdom as a whole, while proportionately fewer men were being prosecuted. The British Crime Survey showed that in 2005 almost half of women in the United Kingdom had experienced domestic violence, sexual assault or stalking. And research by Professor Liz Kelly for the Home Office showed that, in the case of rape the conviction rate had dropped to 5.3 per cent, the lowest for thirty years. [24] In Northern Ireland the tradition of militarism and the lack of police legitimacy compounded the problem. RUC figures on domestic violence – acknowledged to be an underestimate – reported that the domestic violence rate more than doubled during the 1990s, from 3326 incidents to 7335 in 2000. By designating these crimes ineligible, the global community restorative justice movement has attracted voluminous criticism. [25]

Community restorative justice, and its capacity to bring tranquillity, is diminished by this lacuna. Its wish to be a resource in the society's transition demands that it be more ambitious – that it should address bigger stuff, the violence that circulates between sexism and sectarianism. That would require a coalition with the survivors of men's violence who name the problem with no name. [26]

All of this could not be more salient to the transition in Northern Ireland. The macho power that circulates around militarism, paramilitarism and community crime, breaks a society's heart. But the term gender is like a ghost, both there and not there in a society's consciousness. So, masculinity is protected from scrutiny, and the blame for violence migrates to *bad, mad and dangerous* men; to the paramilitaries' *armed* men, not armed *men*.

NOTES

1. Neil Mackay, 'Mo's Woes', *Sunday Herald*, 29.8.99.
2. Rick Wilford and Robin Wilson, *From the Belfast Agreement to State Power-sharing*, PSA paper 2006.
3. John Mullin, 'Balance of Terror', *Guardian*, 21.10.99.
4. Chris Marsden, 'Irish Civil Rights Activist Targeted for Smear Campaign', 29.10.99.
5. Henry McDonald, 'Irish Soldier Aided IRA, says ex-Provo', *Observer*, 15.4.00.
6. Graeme Simpson, *Rebuilding Fractured Societies: Reconstruction, reconciliation and the changing nature of violence – Some self-critical insights from post-apartheid South Africa*, Centre for the Study of Violence and Reconciliation 2000.
7. Ibid.
8. Ibid.
9. Community restorative justice first emerged among aboriginal peoples to address the way that orthodox justice, modelled on the British system, accelerated the difficulties of already disadvantaged people.
10. P. Braithwaite, *Restorative Justice and Responsive Regulation*, Oxford University Press 2002.
11. Northern Ireland Council for Voluntary Action, *The Political Vetting of Community Work in Northern Ireland*, NICVO 1990.
12. Kieran McEvoy and Harry Mika, 'Punishment, Policing and Praxis: Restorative Justice and Non-Violent Alternatives to Paramilitary Punishments in Northern Ireland', in *Policing and Society*, Vol 11, 2001, pp359-382.
13. Letter from the Northern Ireland Office to NIACRO, reported in McEvoy and Mika, op cit.
14. Jim Auld, Brian Gormally, Kieran McEvoy, Michael Richie, *Designing a System of Community Restorative Justice in Northern Ireland – a Discussion Document*, Belfast 1997.
15. NIO 1999 Protocol on Restorative Justice, quoted in Kieran McEvoy and Harry Mika, 'Restorative Justice and the Critique of Informalism in Northern Ireland', *British Journal of Criminology*, 42, 2002, pp534-562.
16. David Mahoney, Tim Chapman, Jonathan Doak, *Restorative Cautioning, A Study of Police-based Restorative Cautioning Pilots in Northern Ireland*, NIO Research and Statistical Series, Report No 4, NIO 2002.
17. McEvoy and Mika, 2002, op cit.

18. Lord Clyde, *Second Report of the Justice Oversight Commissioner*, HMSO 2004.
19. Independent Monitoring Commission, Fifth Report, April 2005.
20. Antje Krog, op cit.
21. Dobash and Dobash et al, 'Just an Ordinary Guy', in *Violence Against Women*, Vol 10, no 6, 2004, 577-605.
22. M. Motshekga and E. Delport (eds), *Women and Children's Rights in a Violent South Africa*, Institute for Public Interest, Law and Research 1993, pp3-13.
23. G. Simpson, *Rebuilding Fractured Societies*, Centre for the Study of Violence and Reconciliation, Johannesburg 2000.
24. L. Kelly, J. Lovett & L. Regan, *A Gap or a Chasm: Attrition in Reported Rape*, Home Office Research Study 293, 2005.
25. See Maureen Cain, 'Beyond Informal Justice', in J. Matthews (ed), *Informal Justice*, Sage 1988; K. Daly and J. Stubbs, 'Feminist Engagement with Restorative Justice', *Theoretical Criminology*, Vol 10 No 1, 2006, pp9-28; B. Hudson, 'Restorative Justice: the challenge of sexual and racial violence', in G. Johnstone (ed), *A Restorative Justice Reader*, Willan 2003.
26. Rape Crisis and Women's Aid. Women's Aid runs about thirty premises for women fleeing domestic violence.

13. Mowlam, Mandelson and the policing crisis

The shenanigans of summer 1999 were echoed by the ticking time bomb of decommissioning and demilitarisation. The reform of policing – the bottom line for catholics and nationalists of all hues and classes – was trapped in the crisis.

Downing Street's reading of the crisis showed how little responsibility it felt for nationalist neighbourhoods. This was careless. Downing Street was taking for granted the political interests that were driving both change and peace. Its strategic objective was stability, and this meant the preservation of David Trimble. Ironically, it also meant the removal of Mo Mowlam and the installation of Blair's main man, Peter Mandelson, in Hillsborough Castle – greatly to the relief of David Trimble, who could now talk man-to-man with a Secretary of State. Mandelson's tenure precipitated neither peace nor stability, however, but crisis.

ONE STEP FORWARD ...
From spring to summer 1999 both governments were involved in intense negotiations towards devolved government and a parallel schedule of decommissioning. The new government was to emerge alongside a positive report from the international commission chaired by General John de Chastelain that was overseeing the decommissioning of the paramilitary arsenals. The British and Irish governments had described the next steps in *The Way Forward* and crossed their fingers.

The British government had been under intense pressure from unionism to enforce linkages between the decommissioning of arms and just about anything. Decommissioning had not been written into the Agreement: in a tactical manoeuvre, however, Tony Blair had offered a decommissioning deadline as a last-minute personal codicil to encourage unionism to sign up to the deal. Decommissioning was understood by the majority of the parties to be part of a larger project of demilitarisation. However, for unionism decommissioning was a proxy for the defeat of republicanism, its condition for power-sharing.

David Trimble put forward a pre-emptive demand for a 'credible start to the process of decommissioning ...' Hopes bloomed briefly in July when de Chastelain reported that there had indeed been a credible start, and Sinn Fein committed itself to work for decommissioning 'in accordance with the Agreement'. Blair described this as a 'seismic shift'. But the UUP rejected the steps outlined in *The Way Forward* and then boycotted the formation of the new Northern Ireland government. It was as if Patrick Mayhew's ghost had risen again to say boo! to power-sharing. Thereupon Seamus Mallon accused unionism of 'dishonouring the Agreement', and resigned as Deputy First Minister. Mo Mowlam, still in office at this point, saw that the process had to be internationalised if it was to survive and appealed to Senator George Mitchell, the international mediator, to return.

The timing of Trimble's unilateralism was not innocent. It coincided with the Orange marching season, and Northern Ireland's First Minister was nothing if not an Orangeman. Portadown was at the heart of his constituency, and since the spring he had been preoccupied by the ongoing crisis at Drumcree. Orangemen's right to go where they pleased, and the IRA's duty to disarm, dominated Trimble's agenda in his first year as First Minister.

CRISIS MANAGEMENT

The British government had invested in the idea of a political centre dominated by unionism. But there was no stable centre. And in any case something was gathering sway that would bring its policy of stability to ruin: the fissuring of the dominant bloc and the ascendancy of Ian Paisley, the Big Man, unionism's unmanageable holy roller, whose pleasure in hatred was the force field of anti-Agreement feeling.

When Mandelson arrived in the autumn, the parties were working with Senator George Mitchell on a way out of the impasse. Early in November, with Mitchell's help, the UUP and Sinn Fein reached a deal: the UUP would acknowledge nationalism's right to pursue a united Ireland by peaceful means, and they would participate in a power-sharing executive; Sinn Fein would acknowledge the end of the armed conflict, and, once an executive had been established, the IRA would decommission its weapons under the scrutiny of an interlocutor of international standing. But could Trimble win his party over to this compromise? His apparent inability to lead his party was now the only obstacle to Northern Ireland's politicians beginning the business of governing their own society.

Trimble secured a slim majority of his fellow Assembly members for the deal, but the minority included formidable critics, including his deputy, the maverick John Taylor. At this point Trimble gave up. At a meeting with Senator Mitchell, NIO officials, the Secretary of State and Sinn Fein leaders, Trimble told them he couldn't pull it off: the deal was done for. Mandelson boldly suggested that he himself would address Trimble's Assembly colleagues. He met the grumbling UUP group. He warned them that this deal was as good as it would get for a generation. And he offered them another codicil: 'If the IRA don't follow by decommissioning, I'll stand by you.'

That day fixed the template for Mandelson's management of Northern Ireland. He assiduously 'worked' the unionist leadership, and worked to its timetable. This appeared to be realpolitik, but it put the put the entire peace process at risk. It gave unionism a renewed sense that it was the centre of gravity.

Trimble secretly did his own deal with his party: he offered a personally signed, post-dated letter pledging to resign as First Minister if the IRA did not begin decommissioning by the beginning of February 2000 – four months earlier than the Agreement's May 2000 deadline. This gave the IRA and the interlocutor only two months to come up with a proposal. But it reassured unionists that they could still be masters of their little universe. Predictably, however, decommissioning didn't happen. Demilitarisation had not happened either. Nevertheless, the IRA, harried by the Dublin government, issued a pledge to 'finally and completely put arms beyond use'.

THE IRA'S DOCUMENT – NOW YOU SEE IT, NOW YOU DON'T

The stage was now set for a showdown. On 10 February 2000, the date of the deadline derived from Trimble's timetable, Mandelson spent much of the day planning the suspension of the devolved government. The virtuoso media man toured the television studios, and catching the 6 o'clock news, announced that the IRA had failed to deliver on decommissioning and that he was therefore suspending the Assembly.

By this time, the IRA's proposals to progress disarmament lay on his desk. But Mandelson claimed – inconceivably – that he had not read the document and did not know what it contained. These same proposals had reached the Taoiseach in Dublin early that morning and Downing Street by mid-morning. Ahern and Blair knew what was in the document. There was therefore no way that Mandelson didn't know too.

The IRA text was late and it was limited; it stated that, in the context of the full implementation of the Agreement, it would put its arms beyond use. But it represented a step forward, and was the result of considerable effort by Gerry Adams to win over reluctant republicans.

At about 5 o'clock on 10 February Trimble's office warned Mandelson's office that his resignation letter was about to be delivered. Minutes later, the script for suspension had been drawn up by Blair and Mandelson – Trimble didn't have to resign. The British suspended Northern Ireland's government instead.

At around 6.30 that evening de Chastelain issued a positive response to the IRA text: decommissioning could be achieved. But his statement had been pre-empted by Mandelson. Northern Ireland's first sovereign, power-sharing government was over. The Irish government was aghast – furious with IRA for its procrastination, and with the British government for its unilateral destruction of the new Assembly, and its failure to take its lead from de Chastelain's commission. It was also extremely worried that suspension was constitutionally questionable.

Women's Coalition Assembly Member Monica McWilliams had witnessed these manoeuvres with growing alarm. She complained bitterly that Mandelson had refused to meet with pro-Agreement parties to find a way together of averting the crisis. Mandelson's choreography that day had, in effect, been authorised by unionism. Although the Assembly was the creation of an international treaty between Westminster and Dublin, endorsed by a massive majority on both sides of the border and in Washington, the wishes of all these parties were brushed aside in a destructive gesture that confirmed the subordination of the people, the potency of the unionist veto, and the sovereignty of the British state. Here was a Labour Secretary of State behaving like a colonial Tory, petulant, bullying, with a tendency to take things personally, and a surly impatience with the human rights agenda. His estrangement from nationalism and republicanism was not concealed, and it located him within the orbit of unionism, the NIO and the RUC.

By now Mandelson was looking messy, not Machiavellian. He had designed no exit, and he seemed to be the servant not of the peace process but of the unionist veto and the securocrats. In this crisis the difference between Mowlam and Mandelson was the difference between 'new beginnings' and the 'old tradition'. Mowlam would have kept the process going. Mowlam had understood that the NIO and securocrats were not neutral. Her practice had been to keep the process alive, to keep the protagonists in it, to try to keep them engaged rather than threaten them with ultimatums that created, rather than resolved, crises. After the February suspension, the prospects for decommissioning, demilitarisation and police reform seemed far away. Peter Mandelson was beginning to understand that the link between guns and government was more complicated than the unionist mantra had encouraged him to think. But his alienation from the pro-Agreement parties left him huddled with sceptics and securocrats. While the realpolitik was telling him that disarmament needed to match decommissioning, he seemed unable to release himself from unionist ultimatums.

Just as Trimble was under pressure, the Sinn Fein leadership was under pressure from IRA volunteers, who were waiting for evidence of demilitarisation, and were not alone in feeling sickened by the suspension of devolved government. But Mandelson appeared to take his cue not from dialogue with republicans but from security services files.[1] So, too, it seems, did Tony Blair, who was noticed at meetings deferring to his chief of staff Jonathan Powell for a digest of security services' assessments of what the republicans were up to.

POLICING AFTER SUSPENSION

None of this helped the British government apprehend the depths of catholic disaffection – at all levels – from the RUC. It did not understand the yearning for a new policing culture; it didn't notice just how much policing mattered to everyone who *needed* the new times. Without structural reform and democratisation, there was no way that nationalists would participate in a new police service.

When Patten's policing commission reported in September 1999, as expected it offered a compromise. It did not advocate immediate rescinding of the emergency laws, but it proposed a new police service founded on human rights, marked by a new oath, not to the queen but to human rights and equality and the ethics of the Agreement. It did not propose a purge of bad apples and elements complicit in sectarian murder, but it recommended that the 'force within a force', Special Branch – the counter-insurgency unit – be merged with the Criminal Investigation Department.

Its proposal on recruitment towards a representative service followed the MacPherson Report's recommendation of a ten-year timetable, and suggested a 50-50 recruitment of catholics and protestants (though the commission missed the opportunity to secure gender representivity by an equivalent recruitment programme). The report argued for an acceleration of civilianisation – an approach that drew on contemporary thinking about the demilitarisation of police services. And it proposed that policing boards be able to buy in services – here it was envisaging that neighbourhoods might purchase the services of local community restorative justice schemes. Control over policing was to be vested in a Policing Board – rather than the Secretary of State. The commission was unequivocal – policing had to be rescued from political manipulation. And society had to be rescued from unaccountable policing, so the commission proposed structures of accountability through the Policing Board, which would be made up of Assembly Members, among others, and local policing partnerships.

None of this would have appeared as anything other than exemplary elsewhere, but, bounced by unionist fury, the government lost confidence in renewal, and backed away. Downing Street utterly underestimated the strength of feeling among nationalists and republicans, and among catholics in general. Policing was, for them, the Geiger counter for measuring the government's good faith. Nationalists' participation in the new structures was entirely dependent on police reform.

Policing and disarmament became entwined. The disarmament target agreed in the peace talks was May 2000, and this was also the month when the policing bill was due to be presented to the Westminster Parliament. At the beginning of May, the Irish government, the SDLP and Sinn Fein were led to believe that the policing report would be fully translated into the legislation. On 5 May the British and Irish governments jointly announced 'Proposals necessary to full implementation of the Agreement by June 2001'. On 6 May, the Prime Minister announced that legislation would be enacted by November and the new Police Service of Northern Ireland would be introduced in April 2001. Within a year, Northern Ireland would acquire for the first time in its history a police service acceptable to everyone. Also on 6 May, the two governments, together with Sinn Fein, agreed a process for inspection of the IRA arsenal, whilst the British government would work towards demilitarisation.

Everyone seemed to be embarking together on the long march towards disarmament and democratic policing. Then the policing Bill was published. It was not at all what the policing commission had recommended. Sotto voce, the government had been muttering that the 'security situation' precluded full implementation. But what, wondered Professor Brendan O'Leary, had changed between the beginning of the month and the end?[2] And what had changed between the publication of the Patten Report and the Bill itself? Apart from Mo Mowlam's replacement by Peter Mandelson, that is?

What had been going on was the re-interpretation of the Patten commission to soothe the refuseniks. One of Mandelson's gifts to unionism was to hang on to the old name: RUC would be in the 'title deeds' of the new service. And the 'new beginning' would only apply to the new recruits. The change to a neutral name, and neutral buildings and emblems, for the new service, as recommended by the policing report, was jettisoned. These things would be left to the Secretary of State. That created uncertainty, commented O'Leary, where the commission had created clarity.

Mandelson had made it known in the first few months of his reign that he was not interested in the new equality and human rights oath intended to replace the oath to the Crown, and he was true to his word. The Bill obliged only new recruits to take the human rights oath. The 50-50 recruitment of catholics and protestants over a ten-year timetable was reduced inexplicably to three. Thus there was no way within the foreseeable future that the police would become representative. District Policing Partnerships would not be allowed to raise local taxes to support local policing initiatives, and they would not be allowed to purchase services outside police or statutory agencies – that, decreed the NIO, might mean paramilitaries being subsidised by taxpayers. Instead of diminishing the Secretary of State's powers, and freeing policing from 'partisan political control', the Secretary of State's powers were actually increased. And, by excluding anyone with a 'criminal' record from participation in local police partnership boards, former combatants were banned. The powers of the Chief Constable and Secretary of State to block investigations were retained; and the details of the IPC's plan for a Policing Ombudsman were rejected.

The government also rejected the commission's approach to policing as 'collective community responsibility'. That, commented criminologists Paddy Hillyard and Mike Tomlinson, not only squandered community initiatives; it also eschewed the potential to dispense with the 'them' and 'us' polarisation which had prevailed during Northern Ireland's more or less permanent state of emergency.[3] Policing Board membership, instead of being organised to preclude partisan control, was to be skewed to give unionism the power to veto inquiries. The Bill gave the Secretary of State the power to veto the Policing Board, and the Chief Constable the power to reject reasonable requests from the board and to prevent it from launching inquiries into police practice before the legislation came into effect. This amounted to an amnesty.

O'Leary explained the radical discrepancy between the Report and the Bill as the work of Mandelson and the NIO, who 'mischievously used their textual warrant' to re-write a creative compromise between nationalism and unionism, which they'd misread as a nationalist policing report. The ferocity of this critique of 'Britannia's perfidy' was indicative. When Blair appealed to Clinton for support on policing, the President is reported to have told him that the outcome of the proposed legislation would be like policing Alabama with an all-white force.

Just as equality and human rights defenders had to mobilise during the summer of 1998 to preserve the spirit of the Agreement that was lost in translation, so they now had to throw themselves into the defence of acceptable policing. The ranks were formidable: the Ombudsman, the Police Authority, the Women's Coalition, Sinn Fein, the SDLP, the Irish Government, the Catholic Church, the Human Rights Commission, CAJ and the human rights community; they all lobbied the government. Washington also pitched in. The SDLP tabled 44 amendments to the Bill in parliament. Sinn Fein identified more than 75 significant discrepancies between the Report and the Bill,

The day before the legislation was to be blessed by the Lords on 15 November 2000, the policing commission's expert on policing reform, Professor Clifford Shearing, wrote a searing critique: the Bill had rejected the commission's crucial conception of 'policing' – as distinct from the 'police' – and narrowed its focus to an institution rather than a public practice. Thus it had also restored institutional exclusivity, rather than expanded collective responsibility for policing. This distinction was vital to the transition. The commission had proposed operational responsibility instead of the traditional doctrine of operational independence; this was vital to transparency and human rights. But the Bill completely eviscerated these proposals, said Shearing.[4] However, in spite of all the opposition, the Act was passed.

Mandelson had utterly underestimated the mass catholic experience of the RUC: it was an experience that transcended class and political alignment; it was in the waters. Instead of helping unionism to adjust to the new times, to change its aspirations, Mandelson had tried to salvage unionist ambitions and pride. He therefore presented himself as unionism's broker, and not as the Agreement's advocate.

Catholics of all allegiances refused to endorse the new service, and all the nationalist parties refused to participate in the Policing Board. Mandelson had succeeded in totally alienating catholic/nationalist sensibilities, while simultaneously failing to satisfy the unionist refuseniks. In the New Year Mandelson lost his job when fresh scandal forced his second resignation. Policing reform languished. It took six months before a specially convened summit in Weston Park, an English stately home, found a breakthrough. Unionism expected decommissioning to top the agenda at the summit. But this time it didn't. Policing defined the priorities of the Weston Park Declaration of 2001. At last, it seemed, Tony Blair had been persuaded that policing was of the greatest importance to catholics, to their parties and their churches. If their concerns were not met, they would not endorse the new policing arrangements.

The Declaration announced that more of the policing report would be implemented. Nationalists' long-standing grievances about collusion between state forces and loyalist paramilitaries would be addressed. Somehow, however, both the SDLP and Sinn Fein failed to seize the time and commit Britain to an inquiry. Blair merely agreed to invite a judge of international standing to inquire into whether certain cases warranted public inquiries. He promised to publish the judge's reports. But Blair was buying time. The government only needed to consult its own archives to find evidence of collusion, commented Jane Winter, director of British Irish Rights Watch. In spite of these weaknesses though, the significance of the Weston Park Declaration was that it drew the British government into daylight as a contributor to the conflict.

NORTHERN IRELAND AND LABOUR'S POLITICS
At this point it is worth pausing to review the different approaches of Mo Mowlam and Peter Mandelson as they refracted the contradictory forces struggling for sway within New Labour. The approach of Mowlam, which succeeded in opening up pathways to dialogue, was completely different from that of any of her predecessors or successors. It is therefore worth considering whether, had her approach been continued, many of the problems outlined in this book could have been avoided. Fundamentally, Mowlam understood the nuances of inclusivity. She believed in the political 'centre' – not least to preserve unionism's presence – but never thought it exhausted the cast of players.

Mowlam's social progressivism animated her approach to Northern Ireland, and her efforts to represent all its people in the peace process. This distinguished her from her predecessors, and from the new Assembly's First Minister, who performed unswervingly as a *unionist* First Minister; and it was in complete contrast to Peter Mandelson, whose authoritarian populism found strength in the security state and led to the breakdown of the peace process.

Mowlam and Mandelson represented a fundamental cleavage in the New Labour project. Mowlam brought feminism, social progressivism and a left-leaning pragmatism to the tone and style of New Labourism. She was opposed to New Labour's adoption of a 'new imperialism'. Like Labour's first Foreign Secretary Robin Cook, and International

Development Secretary Clare Short, her politics was guided by a progressive 'ethical dimension'.

The presence of more women in the House of Commons than ever before after the 1997 general election was a noticeable feature of New Labour's vaunted modernity. This was a gift to New Labour from the irrepressible activism of Labour feminists during the 1980s and 1990s. This, however, was not the kind of modernisation that propelled the Blair court, and feminism was jilted by New Labour in government. Mowlam personified the shift away from the christian moralism – not to say misogyny – of the men's movement that ran New – and Old – Labour. She was an academic, with a relaxed (rather than religious) approach to morals and a pragmatic commitment to social justice. She admitted to having lived a 'messy' personal life before her partnership with Jon Norton. She was renowned for indiscriminate cuddles. She acknowledged that she'd smoked cannabis and that, unlike President Clinton, she'd inhaled. And she was game: she appeared hilariously on Graham Norton's camp comedy TV show in 1999 descending a stair-case escorted by two golden men dressed only in loincloths, to officiate at the marriage of two dogs. Though passionately New Labour, she was also in many ways its antithesis.

The macho megalomania of New Labour's leadership guaranteed that women's impact on the archaic and rowdy culture of the Commons was negligible. Regimented in the power-dressing livery of New Labour's dress code, these new women MPs were dubbed 'Blair's Babes'. Mo Mowlam and Clare Short broke with these constraints, and they were to pay for this eventually with their political careers.

The appointment of Mowlam as Secretary of State brought an unprecedented change of tone to the peace process in Northern Ireland. Mowlam was unusual. She was a fully engaged Minister deter-mined to make a difference. She also already knew the territory. After her death even David Trimble affirmed her early commitment to inclu-sivity in her contacts – this was something new. The NIO had traditionally dominated local politicians, and could also over-ride appointed Ministers for Northern Ireland, who often had only a fleet-ing, and sometimes reluctant, responsibility for their posts. This happened less when Mo Mowlam was in office.

Her raunchy vernacular and affectionate manners extended not only to the aristocrats who sojourned at Hillsborough Castle, but also to the woman in the street, and to former combatants among both loyalists and republicans; she believed that they too had to be engaged in the settlement and the new polity. She acquired a reputation as a raggedy saint for a population habituated to towering patricians, dispatched to do time in Northern Ireland. She was unprecedentedly popular – though not to the liking of patriarchal, conservative unionism, which had sheltered itself from the power of women – or to Blair, the jealous god of New Labour.

Mowlam was the first Secretary of State who was not sequestered among securocrats and civil servants – though she sometimes seemed unable or unwilling to assert her power against the hostile NIO, who were not above leaking or briefing against her. Her chutzpah was exemplified by her readiness to go where other Secretaries of State had feared to tread, whether it was a community centre in the republican inner city Falls, or the neighbouring loyalist Shankill – both of them hard inner-city neighbourhoods, the pauperised locales that fielded foot-soldiers in the armed conflict. This confidence was consummately expressed by her visit in 1998 to the Maze Prison, to meet loyalist prisoners who were turning against the peace process. As she later wrote, 'It was the act itself that held the meaning for them'.[5] She did not recoil from the scorned body. Mowlam supported the equality and rights agenda within the novel culture of governance that developed during the peace process. When it was diminished in translation to legislation by the NIO, she lent her support to the struggle for its restoration. The same struggle met policing reform. But by then there was no Mowlam.

NEW MAN – OLD TIMES

Peter Mandelson was a kingmaker in beau Blair's court; some regarded him as 'the prince of darkness', a malevolent and petulant fixer; to others he was a witty and cosmopolitan exponent of the short-lived Third Way. Mandelson had designed Neil Kinnock's audacious 1987 election campaign, and went on to become Tony Blair's adviser and MP for Hartlepool. Mandelson and New Labour's pollster Philip Gould were perhaps the most devout exponents of the populist discourse of New Labour, and its embrace of a post-Thatcher universe. Mandelson was also a conspirator, a man possessed by political ambition who, according to friends, 'wanted to rule the country'.[6]

Though Mandelson was gay, and enjoyed life in a public/political milieu transformed by gay activism, progressive sexual politics was not a noticeably vociferous part of his portfolio. He did not use his power at the heart of the Labour machine to reciprocate the gay vote with reform of homophobic institutions (though Labour began to make good in its third term). His power depended on the patronage of the leader; his unpopularity in the party was legendary. According to his biographer, Donald Macintyre, as Secretary of State for Trade and Industry he had succeeded by reassuring business that 'his sheer presence was a guarantee against the return of the left, or even old Labour'.[7] Mandelson was not interested in the new social movements. He was in many ways a traditional deal-making politician.

Mandelson's appointment to Northern Ireland was represented as a gift to unionism. His regency at Hillsborough, though brief, proved to be devastating, a regression to *the ancien regime*. His rapport with the security state was not untypical of previous secretaries of state, but after Mowlam's recognition that the security system was a contributor to the conflict, his methods startled everyone outside the unionist establishment. In contrast to Mowlam, Mandelson freely asserted New Labour's impatience with the equality and human rights discourse, and with Northern Ireland's lively NGOs and social movements. His main aim, it seemed, was to sustain Trimble's leadership of the perilously fractured UUP, and escort the reluctant party towards participation in power-sharing, devolved government.

It fell to Mandelson to manage policing reform and demilitarisation. This was always going to be difficult. Many participants were exasperated by the IRA's cliff-hanging refusal to decommission without simultaneous demilitarisation by the British, but they were also shocked by Mandelson's dilution of policing reform. And the pro-Agreement parties were aghast at his estrangement from their communities.

NOTES

1. Donald Macintyre, *Mandelson and the Making of New Labour*, HarperCollins 2000, p577
2. Brendan O'Leary, *The Past, Present and Future of Policing and the Belfast Agreement*, address to Pat Finucane Centre conference, Derry 2001.
3. Paddy Hillyard and Mike Tomlinson, 'Patterns of Policing and Policing Patten', *Journal of Law and Society*, 2000.
4. Clifford Shearing, 'Patten has been gutted', *Guardian*, 14.11.00.
5. Mo Mowlam, *Momentum*, Little Brown 2000.
6. Donald Macintyre, op cit.
7. Ibid, p515.

PART V

COLLUSION

14. Killing Finucane: cruel timing

A symbiotic partnership between the British securocracy and the loyalist militias thwarted any prospect that the question of justice might attract the same transcendent coalitions that had found expression in the Agreement. This book's argument is that the state itself sponsored sectarian terror and fright; that the partnership with loyalist paramilitarism provoked and then prolonged armed conflict. This section is concerned with the scandal of collusion and its implications for the Agreement. Its focus is the assassination of two solicitors. Their murders are exemplars of a larger and longer story of collusion. Their unflinching commitment to the law had attracted the hatred of securocrats, army and police officers and loyalist hitmen. Their deaths exposed the extent to which 'counter-insurgency' had compromised the law itself in Northern Ireland. They were in peril and they weren't protected.

Pat Finucane was murdered in 1989; his killing was the conspiracy's consummate act. Rosemary Nelson was murdered after the Agreement had been affirmed by the people in 1999; her killing was a warning that the deadly partnership was alive and it was active.

These murders synchronised with decisive conjunctures, moments when peace seemed possible: in 1989 the combatants had contemplated a deal. In 1999 the deal had been done. At the moment in the 1980s when the elements of a settlement – socio-economic reform and power sharing – were acquiring political mass, not least among the combatants themselves, the security state's gruesome answer was to re-arm and re-invigorate sectarian terrorism.

These deaths are a scandal. Great public scandals are about open secrets, the stories and lies and misdemeanours and crimes of the powerful; they are about activities that are at the same time transgressive and sanctioned. Scandal is also about the limits of power; it is about how things come to be known, how secrets become open and unsettle the story a society tells about itself. Scandals can be a resource for change. But there is always a risk that the 'radical truth' will be enfeebled, that it will crawl into daylight only to circulate among those 'in the know', becoming yet another open secret, its transformative power diminished because it is simply too big, too systemic, too dangerous.

How and why Pat Finucane had been killed was known soon enough: it was collusion between the police, the army and the security forces, and some believe the trail led to the door of Downing Street. His death belonged to new era of security state sponsorship of terror; it heralded a crescendo of killing that reinstated the projection of the people – rather than the state – as Northern Ireland's problem. This period from 1987 belonged to the enduring history that disabled the Agreement's ability to address justice, and quelled the somewhat pessimistic interest in a truth commission. A violent axis shadowed the 'social alliance' between the protestant working class and the unionist elite, and reiterated the narrative of tribal – rather than state-sponsored – terrorism.

The context was a critical conjuncture: the British government had bowed to internal and international pressure to address socio-economic inequality with greater energy and effect. The government had also been aware of momentum among all the paramilitary movements towards ending their de facto civil war. In 1987 their leaders had mapped the contours of a peaceful settlement. This could not have been more important: it was their exile from the production of the Anglo-Irish Agreement that had guaranteed its failure. Peace could only be guaranteed by the paramilitaries' participation. Within republicanism, Gerry Adams had embarked on a historic journey to find a peaceful solution, and in May 1987 Sinn Fein's Ard Chomhairle, its governing body, affirmed *Scenario for Peace*. The government had not underestimated the impact of these events – indeed, when loyalists plotted to kill Gerry Adams, intelligence intervened: the political elite wanted Adams alive. In 1987 UDA leader John McMichael and UVF veteran Gusty Spence were also canvassing power-sharing as a basis for settlement.

This did not calm Britain's counter-insurgency. On the contrary, it was in 1987 that counter-insurgency was renewed by a focused and ferocious programme of assassination that targeted not only *armed* but *any* republicans. The intelligence and reconnaissance was orchestrated by the security forces, the triggers were pulled by their agents in loyalist militias. The favoured vector was the UDA. The operation was planned by the Force Research Unit and Special Branch. Under the gimlet eye of MI5, the Army's FRU and the RUC's Special Branch operated autonomously and apparently without rules, and between them ran a crowd of agents and informers in all of the paramilitary organisations.

The UDA had been the army's more or less constant confederate. By repute it was less disciplined than the UVF and it was certainly less capable than the IRA. British intelligence, it appeared, preferred its loyalists to be a bit thick.[1] According to a former officer, 'it was one of the worst-prepared, worst-trained rabbles of men I ever had the misfortune to come across'. The FRU galvanised this ramshackle militia. Without the help of the army and the police, 'these loyalists would not have been able to tie their shoe laces.'[2] But *with* their help the UDA was a prolific death squad.

The army's main man in the UDA was Brian Nelson, the conduit through which the FRU channelled its data and profiled its targets. Nelson embodied loyalism's metamorphosis from respectable working-class sectarianism to degenerate militarism. His father had disapproved of the son's preference for Paisleyism and the army rather than the shipyards. Nelson's reputation was established when in 1973 he was jailed following the death of Gerald Higgins, a catholic known as an active peacemaker between catholic and protestant community leaders. Higgins had been kidnapped by Nelson and his UDA friends, and taken to a Shankill club, where they beat him, set his hair on fire, soaked his hands in water, attached electric wires and sent electric shocks through his body. When Nelson tried to dump Higgins outside, the gravely injured man put up a fight and this alerted soldiers patrolling nearby. Nelson was arrested and jailed for seven years, but he was back on the streets by 1977, and in the early 1980s his startling qualifications made him very attractive to British counter-insurgency. He was recruited by the FRU and, under the stewardship of MI5, organised a massive arms deal in South Africa at the end of 1987 that was shared between the loyalist paramilitary groups.

The FRU set up Nelson as its intelligence officer. For years the official version was that Nelson delivered intelligence to the security services. He did that, but it is obvious, however, that Nelson was also a recipient: he was the conduit for information derived from thousands of military and police files; his task was to process it and present it to UDA death squads. 'Day after day', he sat in the UDA headquarters collating intelligence material on the computer, controlled by UDA leader John McMichael.[3] Everything came from military intelligence or the RUC. Nelson burnished his reputation and the security forces finessed their control.

TARGETS

Dermott Hackett

One of the first targets was the driver of a bread van journeying around a familiar delivery route in County Tyrone on 23 May 1987. He was 40-year-old Dermot Hackett. A dozen bullets were fired into his van, and his body slumped over the wheel; the engine was still running when another driver on the road stopped and discovered him. One of Hackett's cousins was an SDLP leader on Omagh council, but his own values were expressed in support for the St Vincent de Paul charity. However, Hackett appeared in the security services files. He had objected to harassment by the RUC after he'd been questioned following the shooting of a security officer. His delivery round had taken him in and out of the vicinity, and it had been noticed. His objections got him into the RUC's records[4] and then into the UDA files collated by Brian Nelson.

One of his killers was Michael Stone, who became notorious for his spectacular bid to kill off the republican leadership at Milltown Cemetery in 1988.[5] He described himself as a solitary vigilante, a 'freelance gunman'. But he was more complicated, he was a UDA man and a British agent. Almost two decades after Hackett's death, he agreed to meet face-to-face with his widow, Sylvia Hackett in the BBC's 2006 television screening of encounters between survivors, relatives and paramilitary perpetrators, *Facing the Truth*. Sylvia Hackett was tenacious: why had he killed her man, who just been a person, a catholic? He was 'in the files' said Stone. In his autobiography, Stone said, 'I had seen his intelligence file'.[6] The encounter with Sylvia Hackett gave Stone another fifteen minutes of fame, but he gave her nothing. He would not answer her key question: where did the files come from?

Alex Maskey

Alex Maskey was a republican target whose death warrant was licensed solely by his public *presence* – he had been elected to Belfast City Council in 1983, the first republican councillor in the city since partition. Twenty years after this inflammatory election he became Belfast's first Sinn Fein mayor – and was generally acknowledged to have been its most eloquent and inclusive. He was an outrage – not because he was an urban guerrilla, but because he was a pioneer in Sinn Fein's journey into the institutions and non-violent solutions. His election was not simply symbolic – he didn't get elected to abstain; he worked as a councillor, he made his enemies breathe the same air.

Maskey was the subject of perpetual police harassment; his body was searched, his house was searched. The RUC knew everything they needed to know about Alex Maskey. In October 1986 his home was petrol bombed while his children were inside sleeping. No one was arrested and no protection was offered. The publication in May 1987 of *Scenario for Peace*, a key document in Sinn Fein's search for peaceful solutions, had not made him a candidate for police protection.

Brian Nelson was provided with a detailed description of Maskey's life, including his tendency to rely on the Apollo taxi firm. A replica car was organised and one summer morning it arrived outside Maskey's home. When a man knocked at his door saying he was from Apollo, Maskey warily opened and saw a sawn-off shotgun sticking out of the man's coat. He slammed the door and this probably saved him: 'what did hit me was the remainder of the shotgun cartridge, and bits of wood and the protective glass from the door. That reduced the blast, but it also made it a dirty wound.' Maskey lost part of his stomach, kidney and bowel, but he was very lucky, he was alive. Then the gunman tried to get into the house. 'I caught his forearm in the door and he dropped the weapon. I hit the wall and I bounced back again. Fortunately I was able to keep on my feet, and push the door back.' The man fled, leaving the gun, forensic treasure. But no one was caught or charged with the attempt on Maskey's life. 'I was never told that the car was found, I was never told who was involved, I was never told if anyone was arrested.'

The shooter's version of events emerged years later in Nicholas Davies' book on Brian Nelson – and he appeared to have had the narrative from the horse's mouth. The gunman's flight was unhindered: 'the Force Research Unit had put an exclusion zone in operation on the estate where Maskey lived, alerting the police and any army patrols to stay out of the area'. When the RUC found the abandoned vehicle later that day there were no fingerprints. Maskey's experience confirmed that Military Intelligence and FRU were targeting republicans in general – as against armed republicans.[7]

In the summer of 1988 Maskey was again in mortal danger. Soldiers saw Maskey having Sunday lunch in a Belfast restaurant. Nelson was alerted and scavenged the city for an assassination team. He finally contacted Ken Barrett, one of the UDA's killers, but by the time Barrett arrived Maskey had gone. That evening Nelson contacted his handler, Sergeant Margaret Walshore, and complained that Maskey had got away. 'If he's there next Sunday, he's going down'. He wasn't there, but no one had warned Maskey. The idea that any of the services would have warned him was of course naive: they were all, in one way or another, implicated. Maskey's attempts, with his solicitor Pat Finucane, to secure a serious investigation into the attempted killing were in vain; and they didn't stop assassins trying to kill him.

On 11 May 1993 workers were putting extra security protection into his home. At teatime the worked stopped and his old friend Alan Lundy stayed behind to have a meal with the family. Alex Maskey describes what happened next as his 'darkest moment'. Gunfire exploded in the street, and Alan Lundy fell through the kitchen door, mortally wounded by a bullet through the back of his head. No one was arrested or convicted of this murder.

On 2 January 1994, a time of awful violence before the ceasefires, Maskey's street was sprayed by bullets. A year later Maskey discovered that the police had possession of the gun used during this attack. No-one informed him of this, but it emerged during the trial of Johnny Adair, the first case to attract the new charge of 'directing terrorism'. A rifle displayed by an RUC officer was, it was said, the rifle used in the attack on Maskey's house.

Patrick Hamill

Just after 6.40 in the evening, Patrick Hamill arrived home. His wife Laura was sitting with their baby Catherine on her lap and two-year-old Kelly was playing on the floor. Within minutes of his arrival two armed men knocked on his door, announced themselves as the IRA and asked who he was. When he replied, his wife saw the men, both wearing balaclavas, look at each other. 'One of them nodded, and they shot him at point-blank range.' No one was convicted of Patrick Hamill's murder, but the security forces knew that the IRA hadn't done it, because they had helped to do it.

Years passed, and Laura Hamill learned nothing more about Patrick's death, until the prodigious Northern Ireland journalist Anne Cadwallader came to see her and asked her if she had read the chronicle of Brian Nelson and the FRU. Laura Hamill then read for the first time that they had targeted her husband. The FRU connection made the murder particularly sinister: 'it is frightening when you learn that it all goes back to the government. The soldiers and the police were supposed to protect you, but this was the politics of pick and choose. It struck fear into the heart of the community when somebody who wasn't even political got killed – it means they can pick anybody!'

Francisco Notorantonio

The gun that killed Patrick Hamill was used a month later to kill Francisco Notorantonio. Laura Hamill only discovered this a year later at her husband's inquest. 'My father asked if the gun had been used before, and he was told that had been used in the Notorantonio murder.' The gun was part of the South African arms cache that had been shepherded by MI5.

Notorantonio, a veteran of 1940s republicanism – though he had not been actively involved in politics for years – was elderly and ill. The murder provoked outrage in Belfast. It appeared to be wanton. But FRU whistleblower Martin Ingram knew that he had been sacrificed to accommodate a sectarian attack, and to save a British agent. He was appalled at this, and had a row with his colleagues. One of his officers excused the killing on the grounds of Gerry Adams having been one of his pallbearers.[8] This was mobilised as evidence that Notorantonio was 'involved', and therefore deserved it. Adams's homage to the old man was also regarded by the UDA as collateral evidence that they'd taken out a republican godfather.

Ingram knew that Notorantonio had been sacrificed to deflect Nelson and the UDA from another preferred target, Frederick Scappaticci. The story took the collusion trail into the bowels of the IRA. Scappaticci was Stakeknife, a British agent working inside the IRA. Notorantonio's death was offered by the security forces as an alternative because Scappaticci's assassination could not be contemplated by the securocrats – among other things he was part of a sadistic machine within the IRA that disposed of 'touts' that the British state had decided to discard. He was a member of the IRA's hyper-violent internal security system,[9] and he tortured and killed people suspected of being British agents; he also tortured and killed British agents the British wanted rid of.

Scappaticci was near to the top of the IRA and Martin Ingram rated him as a very important agent, at the same level as Brian Nelson: 'both were involved in mass murder'. Ingram saw the FRU files on Notorantonio before his murder. They were in the Stakeknife files. It was clear the loyalists wanted Stakeknife, and Ingram raised this with Stakeknife's handler. He was assured that the FRU had found a substitute target. Notorantonio was the substitute.

Pat Finucane
On and on it went, as the Joint Intelligence Committee, the svelte impresarios of the terror, met in Whitehall – sometimes with the Prime Minister – signing off on terrorism across the water. The military commanders of the UDA had never been so potent. They'd been tooled up by the South African arms deal, and directed towards targets that they could not have known without the security forces'

intelligence. But the rate of killing did not satisfy the men in suits, and, after a year, they decided that the assassination strategy should be intensified. This was super secret at the time but, thanks to the inquiries by the Canadian judge Peter Cory, and his report on collusion published in 2004, it is now known that at the beginning of 1989 the FRU decided to launch a new offensive, Operation Snowball, and asked Brian Nelson to co-ordinate the targets – 'major republican personalities'.[10]

MI5 and the RUC had briefed the government before the end of 1988 that there were lawyers who were dangerous.[11] This disposition led to the harassment of lawyers. [12] During a special mission, the American Lawyers Committee for Human Rights found that 'almost every solicitor' it met related stories of death threats. [13] More than forty solicitors regularly received threats from the police. British Irish Rights Watch found that in one firm alone 114 clients had relayed threats from the police, about a quarter of them about their solicitors. Pat Finucane had been eyed since 1981.[14] Why?

International observers often noticed how diminished the justice system had become. The legal community in Northern Ireland was muted as an effect of the permanent emergency provisions, and they were unprotected by their professional organisations.[15]After Finucane's killing, the Lawyers Committee noticed these organisations' 'embarrassing silence'. [16] Few defence lawyers ventured into the dangerous territory where politics merged with 'crime'; American colleagues were aware that 'innovative defence lawyers' placed themselves in peril.[17] Pat Finucane belonged to that tiny network. He had been menaced and insulted most of his professional life. He had represented Bobby Sands; he had established civil claims against the police as a 'permanent feature of the legal landscape'; he had represented Sinn Fein in its challenge to the broadcasting ban; and he had represented clients involved in shoot-to-kill cases. After he was murdered his wife Geraldine Finucane said, 'Pat would have represented the people who shot him'.[18] The Finucanes' son Michael, later an eloquent campaigner for justice for his father, reckoned that for loyalists to kill such a defence lawyer 'made no sense':

> It was clear that this was different – there was a lot of fear around in the legal community. In hindsight it had the effect of changing the way that a lot of lawyers did their business – some withdrew from criminal law, some left Northern Ireland. The UN Special Rapporteur said this was an attack on the rule of law, an attack on the legal system; it compromised the right to legal representation of your choosing – that was

probably the effect that was intended. I think it was the intention of the state – they wanted to make the point to people who thought they were untouchable. Within the conflict cauldron the effects were heightened ten-fold.

By 1988 Pat Finucane was doomed. A Security Services report dated 19 December 1988 recorded a meeting of UDA military commanders that discussed 'plans to kill the three solicitors who have represented republicans at recent hearings'.[19] It was the RUC's Special Branch that had mooted the murder of Pat Finucane amongst loyalist paramilitaries. Just how shocking this was, even to them, can be appreciated from the reaction of UDA leader Tommy Lyttle. In an interview with the *Panorama* journalist John Ware, the UDA leader said that he was so astonished when RUC officers had suggested that the loyalists kill Finucane that he checked it out with Special Branch, and his handler had confirmed that the lawyer's death would be 'a bad blow for the Provos'.[20] The sheer audacity of it, and the sense that the assassination of a solicitor would cross an invisible line, was also confirmed by one of the assassins, Ken Barrett: 'it will bring a bag of shite down on us'. But so deep was the antipathy in MI5 and the RUC that in the institutional imagination the line had already been crossed and Martin Ingram reckoned that shooting solicitors carried no implications for them: 'Finucane was just another body'.

Three weeks before Finucane's death, police officers intruded upon an interrogation of UDA men who were part of a group of West Belfast killers known as 'the military men', and mulled over 'the treble': three solicitors they wanted dead, one of whom was Finucane. By the end of 1988 everything was in place: the UDA had a portfolio of targets, the police, army and security forces planned their manoeuvres, and they had their political warrant. Everyone involved knew what was going to happen. Indeed the rumour that a 'controversial' and 'big' hit was forthcoming was circulating among excitable Orangemen,[21] as well as Special Branch and FRU members, whose shared membership of an Orange Lodge created an arena for unguarded chatter and relieved everyone of any suspicion that they belonged to something as unseemly as a criminal conspiracy.

Intimations of murder fell from the mouth of a minister, Douglas Hogg, in the House of Commons on 17 January 1989 during a Parliamentary debate on the Prevention of Terrorism (Temporary Provisions) Bill, when he repeated the security forces' script about lawyers:

I have to state as a fact, but with great regret, that there are in Northern Ireland a number of solicitors who are unduly sympathetic to the cause of the IRA ... one has to bear this in mind.

His statement instantly brought the SDLP MP Seamus Mallon to his feet:

That is a remarkable statement for a minister to make about members of a profession who have borne so much of the heat in a traumatic and abnormal situation. Such words should not be said without the courage to support them.

The minister refused to support them. MPs were aghast and Mallon warned that this statement was tantamount to a death sentence.

Nelson reconnoitred the neighbourhood. Special Branch informer William Stobie, the UDA quartermaster, arranged the delivery of the guns to be used to kill Finucane, and passed on what he knew to his Special Branch handlers. The neighbourhood was cleared by the security forces, enabling the killers safe passage. The assassins hijacked a car, arrived outside Finucane's detached house in a middle-class enclave of North Belfast, and walked through the front door while the family were having dinner in the kitchen. Patrick Finucane was shot at close range, in front of his wife and children, and while his body lay on the floor one of the assassins stood over him and fired bullets into his face. Then they left.

In summer 1989 the Law Society of England and Wales launched the first investigation into the death, by Geoffrey Bindman and Jane Deighton. They concluded that in the context of armed conflict, Finucane had been targeted because he was challenging the state apparatus. He had 'adroitly used the judicial mechanisms to force the state to justify itself'. But for a decade after this, despite scandalous revelations of collusion, nothing more happened to clarify what had happened to Finucane. There was no contact with the Finucane family – the witnesses – or with his colleagues, who were familiar with the trail of threats.

The facts about Northern Ireland's first lawyer to be murdered might have remained interred in the secret records of the intelligence services had it not been for the UDA's own reckless confidence that their symbiotic relationship with the security forces was the same thing as legitimacy and a public mandate. The generous delivery of secret intelligence files was revealed by the UDA itself during a public row over its reliability in 1989. Stung by the scandal surrounding the killing of Loughlin Maginn, a young catholic, the UDA defended itself by claiming to have had its information on Maginn from a higher author- ity – a top secret security profile. To prove a point about the contested republican affiliations of its victims, the UDA invited the indefatigable Belfast journalist Chris Moore to see their cache of confidential files from the security services. The UDA released a flood of documents, all from sources within the RUC or various British intelligence agencies.

CHANGING THE STORY

It was these revelations that triggered the Stevens inquiry into collu- sion. It started not with a mystery nor a murder, but with the UDA's amazing admission. That gesture instantly jeopardised Britain's repre- sentation of itself as a neutral arbitrator between warring tribes, the defender of democracy and the law against primitive warlords. This was a story Britain had been telling itself over and over. Indeed the strategy had acquired the status of a doctrine, famously theorised during the anti-colonial struggle by Frank Kitson, then a young army officer, later stationed in Northern Ireland. According to this doctrine, resistance to colonial power could always become 'a potential state of insurgency'. Counter-insurgency would therefore enlist gangs to counter the purported insurgents.

But once the gangsters disclosed the partnership, Britain's old narra- tive – that it was caught between atavistic celts – was threatened by a new narrative, that it was a hydra, it was everywhere, causing mayhem. Now men whose class had produced them as masters of the universe, who still performed at Stormont like colonial viceroys, found their reputation imperilled by men for whom they could only feel contempt. Having given the franchise for killing republicans to men they could only regard as servants, as native rabble, the Crown had been forced by the mob to call in the top men, including the Attorney General himself, to scotch the story.

The UDA's publication of the intelligence profiles signified that these marginalised men regarded themselves as by no means the scruffy lackeys of superior beings. Within their communities their militarism allowed these men to assert their masculinity as mastery and martyrdom. They saw themselves, as the UDA's west Belfast 'military men' in C Company sang it, as *Simply the Best*. Access to the means of violence had given them power, and the circulation of the means of violence between the state and the paramilitaries made them indispensable partners. It announced their equality. Leaders of loyalist paramilitarism could certainly see themselves as the match of the RUC and MI5 and the toffs who ruled the place. Nelson's generation had jettisoned the deference of their fathers for the intoxicating pleasures of another kind of power. The redistribution of violence produced these men, therefore, as both lawless and sponsored by the state. Just as their fathers' generation enjoyed respectable power over their community, so these men used their secretive and segregated nexus to en*gender* regimes of dominion. Violence loitered in everyone's imagination. It always had done, of course, but in the context of armed conflict violence it gave them a sense of omnipotence.

The state's stewardship of an assassination strategy did not subordinate these otherwise marginalised men; it empowered them – they were bosses, they pulled the triggers. It compromised both the state's monopoly of the lawful use of violence and its monopoly of morality in the national narrative.

NOTES

1. In 1975, according to Colin Wallace's evidence to the Barron commission of inquiry into the Dublin-Monaghan bombings, the army had tried to split off the UVF from its thinkers.
2. UTV 2001, *Justice on Trial*.
3. Coogan, op cit.
4. Nicholas Davies, *Ten-thirty-three: The Inside Story of Britain's Secret Killing Machine in Northern Ireland*, Mainstream 1999.
5. M. Stone, *None Shall Divide Us*, John Blake Publishing 2004.
6. Ibid, p19.
7. Davies, op cit, p137.
8. N. Davies, *Dead Men Talking*, Mainstream 2005, p88.
9. M. Ingram & G. Harkin, *Stakeknife*, O'Brien Press 2004, p223.
10. P. Cory, *Collusion Inquiry Report: Patrick Finucane*, 2004.
11. *Daily Telegraph*, 10.5.99.
12. Lawyers Committee for Human Rights, *Human Rights at the Crossroads, Human Rights and the Northern Ireland Peace Process*, New York 1996.
13. Lawyers Committee for Human Rights, *Human Rights and Legal Defence in Northern Ireland*, New York 1993.
14. Cory report, op cit.
15. K. McEvoy & L McGregor, *Transitional Justice from Below*, Hart 2008.
16. Lawyers Committee, 1996, op cit.
17. Lawyers Committee, 1993, op cit.
18. Lawyers Committee, 1993, op cit.
19. Cory report, op cit.
20. J. Ware, 'Time to come clean over the army's role in the "Dirty War"', *New Statesman*, 14.4.98.
21. Davies, 2005, op cit, p11.

15. The investigation – how the story came to be told

John Stevens was not the first English police officer called in to Northern Ireland to investigate counter-insurgency controversies, but he stayed the longest: he was a safe pair of hands. Stevens had not been invited to investigate murder. He had been asked to look at collusion. However, for many years it was assumed that he was also investigating Finucane's death, and he confided that he knew 'absolutely' who had killed him. But he was not investigating the killing – because he'd not been asked to. 'It was our remit to find out who was colluding with whom', Stevens wrote in his memoirs, but not who was killing whom. So, what was Stevens' real remit? The effort to wrest evidence from those 'in the know' for the information of those with a need to know – the people – provided some clues.

Brian Nelson and his networks' involvement with the intelligence agencies was swiftly uncovered when the Stevens team trawled through the UDA's treasure. Perpetrators were identified, raids were organised, illegal arms kept by UDR soldiers were found – including the Browning pistol used to kill Pat Finucane. Within a few weeks of the start of the investigation, Stevens told Special Branch that he had found Brian Nelson's prints. But still there was apparently no murder inquiry. And Stevens's inquiries into Nelson were instantly blocked. Officers foraging in the RUC's files revealed the intelligence card on him, however, which – under duress – the RUC handed over. The team was told that it could not interview Nelson. They then went to the top and, under pressure, Chief Constable Hugh Annesley reluctantly agreed. New raids were planned on Nelson and his cohorts. But then the investigators received a warning worthy of the *Godfather*. Fire wrecked the investigation's incident room, even though it was located in an RUC building, alarmed and under 24-hour guard.[1] And then Brian Nelson disappeared – whisked away by FRU the night before he was due to be interviewed. The FRU also impounded the inquiry's database.

Stevens now knew that he was not supposed to be taking the investigation seriously. By the time that Nelson returned and – to the FRU's chagrin – began talking about his relationship to FRU and the conspiracy to kill off republican activists, the inquiry found itself in a quandary. The official records of the relationship contradicted Nelson's story. The documents made available to Stevens were not the originals, but edited, stilted, staged conversations between Nelson and his handlers, intended to show that Nelson, not they, was providing the intelligence. The Stevens team had been conned.

After many further obstacles had been put in his way, Stevens published a summary report in 1990 that concluded that collusion was 'neither widespread nor institutionalised'. He said he had not uncovered evidence that would 'substantiate' allegations of police collusion – though there had been 2000 documents in circulation, and some of the leaked material came from police files. The investigation resulted in the arrest of 94 people, the prosecution of 47 and 183 convictions, but these were mainly on minor charges such as 'the possession of documents likely to be of use to terrorists'. 'Strikingly, not one of the prosecutions was of an RUC officer, despite the fact that some of the leaked material was from police files.'[2] The Lawyers Committee learned from Stevens himself that he had not followed every lead in the Finucane case. His report was turned over to the RUC and his vast archive was kept under lock and key.

Brian Nelson eventually appeared in court in 1992. He pleaded guilty to 20 counts, including five counts of conspiracy to murder, and two of aiding and abetting murder. There was no charge of conspiracy to murder Patrick Finucane. The senior law officers in the land had intervened to minimise the charges against Nelson, to edit the Finucane case out of the charge sheet, and to stop Nelson saying anything in a public arena. According to one of Northern Ireland's most respected journalists, David McKittrick, Nelson's role, and his fate, had been discussed between the Director of Public Prosecutions, the RUC and the army, and there was no question of letting Nelson take the stand, disclosing his activities and his allies.[3] The Attorney General, Sir Patrick Mayhew, had taken control of Nelson's trial. The FRU's commanding officer, Gordon Kerr, appearing as Colonel J, insisted that Nelson's motivation had been to 'save lives'. And, sentencing Nelson to ten years in prison, Lord Justice Basil Kelly commented: 'he had passed on possibly life-saving information in respect of 217 individuals'.

This notion was absurd, but it discombobulated the collusion story. However, collusion, by definition, implies a dispersal of control – the security forces could not stop the conspirators talking, they couldn't stop journalists and human rights campaigners listening and trying to

tell the story. And they could not stop Finucane's widow Geraldine
from seeking justice. Slowly, the state's fortifications were penetrated.
This is how it happened.

If the criminal court was a closed circuit, civil proceedings seemed
to offer Geraldine Finucane a way to call Nelson and the Ministry of
Defence to account in the early 1990s. She sued them. Nelson's
response was to threaten to expose the FRU if he was forced to come
to court. That and the BBC triggered what came to be known as
Stevens II. At the same time the eminent *Panorama* journalist John
Ware broadcast an historic intervention into the collusion scandal.
Ware had been surprised at the lack of response to the UDA revelations
back in August 1989. He felt that it should have provoked a political
crisis: ministers should have been recalled, it was political dynamite.
However, Stevens I had effectively closed down the story. Ware reckoned that there was more to be revealed and decided to look for it. He
met with Tucker Lyttle, who told him that RUC officers had proposed
to UDA volunteers that Finucane should be killed.[4] Ware also met
Nelson, who enthusiastically showed him photographs and computer
printouts of security services data. Ware also got access to his journal –
to Nelson's chagrin – and its revelations about the Finucane conspiracy.
This was an amazing cache. Ware's *Panorama* programme broadcast in
1992 what the Attorney General, the secretary of State and the DPP had
tried to censor: that the FRU was a law unto itself; that Nelson, over-
seen by MI5, had re-armed the loyalist paramilitaries; that Nelson had
been implanted as the UDA's intelligence officer; that the FRU operation was the army's attempt to recover ground ceded to the RUC under
the principle of police primacy; that 'Colonel J' had been prepared to lie
about the FRU's complicity in murder; that Nelson had distributed
Finucane's photograph a few days before the killing; and much more.

The journalist believed that this broadcast would be a watershed.
But it wasn't. Again nothing happened. The DPP did not feel moved to
use its powers to order an investigation into the murder and the larger
evidence of conspiracy to kill.[5] The DPP and Stevens had access to
Nelson's journal, his prints, the hoard of RUC and intelligence data,
and yet still there was no prosecution, and no explanation for no prosecution. Stevens believed he had evidence implicating RUC officers.
He produced a second report on collusion, delivered it to the Chief
Constable, and that was the end of that. Nelson was not obliged to
rehearse his story again and the FRU was not called to account.
Nothing was made public.

Stevens later told the Lawyers Committee that he had fully investigated Nelson's activities and he knew 'absolutely' who had killed

Patrick Finucane. But if Stevens himself was not able or willing to reveal the modus operandi between the security services and the UDA, the evidence he had gathered gradually trickled into the public domain. John Ware published an account of the attempts to sabotage and silence Stevens. It was revealed that the Stevens team had compiled a report – kept from the public – setting out the evidence of FRU collusion in targeting republicans, but that the DPP and Sir Patrick Mayhew had decided not to prosecute those involved. The evidence that was slowly surfacing from the Stevens investigations gripped the Finucane family – even though Stevens had never communicated directly with them. 'The material was compelling,' recalled Michael Finucane. It was edge-of-the-seat stuff'.

STORIES FROM THE DARK

Witnesses kept talking about the Finucane murder. Some were talking out of fear, some out of frustration or fury. FRU intelligence officer Martin Ingram confirmed that Tucker Lyttle, the man who had revealed the UDA's cache of police data, was a police informer. Lyttle also revealed to John Ware that it was Special Branch that had first suggested killing lawyers. Lyttle had been in charge of both Brian Nelson and William Stobie – a Special Branch informer and UDA quartermaster. Stobie was ultimately to become the only one of the perpetrators to support the movement for a public inquiry into collusion and the Finucane murder.

Before Finucane was killed Stobie had told Special Branch that a top republican was likely to be shot, and had alerted them to the location of the guns used. And when he later showed that he was prepared to expose the conspiracy, his own life became imperilled. (He was finally killed in December 2001.) The figure of this small round man with a big bald head was to become familiar in Northern Ireland. His story exemplifies the way that witnesses were silenced and the story was squandered.

In 1990 Stobie shared his story with two Northern Ireland journalists. It was part of his personal protection plan. One of them was the prodigious reporter Ed Moloney, who agreed to reveal nothing unless on Stobie's say-so, and kept his confidence for the next decade. The other was Neil Mullholland, who became a Northern Ireland Office press officer and spilled the story to the RUC. After this Stobie was arrested and in January 1991 he was due to go on trial, charged with firearms offences. However, in spite of the existence of strong evidence against Stobie, the Director of Public Prosecutions offered no evidence and asked the court to acquit him. The likelihood is that Stobie had threatened to expose what he knew about the Finucane murder in court and the DPP's actions prevented him talking in a privileged public arena.

Around this time, but in a completely different context, another of the conspirators, Ken Barrett, a Belfast loyalist with a career during the conflict as a serial killer, had been boasting about the Finucane murder. His reason for breaking his silence was fury: he'd recently been stood down by the UDA/UFF after they'd caught him siphoning off funds. Barrett contacted a CID detective, Johnston Brown, who was rather well known for investigating loyalists' criminal activities. Brown organised a rendezvous on 3 October 1991, accompanied by an officer from Special Branch, the specialist – and autonomous – counter-insurgency branch. During their taped conversation Barrett swanked about killing Finucane, and provided convincing details to back his story.[6] Brown believed that Barrett's admission cleared the RUC of allegations of collusion in the murder and wanted to pursue the case. He expected the Special Branch man to find a way to do it. But he was wrong. After Barrett left the car, the Special Branch man told him to 'move away' from the case. Special Branch already knew about Barrett, he said, 'we know all about it'. And he confided in Brown that he himself was currently being questioned by the Stevens inquiry, about his relationship to William Stobie. In other words, as Brown later realised, his colleague was in fact implicated in the very allegations of collusion that he had hoped to dispel. At that time, however, Brown had no idea what the officer was talking about. The tape was transcribed, but Brown was warned categorically: this would go no further. In fact, 'Barrett was to be accepted into the fold as a Special Branch agent and that was it'. Brown had already agreed to meet Barrett again on 10 October and again Special Branch joined them. Brown was ordered: no questions about Finucane. This time Special Branch took charge of the interview – also taped – and Barrett instantly chattered about two murders that had been committed that night. But there was no talk of Finucane.

The argument about what to do about Barrett subsequently went to the highest echelons of the RUC: everyone with any power to do anything about the murder knew about it, and thereafter tried to ensure that the knowledge remained within their select circle. Brown was blocked and Special Branch recruited Barrett to work for them.[7] Brown himself was now subjected to intimidation. In 1994 the harassment took the form of a letter sent to the UDA office that falsely accused Brown of exposing loyalists to republicans. But the letter was spotted by William Stobie, who passed it to an RUC detective, who passed it on to Brown. The two men didn't know each other, but Brown credited William Stobie with saving his life.[8] None of this had been allowed to go anywhere near the Stevens inquiry. Stobie was silenced – for the time being. Brown, too, was silenced for the time being.

THE THIRD STEVENS INQUIRY

It was a decade after Finucane's death that the British and Irish governments were given a dossier that finally detonated their inertia. On the tenth anniversary of Finucane's death, British Irish Rights Watch director Jane Winter, a cool, scrupulous inquisitor, delivered the dossier, detailing exhaustive evidence of collusion to the British and Irish governments. Her sources were impeccable. Her dossier made it impossible for the government to continue to dissemble because she had witnesses' evidence and hitherto unpublished documents. Her demand was simple and large: the government must order a public inquiry into the evidence that 'agents of the state have been involved directly and indirectly in the murder of its citizens, in contravention of the law and all international human rights standards.'

The Irish government was unequivocal – Justice Minister Liz O'Donnell wrote to the British government insisting on that a public inquiry should be set up. But Secretary of State Mo Mowlam faltered: she gave the dossier to RUC Chief Constable Ronnie Flanagan to decide what to do. His response was to bring back Stevens, recently elevated to be the Metropolitan Police Chief Commissioner's number 2 at Scotland Yard. The Labour government had not been responsible for the conspiracy. Downing Street might have felt that investigation of the scandals of the past could empower the new beginning. But it didn't. Instead it instigated a third inquiry by Stevens.

Jane Winter noted that the government had never denied the evidence in her dossier. But it reached to the law to safeguard the state's secrets. As more evidence came out, its response was to try to prevent its publication. The journalist Nicholas Davies had already been subjected to a High Court injunction to stop his book *Ten Thirty Three*, the story of Nelson, the FRU, and the Joint Intelligence Committee, and based, he said, on senior intelligence sources.[9] At the end of the decade more confirmation was broadcast. In 1999 Peter Taylor's BBC series, *Loyalists*, aired the loyalist combatant Bobby Philpott's brash admission: data had been flowing from 'all branches, RUC, army, UDR'; information on targets arrived 'daily'. 'I was getting so many documents I didn't know where to put them ... intelligence reports, photos, what colour socks republicans were wearing...' Evidence was running from all directions.

As soon as Stevens III got under way, the state again tried to censor the story. Instead of being protected as a vital witness, William Stobie was charged with Finucane's murder. True to his promise to tell the story, Stobie gave Moloney the go ahead to publish. Stobie's story ran in the *Sunday Tribune* in June 1999, based on the notes Moloney had kept since 1990. Within weeks Moloney was himself arrested under the Prevention of Terrorism Act and ordered to hand over his notes. This was a critical moment in Northern Ireland politics. Mo Mowlam was besieged, the Patten report was pending, the unionist and police establishment were organising. Collusion could have been an arrow fired for reform. It wasn't. The effect of Moloney's arrest was to render *sub judice* any discussion of the Finucane murder. The prosecution of Stobie and Moloney removed the scandal from the debate on the Patten commission; it discredited and discouraged important witnesses; and it was a warning to anyone else who might be inclined to blow the whistle. Defence Secretary Geoff Hoon, a robust guardian of the securocrats, defended Moloney's arrest. He told the House of Commons that the journalist's notes were vital evidence *against* Stobie. But it had all been in the possession of the court in the 1991 hearing – and police evidence revealed that Stobie had been interrogated by the RUC 32 times in 1990. Why, in any case, was Stobie being treated as a suspect not a witness?

The case became a *cause celèbre* and ultimately Moloney triumphed. In October 1999 the High Court overturned the order to disclose his notes. But the case raised new questions: if Stevens was supposed to be investigating collusion in the Finucane killing, why muzzle Stobie? Why was a journalist being silenced?

On 12 December 2001 Stobie was acquitted of the murder. As he emerged into daylight – and danger – this ill-educated man who still lived near his mother, who had just decorated the flat he shared with his partner, made a remarkable announcement: he proposed a public inquiry into the role of the Stevens inquiry, the police and military intelligence in his prosecution. He knew his life was at risk. He'd already been shot by the UDA. His solicitor Joe Rice had asked that he be offered protection under the Key Persons Protection Scheme. By now the Secretary of State was Peter Mandelson, and he turned Stobie down. Less than a week later he was dead. He was shot walking down the path outside his home. The Red Hand Defenders, a UDA flag of convenience, claimed his death was 'for crimes against the loyalist community'. The UDA spokesperson who offered the explanation was John White, a man who had been jailed for life following a weird and sexually sadistic sectarian murder, and released under the Good Friday Agreement. He had also been outed as a Special Branch informer.

According to White, Stobie's words had undermined 'the credibility of the RUC and the Northern Ireland entity itself'. White was, of course, correct.

Ed Moloney reckoned that since the UDA was thoroughly pene-trated by the security services, there ought to be a question mark behind the role of the authorities in Stobie's death. 'Did someone, somewhere in the intelligence apparatus know it was planned and let it happen?'[10] This is what John Stevens had to say about William Stobie: 'he was foolish enough to stand up and say he thought there ought to be a public inquiry into the Finucane shooting'; that would have meant that suspects would have been questioned, 'just what the UDA didn't need'.[11] When the UDA 'went and shot him in his driveway, that was the end of Stobie, and of our inquiry into him'. That was all Stevens had to say about the extraordinary life and death of William Stobie.

When Stevens was called back to Northern Ireland for his third inquiry, Johnston Brown reckoned it was time for another conversa-tion in a car with Ken Barrett. Brown was a confident cop, a tanned, strong, handsome man with unflinching blue eyes. He was not involved in counter-insurgency, he was a crime cop, but his territory was loyalism and inevitably, from time to time, brought him into contact with paramilitaries. His knowledge of the Finucane case provoked a crisis for his bosses: CID could not countenance a chal-lenge to Special Branch. But Brown would not go quietly. So his records were handed over to Stevens, and in April 1999 he was summoned to see the Stevens III team at its suite in the RUC's complex at Carrickfergus. He sat in a sweltering office for a day while detectives interrogated him about his interviews with Barrett, and especially that confession recorded at a busy roadside on 3 October 1991. He returned to Carrickfergus the next day, and the detectives presented him with a statement to sign. Suddenly he understood: he was being treated not as a witness but as a criminal suspect. Special Branch had got to Stevens. Brown was told that there was no Barrett confession. He was devas-tated and asked if he could hear the tape himself. Sir John Stevens agreed, with little grace. 'When he is finished', Stevens told the detec-tives, 'seize his notes and exhibit them'. Brown was humiliated. 'He obviously did not believe me', he recalled. When Brown listened to the tape he heard Barrett, amidst the fuzz of traffic, talking about two murders, committed that night. Brown instantly contacted the RUC's record-keepers and they confirmed that these two murders had happened on 10 October – a week *after* the date of Barrett's confession. Now Brown understood: the tape had been switched. Stevens had the *second* interview, not the taped confession. The second interview had been set up to create a substitute tape in which Barrett had said nothing. The trick had almost worked. Stevens had been persuaded. It was only Brown's persistence that had exposed it. The Stevens team then ordered up the original 3 October tape from the RUC archives and heard the confession.

Inexplicably, in his own chronicle of his inquiry, Stevens paid no homage to Johnston Brown. In an account that is so ungenerous as to amount to hubris, Stevens complained that: 'Brown then complicated matters still further by saying that he had been undermined by the Special Branch, who took Barrett over as an agent'.[12] Here was Britain's top cop, who had been personally thwarted at every turn by the Special Branch, still apparently protecting it, and still saying that he found it 'very hard to know what to believe'. Without acknowledging Brown's discovery of the switched tapes, and his determination to bring Barrett's admission to light, Stevens describes his own investigation of Ken Barrett. His team checked whether his prints appeared on the Brian Nelson cache of documents, and they did. And they then interviewed Barrett, who denied everything. That was that – it was an interview masquerading as an investigation. The DPP decided there was insufficient evidence to prosecute. This was the contribution of Stevens and the DPP.

In 2001 Johnston Brown, now no longer a detective, began to tell the public about Ken Barrett's confession and the Special Branch disposal of it. He appeared in *Policing the Police*, a documentary broadcast on UTV in May 2001. The programme investigated both the murder of Finucane and the anomalous immunity given to Special Branch by the secret guidelines. It shamed not only the RUC but the Stevens team. John Ware then picked up the gauntlet, and a year after the UTV broadcast the *Panorama* team tracked down Barrett, by now a very frightened man. Barrett was clear about the intentions of the security services: 'they're not passing us documentation to sit in the house and read it,' he said. 'They are passing us documentation because they know what's going to result.' He then explained that the UDA's C Company warlord Jim Spence had orchestrated the Finucane execution. Spence had 'set it up', and Finucane had been shot by a 38 Special. Barrett had been surprised at the proposal to kill Finucane: 'you can't start whacking solicitors ... you'll bring the peelers down on us like a bag of fucking shite...' [13] But, of course, no such thing had happened. The murder had outraged everyone committed to the politics of human rights, but not the peelers: Finucane had been on their assassination wish list.

Only after that *Panorama* programme was screened – and provoked by the evidence offered by Brown, by journalists, and finally by Barrett himself – did Stevens III mount the investigation that the police could have initiated at the beginning. Stevens organised an audacious snare – Barrett was encouraged to apply for a job as a driver in a phantom firm staffed by undercover police officers. It was to these officers that he boasted again that he'd killed Pat Finucane.[14] Finally he was prosecuted: on 13 September 2004 he appeared at Belfast Crown Court and pleaded guilty to terrorist offences and the murder of Pat Finucane. His plea guaranteed that the case was, so to say, opened and closed. The evidence was not heard. The truth was tidied away.

FROM THE FRU INTO THE LIGHT

Jonty Brown had exposed police collusion from within, but it had not been allowed to impinge on the debates roaring around reform of the RUC. It was this erasure of the security forces' culpability that provoked Martin Ingram into contacting the press in November 1999 to tell the FRU story, though injunctions prevented much of his story from being published. And while Brown was trying to get a hearing in the Stevens inquiry, so, too, was Ingram.

Ingram worked on the loyalist desk in the FRU. He had not approved of the direction of the unit's work after the appointment of new boss Gordon Kerr in 1987. He thought that Kerr's interpretation of the targeting policy had gone beyond what was acceptable:

> nobody has license to kill. The FRU was never given guidelines, so that allowed a certain amount of in-built leeway. If I provide an agent with information I'm breaking the law, if I ask agents to join the IRA I'm asking them to be agent provocateurs, I'm breaking the law, I accept that. But giving Finucane's details, that's crossing the line. We've already crossed the line of the law, and I'm prepared to cross that line, but I'm not prepared to cross the line which is involvement in murder. That is a line that is sacrosanct.

Martin Ingram confirmed that the fire that had wrecked the Stevens inquiry's incident room had been started by the FRU. However, the Metropolitan Police Special Branch's subsequent investigation was not into the fire, but into Ingram's possible breach of the Official Secrets Act. Ingram was an unrivalled source. Not since the 1970s had a member of the intelligence machine disclosed its motives and modus operandi. His experience on the loyalist desk seemed to vindicate the theory of symbiosis: he reckoned that about half of loyalist combatants were agents, and estimated that two thirds of the members of the unit that organised the murder of Finucane were agents. He revealed his rows within the FRU about Notorantonio and Scappaticci (see p225–6), and he also took the Scappaticci scandal to the Police Ombudsman. What he revealed to the Ombudsman was a conspiracy between Scappaticci, FRU and Special Branch in 1990 to entrap Sinn Fein's spokesperson Danny Morrison.[15] Ingram went to the Ombudsman because he believed that Morrison had been the victim of a miscarriage of justice, which, in turn, shielded many more injustices. But the security forces were beyond the Ombudsman's brief, and the collusion investigation, technically, belonged to Stevens. So, Ingram's evidence went to Stevens. And there it remained, entombed. Ultimately Scappaticci was identified on the internet by journalists, and his sadistic history was described in unprecedented detail by Ingram and journalist Greg Harkin in their book *Stakeknife*

Ingram had been assailed by writs, raids on his home, theft of his documents, and their reappearance in court cases against him. He was used to dirty tricks. But the Finucane case 'demonstrated what was bad about the conflict', he said. 'We fought it on the side of law and order'; that was how the state could take the moral high ground. But the way that Brian Nelson and Frederick Scappaticci worked and were protected crossed the line, and that meant that the state had forfeited the moral high ground.

The *Guardian*'s media correspondent Roy Greenslade noticed that when *Stakeknife*'s scalding revelations were published in 2004, the dominant question the book prompted was not about the state's involvement in the IRA. Instead the revelations were pointed at the republicans with a gleeful howl: 'Ha ha! Gotcha!'. Scandals that should have exposed the state were scripted instead to expose and embarrass the republicans. They were powerless to overturn or unsettle the prevailing perception of life-saving and life-taking, the orthodoxies about what the conflict was for.

It was not until five years after BIRW had presented Mo Mowlam with its dossier that there was finally a conviction in the Finucane case. The BIRW's dossier might have been mobilised during a crucial time in the peace process, to tell Northern Ireland the truth about its security systems and conspiracies between the unionist state and its loyalist servants, and to invoke truth-telling in the work of renewal. But Mowlam had been ejected and the truth-telling process had been quelled; and her successors ensured that the sovereignty of the secret state was secured.

As it turned out, Barrett's prosecution only confirmed the pattern of appearing to do something but not doing it. He was released from prison in 2006. The Finucane family graciously expressed no feeling whatever about this – they weren't interested in him, they said; what they had always wanted was an inquiry into the conspiracy. They were, as Geraldine Finucane had put it, 'not after the men who pulled the trigger but the people who pulled the strings'.

Martin Ingram had encouraged the Finucane family to co-operate with Stevens, but later changed his mind. 'I was wrong,' he said. Stevens had mounted three investigations, and had yet to produce a single member of the security forces for institutional collusion. 'But he did deliver something, he delivered time'.

What had given the Finucane killing such a resonance was the sheer stamina of his family, the commitment of journalists, human rights organisations and whistleblowers to telling the story, the stalwart attention of international NGOs, members of the US congress and the UN, and the Irish government's unequivocal decision to support an international and public inquiry. What did the British government do? It changed the law to tighten its control over public inquiries. And in so doing, it again revealed the great lengths to which the state would go to cover its tracks.

NOTES

1. J. Ware & G. Seed, 'Army Set Up Ulster Murders', *Sunday Telegraph*, 22.3.98.
2. Lawyers Committee for Human Rights, *Beyond Collusion*, New York 2003.
3. David McKittrick, 'Ulster Supergrass Gagged by DPP', *Independent*, 11.10.90.
4. John Ware, 'Time to Come Clean Over the Army's Role in the "Dirty War"', *New Statesman*, 24.4.98.
5. Lawyers Committee, 1996, p22.
6. Johnston Brown, *Into the Dark*, Gill & Macmillan 2006, p180.
7. Ibid, p229.
8. Ibid, p79.
9. Davies, op cit.
10. Ed Moloney, 'NIO Ignored Stobie's Pleas for Help', *Sunday Tribune*, 16.12.01.
11. J. Stevens, *Not for the Fainthearted*, Weidenfeld 2005, p175.
12. Ibid.
13. John Ware, *Licence to Murder*, *Panorama*, BBC 2002.
14. John Stevens, op cit.
15. See Ingram and Harkin, op cit, for a graphic account of the ghastly and complex plot.

16. Another death foretold: 'A special kind of badness'

Everyone knew that Rosemary Nelson's life was in danger. The Secretary of State, the Chief Constable of the Royal Ulster Constabulary, the Prime Minister's office, Northern Ireland's establishment, US Congress and United Nations special envoys. They all knew, not only because she had told them, but also because the inevitability of her assassination had been announced time after time. Death threats by police officers had been transmitted via her clients for years. These had been investigated by the police, and the police had been chided for their unsatisfactory investigations. During the complaints process, the ICPC had learned that police investigating the complaints seemed to 'have the same view as the people complained about – that she deserved all she got'. But just as a hitherto limp complaints commission was about to publish a long-awaited and unprecedentedly tough critique of the Chief Constable, Rosemary Nelson was dead.

She was murdered on 15 March 1999, a decade after the Finucane assassination. Shortly after leaving home and setting off in her car, a bomb attached underneath the driver's seat exploded. Northern Ireland first minister David Trimble ventured the perverse suggestion that republicans could have been the perpetrators. Nothing, it seemed, could bend his mind to the lawlessness embedded in unionism. Before the week was out the killing was claimed by the Red Hand Defenders, the Ulster Volunteer Force, the Ulster Freedom Fighters and the Loyalist Volunteer Force.

But there were more specific grudges that made Nelson a known target. Like Pat Finucane and other vigorous defence lawyers, Rosemary Nelson's forensic defence of human rights had attracted the visceral hatred of many loyalists and RUC officers. As the Lawyers Committee for Human Rights had already noted in connection with the Finucane case, lawyers who fought for human rights put their lives in peril. UN Special Rapporteur Param Cumaraswamy had also criticised the legal profession's fatalistic failure to challenge the state about death threats and harassment, and had encouraged lawyers to protest about any threats. Rosemary Nelson was someone who had come forward to give evidence about those threats. In fact when Michael Finucane was in Washington with Cumaraswamy in 1998, he had sensed that Congress Representatives believed that if only his father had publicised the threats against him it might have saved him. 'She did – it didn't', was his comment.

Nelson was not reckless, but she lived in hope that her visibility and the light of public interest would protect her. 'I feared for her', recalls one middle-of-the-road member of Belfast's legal elite. 'We all did.' If Rosemary Nelson felt fear, it was not the face she wore. The power-dressing, chain-smoking, high-street solicitor, the first woman to run a legal practice in her home town of Lurgan, simultaneously warned the world that her life was in danger and tried to live it as if it wasn't. The last time we talked was two weeks before her death – at a conference on the reform of policing in Northern Ireland. She smoked as usual, she smiled as usual, but actually she was afraid.

Her practice handled everything from conveyance to divorce and domestic violence; though she was a catholic herself, her clients included both Protestants and Catholics. She had never been particularly political – if she was regarded as radical, it was her professional rather than political experience that made her so. 'This is a crazy jurisdiction,' she said in 1998 when the death threats were mustering. 'It is life-threatening to be a lawyer here. People come to you as a person who will defend their rights. It's bloody hard saying "You have none".'

Three of Nelson's cases in particular enraged her enemies; they were cases that confronted the shoot-to-kill policy; collusion in deadly force; and the role of the security services in managing the annual sectarian outings at Drumcree. During the summers, when the mighty Lambeg drums announced the Orange marching season, Nelson would work as the Garvaghy Road residents' legal representative in the annual showdown at Drumcree. This was one reason for the threats made against her. A second was her representation of the family of Robert Hamill, a young man kicked to death by a loyalist crowd, watched by RUC officers – a case that came to be seen as Northern Ireland's Stephen Lawrence. A third reason was her representation of Colin Duffy and the family of Sam Marshall.

COLIN DUFFY
Colin Duffy was a man regarded by some unionists as a republican scarlet pimpernel – a tall, dark, handsome republican who had escaped

not only a deadly ambush by loyalists and security services, but also a life sentence for allegedly killing a police officer. Duffy was a wanted man. Rosemary Nelson was his lawyer.

Duffy lived in the Kilwilkie estate, a municipal suburbia within walking distance of Lurgan town centre, its RUC barracks and Rosemary Nelson's high street office. Modest, leafy, quiet, the place was decorated by republican murals and regarded as a republican garrison. In 1993 Duffy was given a life sentence for the murder of a part-time soldier. There had been one witness, a man who said he had been cycling past and saw Colin Duffy fleeing the scene. The man was Lindsay Robb, a well-known UVF man, by then a member of the PUP. In 1995 the witness was himself arrested and jailed in Scotland, for conspiring to run guns to Northern Ireland – following an MI5 undercover operation. Clearly, this meant he was not a reliable witness. Nelson therefore mounted an appeal and in 1996 Duffy was freed.[1]

Less than a year later Colin Duffy was re-arrested and charged with the murder of two police officers who had been shot one night in Lurgan. Twelve witnesses presented themselves to Rosemary Nelson to testify that Duffy was not the killer, and that he had been somewhere else when the officers were shot. The charges were eventually dropped. Nelson reckoned that the RUC was out to get Duffy and decided to ask questions about an ambush on Duffy and two friends, which had taken place in 1990. This had always carried the odour of collusion. It had happened after Duffy and two republican friends had just signed on at Lurgan police station – an appointment known only to them, their solicitor, and the RUC.

Duffy, Sam Marshall and Tony McCaughey had to sign on regularly with the RUC as part of their bail conditions and their appointment was kept secret to protect them – they were, after all, entering hostile territory, and they knew they were under threat from loyalist paramilitaries. The three didn't usually go together, but on this night they had met up before walking together to the barracks. Duffy recognised a red Maestro car following him. He'd noticed it a week earlier, and now he saw it appear at the same bend in the road. 'I made a mental note.' It was as if 'somebody had called the car and said "Duffy's left the house".' Something like that probably had happened – a few days later a neighbour walking his dog came across a black tube with wires hanging out on a railway embankment near Duffy's home, which turned out to be an army camera transmitting pictures of Duffy's home.

The red Maestro appeared again a couple of times before they arrived at the Lurgan barracks. And on their way out they noticed that it was there again, waiting, this time apparently accompanied by a maroon Rover with three people in it. When they approached their estate they noticed the Rover again: 'the car doors opened, two guys got out with automatic rifles and started opening fire. Tony ran back and Sam and I ran up Kilmain Street. Sam was cut down yards after he'd started running'. One of the last things Sam Marshall said was, 'we've been let out to be set up'. Duffy managed to get the number plate into his head and then he ran for his life.

There were several witnesses to all this who had noticed the unfamiliar car. The RUC arrived, one of them Alan Clegg. John Marshall, Sam's brother, remembered that his brother had told him not long before his death that Alan Clegg had said to him: 'next time I see you Sam it'll be in a body bag'. Immediately after Sam's death, said Duffy, they 'came out with the car registration number and ... alleged collusion'. Alan Clegg's name appeared in graffiti on the town's walls.

It was also Alan Clegg who had received the men at police station, but Flanagan appointed him to head up the investigation into the killing. Clegg dismissed all claims of collusion and insisted that the red Maestro had been 'eliminated from inquiries', an assertion repeated by both Flanagan and the then Secretary of State Patrick Mayhew. However, later, in a different case, a California courtroom extradition hearing, Colin Duffy gave evidence on Marshall's death and the red Maestro, and the implications for a republican on being returned to the UK. Clegg was called to give evidence. Questioned about that red Maestro he made an amazing admission: it had been 'part of national security'; and he admitted that the car had been in the vicinity that night, and that 'the vehicle certainly was involved in a surveillance operation'. But more than that he would not say.[2]

Rosemary Nelson represented the Marshall family in their campaign for an inquest for Sam Marshall, but ten years after his death there had still been no inquest – although two men had been convicted of hijacking the Rover and aiding and abetting the death. That trial did not throw light on the red Maestro.

Duffy's belief was that the important question to ask about Rosemary Nelson's death was: who feared Nelson most? It was not loyalist paramilitaries, but the RUC. 'They blamed her for my release. She knew there was a growing hatred of her. It is not usual for solicitors to challenge the RUC on every single detail. Rosemary Nelson was very inquisitive and determined.'

ROBERT HAMILL

It was to Rosemary Nelson that the family of Robert Hamill turned, after he had been kicked to death by a loyalist crowd in Portadown in

1997, under the eyes of four armed RUC officers. Arrests were made, but charges were later dropped. (The case was taken up by Northern Ireland's new Police Ombudsman, and she later announced seven arrests, among them an RUC officer.)

Robert Hamill was a young catholic man, who lived with his partner Caroline Maguire and their two young sons, Shane and Ryan. He worked on building sites and played Gaelic football. On a balmy April night a few days before the 1997 general election, he went with his cousins Joanne and Siobhan Girvan and some other friends to a dance at St Patrick's Hall. The area where the hall was situated had previously been a catholic neighbourhood, but now it was marooned in hostile territory. When they decided to go home they called a taxi, but they couldn't raise one. It was only a short walk home, and they decided to risk it. They had noticed an RUC Land Rover parked in Portadown's main street, which seemed to offer protection. After more than a dozen recent incidents, the RUC had stationed the Land Rover in the town centre. This vehicle could have been a safety beacon, but it was positioned oddly – its location guaranteed that there was only restricted vision of the danger zone from inside. The Hamill group did not realise it, but the vehicle's orientation announced the ambiguity of its presence: it appeared to promise protection to catholics, but to protestants out on the razzle – a public pleasure which included attacking catholics – it offered the protection of both being there, and yet not being there, seeing and not seeing. In fact, a man had already approached the Land Rover a few minutes before, and had warned the four armed officers inside to be on the *qui vive* because there were loyalist crowds in the town and people would soon be leaving St Patrick's Hall en masse and walking into trouble. But the officers continued to sit and wait in their vehicle.

Suddenly, one of the Hamill group saw 'a large crowd of Protestants coming towards us – they started calling us Fenian bastards'. 'And then, "Get them, get them"'. And then they saw the crowd drag Robert Hamill to the ground. 'He was doing his best to protect himself ... they were all booting at him and shouting "Kill him".' According to one witness: 'I can say for definite that the RUC would have seen what was going on and made no effort to give any assistance to the injured men.' One woman 'banged the back of the RUC Land Rover, pleading for help. The RUC ignored her'. It was only when the ambulance arrived, another witness said, that the officers got out of their Land Rover and stood in front of the crowd. The RUC station was only a couple of minutes away from all this. Hamill and another cousin, Gregory Girvan, who had also been attacked, were taken to hospital. No arrests were made and the four officers in the Land Rover went off duty after the incident without making statements about it. The crime scene was not made secure in any way until the next morning.

It soon became clear that Hamill's condition was serious. Eleven days later, on 8 May, Robert Hamill died. His sister Diane, small, dark and calm, now emerged, from her own very private life, to become her brother's herald; her mission had become the quest for justice.

The case had many similarities to the murder of Stephen Lawrence – except that the police were present in Portadown, watching while the blows were struck. As Robert Hamill lay dying in hospital, the police versions of the attack changed dramatically. The early version, based solely on police sources, suggested gang warriors who overwhelmed plucky police officers; the later version, enlightened by civilian eye-witnesses, described an unprovoked sectarian attack. During the Drumcree marching season in 1997 the legend 'We Got Hamill' appeared on a bridge. A Loyalist Volunteer Force pamphlet being sold in the town centre declared support for the 'Portadown Six'. It said: 'anyone of us could be sitting in your place. You have been crimi-nalised for defending yourselves against an unprovoked attack. There have been many Nationalist attacks upon ordinary Protestant people at that same flashpoint where Taigs wear a different face at night.' When the 1998 Orange Order parade to Drumcree Church passed by the St John the Baptist Church – where hundreds of people had attended Hamill's funeral a year earlier – loyalists chanted 'Robbie Hamill, ha ha ha' and jumped up and down on the spot, as if they were stamping on Hamill's head. This death was a triumph for them.

There was a criminal trial in the spring of 1998, but only one young man, Paul Hobson, faced a murder change. (He was eventually convicted of causing an affray and sentenced to four years in prison.) As Rosemary Nelson commented, no one expected convictions: there had been no arrests during the attack, and 'the forensic evidence was allowed to walk away'. The police made little effort to collect evidence or find witnesses, and two witnesses who had originally come forward were intimidated into withdrawing or changing their testimony. Nelson took on the case and 'started asking uncomfortable questions about what happened, and why it was allowed to happen', but got no answers.

Meanwhile, another process was rustling around Portadown; two women were wrestling with their secrets and their consciences: they knew there was a conspiracy to cover up the killing, and more, to cover up collusion. The two women were the partners of two men involved that night. One was a well-known martial arts champion at a local gym, who had been part of the killing crowd; the other was a police officer who was part of a group who provided 'protection' at the gym, and he too had been there that night. The two men had provided each other with alibis – and implicated the women in the cover-up. The women went to the police. But the cover-up prevailed.

There was no investigation of suspected intimidation of witnesses, or of any conspiracy to pervert the course of justice. This was during the new era of human rights. This was the moment when the RUC was to morph into the PSNI. But nobody in authority acted as if something sinister had been going on. In 2001 one of the women felt compelled to go to the police again. She was Andrea McKee who, together with her husband Michael, ran the martial arts club. As a result of her evidence five officers were disciplined or suspended. There were no criminal prosecutions, however – or not until Andrea McKee took herself and her now ex- husband to court to confess their part in the cover up. In 2001 they were convicted of perverting the course of justice

By the time the 2001 Weston Park summit agreed that this case should be one of those to be re-investigated by an independent judge, the only people who had been convicted of any charge concerning the killing, or collusion, or cover-up were the McKees. Diane Hamill described Portadown as 'a town with a special kind of badness directed against people of my kind'. According to Nelson, 'Robert Hamill had no politics – he was just content to live, and he wasn't even allowed to do that. He died because he was a Fenian.' When Judge Peter Cory trawled through the evidence he came the conclusion that what he had learned invited a public inquiry into collusion.

DRUMCREE

After the 1994 ceasefires, two centuries of Orange triumphalism hailed a new imperative: if catholics were not to be vanquished by pogrom, by a protestant parliament, or by armed conflict, then the annual appearances of the Orange Order each summer would at least remind everyone of who the place *ought* to belong to – especially the marching rituals blessed from the pulpit at Drumcree church on the edge of Portadown. Catholics had for years been organising their own form of pleasurable dissent in street parties along the route through Garvaghy Road, but in 1995 the political temper of the place had been transformed. Several tenants associations in the area amalgamated to resist the march through their communities, and the Orange Order, finding its habitual parade banned by the Parades Commission, was joined by thousands of unionists in July to try to force their way along Garvaghy Road.[3] Every unionist who was anybody was there among the 50,000 marchers, and the RUC caved in and allowed Orangemen to march, on condition that they did it quietly. And so 1995 came to be seen as a unionist victory, and known as Drumcree One. Every year thereafter the same ritual was re-enacted. Rosemary Nelson became the residents' legal adviser, and another iconic image entered the archives: Nelson, a solitary woman in a summer blouse surrounded by uniformed, armed men. Every July, the gathering of the unionist multitudes at Portadown, 'the very Vatican of Orangeism', became 'a defining trial of its strength'.[4]

In 1998, the year of the Agreement, the Secretary of State and the Prime Minister's office became heavily involved in the negotiations to find an accommodation in Portadown. This was a summer of awesome brutality. Three days before 12 July loyalists torched the home of a catholic woman living with a protestant man in an estate in Ballymoney, an estate where there were only five catholic households. At dawn a petrol bomb was thrown into the house and Christine Quinn's three sons, Richard, Mark and Jason were burned to death. Ronnie Flanagan declared that the catastrophe changed everything, and the Drumcree minister William Bingham told the congregation on 12 July that the Orange march down Garvaghy Road would be a hollow victory 'in the shadow of three coffins'. But the Orangemen didn't budge from their hill by the church. They kept marching up and down, and the summer was dominated by negotiations over parading. In the first two weeks of July there were more than 2200 acts of public disorder; police and soldiers were attacked 615 times, and more than 600 vehicles were destroyed.[5] In August dissident republicans opposed to the Agreement bombed Omagh, killing 29 people. It was the worst single death toll since loyalists had bombed Dublin and Monaghan in 1974 – and in both atrocities the security services were implicated. In September loyalists organised a demonstration to purge catholics from Portadown town centre. A young police constable, Frank O'Reilly, was hit by a blast bomb and later died. He had been born a catholic and was married to a protestant. He was the 301st police officer to die in the conflict, and the last

The new Assembly at last assembled. The Agreement survived, it was still the settled will of the people. But not in Portadown. RUC officers drafted in from outside Portadown complained privately that they were sickened by the sectarian spirit of the Orangemen. 'The hatred is hanging off them', said one officer patrolling the town centre. The Red Hand Defenders circulated unambiguous propaganda among the faithful at Drumcree. One flyer invoked Old Testament fury to defend the destruction of Catholic churches, and another leaflet, headlined 'A Man With No Future', specifically targeted the spokesman of the Garvaghy Road residents, Breandan Mac Cionnaith and Rosemary Nelson, libelling her as a 'bomber', and giving her office address and telephone number. No one could doubt the RHD's intentions. This was a very public death threat.

DEATH THREATS AND THE RUC

Rosemary Nelson had been aware of death threats before this – it was in 1997 that her clients in Gough interrogation centre began to report sexist and sectarian abuse by RUC officers, and a series of warnings predicting her early death. Colin Duffy recalled that she spoke to him of her experience when walking into Lurgan RUC barracks, the sneers, the looks, the attitude. 'She knew there was a growing hatred of her.' Police officers made remarks to her clients about her face – she had a red mark. Duffy remembered comments they made to him about her face – 'isn't she an ugly bastard, she's a real dog, ugly bitch'. 'And then they claimed to me – and I complained about this – that she would have been proud of what I'd done – implying that she wasn't impartial, that she condoned what I was alleged to have done.'

Rosemary Nelson was aware of all the threats, and of the hostility of the RUC in Lurgan. 'Police are telling my clients that I'm not going to be around long, and that I'll be dead soon', she told me a year later. She opened her handbag and brought out a blue envelope, posted on 3 June 1998, with a handwritten note inside saying: 'We have you in our "sights" you Republican bastard. We will teach you a lesson. RIP.' The RUC did not bother to investigate this evidence until after Nelson was dead.

The United Nations Special Rapporteur on the independence of judges and lawyers, Param Cumaraswamy, went to Northern Ireland in October 1997 to investigate allegations of state collusion in threats to the lives of lawyers. After talking to several lawyers, including Nelson, about death threats and harassment, he sought Flanagan's reaction. He was disappointed: 'I came to the conclusion there was a complete indifference by the RUC', he said. When he interviewed the Chief Constable at RUC headquarters he was dismayed to hear him repeat the charge that some lawyers were working to 'a paramilitary agenda', and that he had 'reams of documentary evidence' to back this up. Flanagan denied making this comment, and also claimed to have no recollection of calling Cumaraswamy to protest about its being included in his report. But *Panorama* checked the telephone records, and they confirmed a call from Flanagan's office to Cumaraswamy's on 27 February 1998.[6] The UN report was unequivocal: the RUC had 'identified lawyers who represent those accused of terrorist-related offences with their clients or their clients' cause'. Intimidation of lawyers by RUC officers had been 'consistent and systematic'.

While the international community was expressing its fears for Nelson's safety, what was the British government doing? The death threats were aired during the talks between the Orange Order and the Garvaghy Road Residents Coalition in 1998. These were hosted by the British government and steered by Tony Blair's chief of staff, Jonathan Powell. One of the participants was David Watkins of the NIO. Powell appeared to take the threats very seriously and promised personally to contact the chief constable about the death threats. The RUC offered crime prevention advice. That was that. Ultimately, it also offered protection, but only to two of the people that had been threatened, both of them elected councillors. So the RUC and the NIO get to decide who lives and dies, said Breandan Mac Cionnaith that summer.

The Committee on the Administration of Justice (CAJ) sent security minister Adam Ingram copies of two death threats directed at Nelson: the 'Man Without A Future' flyer, and the handwritten threat of 3 June 1998. Ingram said that he had forwarded this evidence to Ronnie Flanagan, but Flanagan insisted that he had only received one of these documents and that he had not investigated the threats because there was no specific threat to act on.

When the RUC was first invited by the Lawyers' Alliance for Justice in Ireland in 1997 to investigate officers' death threats to Nelson, the force declined. The Independent Commission on Police Complaints did, however, begin a more general investigation, to be carried out by an RUC inspector. This investigation was subsequently found to be so flawed that it created a crisis in its own right. All but three of the 28 officers accused of making or passing on death threats to Nelson had responded to questions put to them with only a few lines of text; and seven used only one word: yes, no or dunno.

The ICPC supervising member appointed to oversee the investigation was a cool, rigorous barrister, Geralyn McNally, who had already supervised one hundred cases. For several months she had warned her ICPC colleagues that the investigation was in trouble, and by the autumn she had concluded that it was at risk of formal failure. At this, Flanagan came up with the idea of a review of the investigation. McNally agreed to this on condition that her own report was published with the review. Flanagan then brought in an officer from the Metropolitan police, Niall Mulvihill, to do the job, and Mulvihill duly gave his reassurance that the RUC's investigator had been 'robust and determined' – and that a more challenging approach would have 'achieved far less'. The ICPC disagreed. What, it wondered, had the investigation actually achieved? There was – and still is – no answer to the main question the investigation should have answered: did the RUC believe that 28 of its officers had threatened Nelson? 'I can't say', Flanagan told me. 'I can't come to a view'. The review was a way of not knowing.

McNally had recognised 'an ill-disguised hostility to Mrs Nelson' that could be judged 'destructive'. Mulvihill, by contrast, thought the 'lads' were just 'peppery' and deemed McNally's criticism to be 'subjective': he seemed to be reviewing McNally rather than the RUC. Furthermore, McNally's report of the original investigation was not documented in the review, as had been promised. Nor was there any public acknowledgement that her comments had led to twenty changes in RUC procedure. Mulvihill's conclusion was that the Nelson case created 'an air of concern wholly at odds with and disproportionate to the actual situation'.

In the week that the ICPC report finally appeared, the 'actual situation' was that Nelson was dead. Within weeks McNally, too, became the subject of death threats.

In 2007 the Police Ombudsman was finally able to publish the results of her investigation into CAJ's complaint that the government and the RUC/PSNI had failed to respond to its red alert. The Ombudsman upheld the complaint: the police had not acted upon an 'inherently dangerous death threat'. The RUC claimed that it had not received all the documents from the NIO. But it had been aware of them, said the Ombudsman, and had not made the effort to get hold of them. At first the documents were not in the relevant file. When the investigators returned, they were in the file. The Ombudsman was never able to discover why.

THE INVESTIGATION

Flanagan drafted in an English police officer, Colin Port, to direct the investigation into Nelson's death. He had no alternative, since RUC officers had been implicated in making death threats against her. However, Port agreed to include RUC officers in his inquiry team. He maintained that they were needed for local police intelligence. But the effect was to forfeit local people's goodwill and intelligence. Many simply refused to talk either to the RUC or to Port's investigators. Instead, more than fifty people gave their evidence to the Pat Finucane Centre, a human rights group in Derry.

These witnesses recalled that in the months before Nelson's murder, there had been an intense security presence around the area where she lived – helicopters, Jeeps, foot patrols and roadside checkpoints. On the day before her death the area was 'saturated' with helicopters swooping and hovering overhead, some of the time using an image intensifier as if searching for something below. Just hours before the explosion, witnesses noticed more patrols nearby, as well as a dog van and officers wearing boiler suits waiting by Jeeps near the Lurgan RUC barracks – one officer was later recognised at the murder scene. Some observers who rushed to the bombed car say they were astonished to see RUC officers arriving 'very slowly' and 'almost nonchalantly'. Many witnesses reported seeing officers smirking or laughing. One said they were 'jubilant, jovial, almost celebratory'. Other observers, however, reported that the RUC men were both prompt and professional.

None of the security personnel questioned by Port's team offered any information about the helicopters so noisily present above Nelson's home. There seemed to be no system or protocols disciplining the security services' use of helicopters or video equipment. Video tapes might be stuffed in soldiers' lockers or thrown away. In so chaotic and casual a context, 'anything can happen', said one investigator. With Royal Irish Regiment[7] soldiers up in the air and thick on the ground, it would not have been difficult for a soldier reconnoitring Nelson's home to alert the bombers to the return of her car from a family weekend break. Port's investigators found that one of the helicopters had been up over Lurgan using its cameras at around dawn on the day of Nelson's death. Adrenalin and anticipation greeted this discovery. Only to be followed by disappointment: amazingly, the tape had been wiped. Port's team came up with a number of people who were implicated in various aspects of the case, including two special branch informers, but no one was prosecuted for the murder.

One of the suspects was a preacher who claimed to be a leader of the RHD. The preacher was one of three RHD men interviewed by *Irish Independent* journalist Martina Devlin less than a week after the murder. The men had claimed Nelson's death for their organisation and broadcast their ambition to wage holy war and to bomb Dublin. The preacher told Devlin: 'There are car bombs in place in the North, ready to move across the border ... if we can put a bomb under Rosemary Nelson's car, we can put one in Dublin, believe me.' Still the RUC did nothing. This preacher already had a long association with hate campaigns against Catholic churchgoers. In the autumn of 2000 a rocket launcher was found in his car and he was jailed for a hefty ten years for possession of weapons. When the police searched his home,

Port's team took his computer and found documents referring to Nelson.

Port's team also arrested a young Royal Irish Regiment soldier, Ian Thompson, who had left the regiment shortly after Nelson's murder. His home was adorned with a poster of the LVF's martyr Billy Wright, and stuffed with neo-Nazi Combat 18 material. In March 2001 he appeared in a Belfast court charged with possessing weapons – he had an Uzi machine gun, explosives and a sawn-off shotgun. At the trial, Mr Justice McLaughlin was shown loyalist and neo-Nazi documents that had been among Thompson's possessions – including frightening references to Nelson. McLaughlin stated that there was 'some material in these depositions that would make the blood run cold': 'there are remarks made about Rosemary Nelson which have no place in any decent society'. The former soldier was jailed for nine years for possessing weapons. But Thompson still refused to comment on suspicions that he had reconnoitred Nelson's neighbourhood before she died.

Five years after the murder, in 2003, a loyalist prisoner, Trevor McKeown, claimed while in prison that during a murder interrogation that had taken place before Nelson's death he had been approached by police officers and offered details of her address. The officers he identified were among the 28 men investigated by the ICPC. They, however, denied McKeown's allegations.

The Port investigation focused on the prolific assassins – thrown up by intelligence – in the thoroughly penetrated LVF. It mounted a massive surveillance operation and engineered employment in England for William James Fulton. Fulton's brother Mark 'Swinger' Fulton was another suspect, who, the police believed, had guided Rosemary Nelson's murder. Mark Fulton had taken over the leadership of the LVF after Billy Wright's murder in prison, and he, too, died in prison in 2002 – allegedly by suicide. Jane Winter expressed grave concern that such an important witness in both the Billy Wright and Rosemary Nelson cases should have met a violent end in prison.

William James Fulton and his partner Muriel Gibson finally appeared in court in 2006, on scores of charges deriving from thousands of hours of surveillance evidence. The trial was the longest in Northern Ireland's history and at the end of it Fulton was convicted of 48 terrorist offences, including murder. However, Rosemary Nelson's murder was not part of the trial.

And yet it was a spectre haunting the courtroom. Port's decision to employ local RUC intelligence was returning to haunt him: in May 2006 Robert Bogle, a chief inspector in the RUC who was part of the Rosemary Nelson inquiry management, was accused of colluding with the LVF, and, according to bugging transcripts, of doing 'favours' for Fulton. Bogle had a vital role in the inquiry. He had been in charge of summarising and interpreting and responding to the millions of words of surveillance. He insisted that he was not involved with the LVF, and that his professional contacts did not amount to collusion – and had, in any case, been disclosed to the Port inquiry. Port had complete faith in him.

Suspicions of collusion between loyalist dissidents, RUC Special Branch and serving members of the military were always in the investigators' minds, though they found no forensic evidence to make a conspiracy theory stand up. Nevertheless investigators privately had no difficulty in endorsing the broader definition of collusion – turning a blind eye or conniving in acts of violence – adopted by Peter Cory in his inquiry; and they remained unsettled by the fact that neither the police investigation nor Cory's inquiry had been given access to any security service file on Rosemary Nelson.

Ultimately there was no prosecution in the case, and there was no report from Port's team – though it was confident that its conduct of the case was, itself, the record. However, into that empty space floated the Unionists' discredited hypothesis: that republicans had murdered Rosemary Nelson. Port had considered it and, in the absence of any evidence, rejected it. Flanagan had also rejected it. But none of this mattered; its advocates didn't need evidence. The hypothesis, buoyed by bigotry, offered an irresistible alternative to collusion.

There was always an aura of obscenity around Rosemary Nelson's assassination, an intimation of 'the proximity of evil', said Martin O'Brien. 'And I don't say that lightly.' The investigators were not alone in their sense that the silence enveloping her death was eerie. It was, suggested Jane Winter, 'a kind of *omerta*'.

NOTES

1. Lindsay Robb was jailed for ten years for gun running. He was released in 1999 and murdered in Glasgow in 2006.
2. By then Rosemary Nelson was dead and some of her cases, including that of Duffy, had been taken over by another lawyer, who had also received death threats, Paidragain Drinan.
3. For the role of Billy Wright in the protest see p22.
4. Chris Ryder and Vincent Kearney, *Drumcree, The Orange Order's Last Stand*, Methuen 2001.
5. Ibid.
6. Panorama, *Careless Talk*, 21.6.99.
7. The Royal Irish Regiment, a counter-terrorism force, was formed in 1992, with the merging of the UDR and the Royal Irish Rangers.

17. A tale of two texts

OFFICIAL KNOWLEDGE

Ever since Douglas Hogg's parliamentary semaphore had signalled Finucane's death, the murder had unleashed a contest between kinds of knowing. Downing Street knew who'd done it, and also that Downing Street – as on Secretary of State put it – 'was up to its neck in it'. The political struggle was about how to wrest that the open secret into official and popular knowledge, how to transform a medley of suspicions, intuitions and experience into the national narrative.

Unlike the perpetrators in the murder of Rosemary Nelson, who said nothing, in the Finucane case there were insiders who talked: a few killers, former soldiers, police officers and paid agents of the Crown. They had told their stories to human rights lawyers and to journalists. But that archive of *popular knowledge* was not allowed translate into institutional knowledge. Parliament was not recalled. The revelations did not create a crisis for the state. No one was called before a parliamentary or public tribunal. No one was named and shamed in a public arena. No one was obliged to explain these assassinations as the work not of rogues, but of a regime.

No debate was allowed, therefore, about the implications: without the partnership, the state's sponsorship of the protestant warlords, would armed conflict have continued in Northern Ireland? What would have happened to sectarianism had the state not sponsored it?

In 2003 two kinds of texts were produced which had the potential to transform popular knowledge into official, institutional knowledge, to vindicate political suspicion and make scandal shake the state. These were the Stevens III inquiry and the Cory collusion reports. Both these reports confirmed institutional collusion. Colin Port's investigation into the Rosemary Nelson case had not produced any dossier or prosecution in which there was an explicit charge of her murder, but there had been several prosecutions arising from it in which the defendant was also a suspect in the murder. Port's inquiry undoubtedly confirmed Cory's wider definition of collusion.

Stevens III and Cory reconnoitred the same landscape, they were asking the same questions, and they were reaching similar conclusions. Stevens reported how many documents his team had amassed, how many suspects had been interviewed; Cory's chronicles disclosed the documentary trail – the security services' records, from police and army intelligence, the evidence therein of collusion. But both Stevens and Cory disclosed a murderous political project that went all the way to the door of Number Ten. They should have been political detonators. Certainly, they implied a new politics of disclosure.

The reports were presented to the government. But the prime minister did not publish Cory, as he'd promised. In fact they were only published in April 2004, under pressure from the Irish government – which had already published them anyway. Both concluded that there was prima facie evidence of institutional collusion that reached to the highest level. Despite their differences, oddities and redactions, both texts gave the government the opportunity to do what the 'new beginning' demanded of it: disown collusion and create the conditions for naming and shaming and changing.

STEVENS III

When Stevens III was published, in April 2003, it was still the case that no one had been prosecuted for the murder of Pat Finucane. And yet in 1995 the Stevens team had told lawyers that he 'knew absolutely' the identity of the killers. So, what had Stevens been doing all this time? And why had there been no prosecutions? It was only after he was brought back in 1999 that he admitted that: 'At no time was I given the authority by either the Chief Constable of the RUC or the Director of Public Prosecutions to investigate the murder of Patrick Finucane.'[1] So, what were the Chief Constable and the DPP up to? And what, for that matter, was the government up to? They had rendered Stevens a *virtual* murder investigation – which had undoubtedly gathered a vast, dangerous archive, but could never share what it knew.

The publication of Stevens III (or rather its summary) was heavily media managed. Its impact was minimised and a soft landing ensured. Challenging questions were quelled. Reporters were encouraged to think that there were to be interesting arrests ahead – perhaps a score or more members of FRU, including Gordon Kerr (Colonel J in the Brian Nelson trial), now a diplomat in China; they were looking forward to something that had never happened before: a collusion trial, with low-life warlords and gangsters sitting in the dock with army officers and security chiefs. Stevens was presented as a hero. The spin garnished Stevens's dossier *manqué*. But what appeared to be a promise of prosecution was already an intimation of failure.

The Stevens summary offered an inventory of 9,256 statements taken, 1 million pages of documents recovered, 144 arrests and 94 convictions.[2] Awesome, it seemed. Except that the convictions concerned only charges of possession of documents and weapons. There was no conviction for the murder of Pat Finucane, no charges of conspiracy or 'directing terrorism'. The Brian Nelson inquiry had finally led to 20 former FRU members being interviewed by Stevens III – after determined MoD resistance – and the discovery of the prints of 81 other individuals on documents to which they had had no lawful access. Only six of these were convicted however, and none, of course, were FRU members. The report offered much less than it had appeared to promise.

The threats to Finucane by RUC members alleged in the BIRW report *Deadly Intelligence* had been investigated but none could be 'substantiated'. Could lives have been saved if agents had acted differently? Yes, said Stevens. Were agents unlawfully engaged in murder? Yes. The summary concluded that 'informants and agents were allowed to operate without effective controls and to participate in terrorist crimes'.

The team had been led by the documents to 'informants and agents' – their fingerprints littered the pages. The Stevens III team let it be known that 120 paramilitaries had been interviewed, and that 108 of these had been paid agents of the Crown.[3] The documents that had been offered as vindication by Tommy Lyttle all those years ago in 1998 – which had prompted Stevens's first invitation to Northern Ireland – indicated systemic collusion. Wasn't the larger question, then, how deep, how wide and how high? These were questions that the Stevens III summary left unanswered.

The briefings to journalists before publication, nevertheless, did broadcast Stevens's dramatic u-turn new conclusion: there had been institutional collusion. But these new words did not actually appear in his published summary. Still, the *Financial Times* reporter felt moved to say, 'The Stevens III conclusions, and there is no exaggeration here, are horrifying.' The FRU, 'reporting direct to the senior military commander of Northern Ireland, colluded systematically with loyalist terrorists in the murder of republican sympathisers.'[4] There was something of the Contras, or the Sicilians, about it all, as if Britain had become another country. Writing in Ireland's *Sunday Business Post*, Tom McGurk commented that Stevens implied murder with a 'near impunity' that 'beggars belief'. There had been a 'deadly pogrom' that – if Stevens's report was 'as is anticipated' would open up 'a vista so appalling that the post-war liberal and democratic state should be shaken to its core. The private briefings had given Stevens the man the political élan that the text available to the public precisely lacked. But the system did not quake. The official text had been muted by months of wrangling with the intelligence and MoD hierarchy.

Stevens's cachet blessed the appointment of a new Chief Constable in Northern Ireland. The new man was none other than Hugh Orde, Stevens's operational lieutenant during the Stevens III enquiry. Politically, therefore, the report represented a kind of rapprochement. It was now Orde's mission to create policing for all the people, and more particularly to do something about Special Branch, the 'force with the force' that had been criticised by the Patten commission

The Stevens report asked the question that was the key to the great debate about policing: 'were both sides of the community dealt with in equal measure?'. The answer was three crisp words. 'They were not.' Stevens also acknowledged that loyalists and security services colluded to kill catholics. But although Stevens had travelled a long way to reach his collusion conclusion, he still gave the impression that the problem was exceptional, not systemic. And yet he disclosed with 'great disquiet' that the Ministry of Defence had withheld documents from his inquiry. These documents – army files – had been revealed only six months earlier (actually, as a result of Cory's tenacity in 2002); and they showed that MI5 had participated in collusion, despite its denials in 1990. The summary wore the evidence of political pressure in its omissions, failures and its grandiosity. What Stevens III offered was reassurance. It implied that the job had now been done: Stevens had his right-hand man in the top job, recommended reforms were being implemented, and baddies had been identified and prosecuted. It participated, therefore, in the rhetoric of the British as peacekeepers.

Deals had been done. The open secret remained an official secret. No politicians, army officers, security mandarins or police officers had appeared in any public arena to explain this scandal. Furthermore, the Stevens III report did not disclose its own history – that the inquiry had been thwarted, the text had been scarred, its words mangled during savage diplomatic wrangling; that it had been trapped in a historic battle between the police and MI5 about power and responsibility. In fact, by the time Stevens III was published MI5 was winning that war; it had been promised control over security in the new Northern Ireland. In the 'new beginning', the government had decided that the securocracy would be sequestered in MI5, safe from public scrutiny.

William Stobie's evidence had helped in the arrest of a dozen suspects on suspicion of Pat Finucane's murder. But none were prosecuted. The reason? The absence of 'admissible evidence'. But two of the conspirators had talked and talked: Brian Nelson and William Stobie. Nelson had been controlled; and Stobie had been killed. Tommy Tucker Lyttle had also talked. He was also dead. Hugh Orde claimed that the Stevens inquiries always tried to follow the evidence. But Stevens had spurned the evidence given to him by detective Johnston Brown (see pp239–40). And he had been provoked into pursuing Ken Barrett only after two television documentaries had exposed him as an admitted assassin.

The text's inventory of convictions gave the impression of prosecutory zeal thwarted by the rigours of the prosecution process. But the report did not explain the role of the Director of Public Prosecutions. Nor did it account for the impact of the Attorney General's seizure of the Brian Nelson prosecution, the intervention of the Secretary of State into that case, and the falsehoods of 'Colonel J'. It did not explain the destructive treatment of William Stobie. It did not explain why Ed Moloney had been charged under the Prevention of Terrorism Act, or Martin Ingram had been charged under the Official Secrets Act.[5]

The Finucane family was scathing about Stevens III and the idea that something 'went wrong with the system'; that there had been a lack of 'effective controls'. Michael Finucane, now working as a lawyer in Dublin, argued that nothing had gone wrong: 'The system worked exactly as it was intended and, in the British government's eyes, it worked perfectly.' The loyalists and the security services were just 'different departments, same bureau'. The evidence given to the British and Irish governments by BIRW and the Finucane family had in fact done some of the work for the Stevens inquiry: it had provided an analysis for the first time of 'the collusion machine'. In Michael Finucane's view, there had been a policy: to harness the 'killing potential of the paramilitaries, to increase that potential through additional resources in the shape of weapons and information and to direct those resources against selected targets so that the government could be rid of its enemies ... Simple policy. Simple operation. Simply chilling.'

THE CORY REPORT

Judge Peter Cory's texts did what the Stevens report did not do: he let the archives speak. He published the narrative in its raw state, and allowed himself to be the medium through which the public could access some of the records of the matrix: the Secret Service, MI5, the FRU and Special Branch. All of the security services were implicated in the murder of a lawyer: a direct hit against democracy and the rule of law. All of them were running agents in the loyalist paramilitary organisations, and they were all recording their relationships. Cory gained access to MI5 records that had been kept from Stevens for a dozen years. Cory vindicated Jane Winter's counsel when BIRW had handed over its dossier to the government, when she had told Whitehall that all they needed to do to find out what was happening was to consult their own documents.

Cory did something else that Stevens did not do: he followed the evidence. It was all there in the army, intelligence, secret service and police archives, tons of documents – records of telephone conversations, assessments, profiles, all of it circulating up and down, between the safe houses, bars and Orange Halls of Northern Ireland and across the water to the Embankment. The question he asked of the evidence was whether it indicated collusion – by omission or commission – and connivance. Cory followed the papers, not just the people; his report did not have to protect the records of the security services, and therefore he did not depend on confessions. Confessions might narrow the field of vision to the person of the perpetrator, but Cory was interested in opening the window onto the perpetrator's place in a larger system.

Cory cast doubt on the Stevens/DPP claim that there was insufficient admissible evidence to prosecute the paramilitaries and security services (though, inexplicably, Cory redacted from his text swathes of documents from the William Stobie prosecution process – in the course of which Special Branch is believed to have named many names – which revealed not only that Special Branch could identify the perpetrators, but also that it was working with them. Evidently, even Cory could be constrained.) Cory also assessed the input of the military during the Brian Nelson trial. The army's records showed that the military were pleased with Nelson. Contrary to Gordon Kerr's claim on *Panorama* that the FRU had been worried about Nelson's excess of enthusiasm, the records revealed to Cory that, shortly before Finucane's murder, the army was 'anxious to have Nelson rise higher and have an ever greater influence'. Cory also asked himself why Colonel J had defended his evidence as a 'script' that had been vetted by 'the authorities'. Why would a script have been necessary, he wondered. He also found that the army had reminded Nelson that he should have obeyed advice and refused to give evidence to the Stevens inquiry; and that the General Officer Commanding in Northern Ireland had congratulated Colonel J for his testimony, reassuring him that, though the trial had drawn unwanted attention to agents, his comments had addressed 'the institutional rather than individual', and therefore had helped to keep 'existing critically important personal relationships in Northern Ireland undamaged'. Collusion, concluded Cory.

Cory discovered documents showing that the Chief Constable and General Officer Commanding had decided that Stevens would get no access to intelligence material. That explained why the FRU seized Nelson's intelligence dump, and it explained how it was only the evidence trail – the documents made public by the loyalists – that had led the Stevens team past the acts of concealment.

Cory also disclosed that, as early as 1981, when Pat Finucane was representing Bobby Sands, the Secret Service had discussed with Special Branch the 'very real and imminent threat' to his life, but had decided that any intervention would compromise their agents. After his death in 1989 the Security Service was aware that two other solicitors were under threat, but the record showed that its only concern was that their murders might 'provoke retaliation'.

FICTION IN THE ARCHIVE
The historian Natalie Zemon Davies has put forward the notion of 'fiction in the archive', and this is an apt description of the records of the security services in Northern Ireland.[6] The Cory report's authority derived from the records. Yet these were simultaneously a record and a fiction – the syntax and the scripting were pre-emptive, written in anticipation of risky exposure; and the originals presumed a disposition in the reader that had already demonised the perceived enemy. And so, in a sense, the record assumed the great constitutional unsaid: that this was war, and that that there was among British citizens an enemy that deserved to die.

The 'fiction in the archive' was most transparent in the record of the FRU discussion following the attempt to assassinate Alex Maskey in 1987. The record reports that FRU officers were told by a senior officer:

> You must have heard that the RUC Special Branch are making allegations that Military Intelligence could well have been involved in some way with the shooting. Now of course we all know that this is not true and has nothing whatsoever to do with the FRU. As far as we know this shooting was probably the responsibility of the UDA … we have contacts within the UDA but unfortunately, we do not always know when they are planning an operation.[7]

The implication – critical to the way the matrix represented itself – was that the UDA was autonomous. But the UDA was, to all intents and purposes, an 'auxiliary' of the security services. The story in the records was constructed around agencies' contacts with the UDA. It was not the story of the agencies themselves, nor of the political culture that gave them their mandate. The Stevens inquiry, and Cory, were invited to address *acts*, not *cultures* of collusion. Cory had endeavoured to widen his aperture, and to consider cumulative activities suggestive of collusion or connivance. It was this that released his inquiry from forensic myopia concerned only with acts and allowed him to look at a bigger picture. Nevertheless he remained focused on a series of acts, not a system.

Cory commented that Douglas Hogg's comments in Parliament showed that: 'Both military and police intelligence fundamentally misconstrued the role of solicitors'. This was a grave charge against the political culture. Clearly, Cory concluded, the security services implicated in the killing were 'not bound by the law and were above and beyond its reach'. Government departments were prepared to 'participate jointly in collusive acts in order to protect their perceived interests'. Cory's importance was that, for the first time, he made public the chronicle of the relationships between loyalists and the security services that was filed in the National Archive. This was a mordant critique of British democracy.

THE RECEPTION OF THE REPORTS

The fate of the Cory report instantly exposed the limits of the – albeit reluctant – new politics of disclosure. The government had two options: containment in the service of continuity; or revelation in the service of change. The reports could have been mobilised *pour encourager* Unionists to confront the illegality, as well as the illegitimacy, of the project carried out in their name. But that would have obliged the state to first submit itself to a new dialogue with its past.

The prime minister was mentored in foreign policy by the intelligence establishment.[8] His undoubted commitment to the peace process could not withstand the interests of the Joint Intelligence Committee, the conduit between the intelligence services and the government on Iraq, as well as Northern Ireland. His 'war on terror' had been conceived with the JIC. How could he now call the JIC to account for its deployment of terrorism in Northern Ireland? Even if he had wanted to, no Labour Prime Minister could expect to survive such a profound rupture without an alternative magnetic field from which to operate, in other words, without the confidence to mobilise the scandals to ignite change. This was 2003. It was the year that the Prime Minister and the Cabinet and the Joint Intelligence Committee were enmeshed. It was not a time, an era, or a regime, that could tolerate a critique of traditional power – a power that had not been above destabilising Labour governments in the past.

When the government received Cory's report, it first refused to publish it, and then introduced new legislation to quell its implications. The Inquiries Bill, Blair's response to Cory, was quickly shoved through a compliant Parliament to enable the diminishing of any Finucane inquiry by ceding to government the powers that otherwise would have been vested in the inquiry itself, and its chairperson. A galaxy of human rights organisations protested at this. The US House foreign affairs chairperson, Congressman Chris Smith, was among the protesters. 'A public inquiry into Finucane should be no-brainer', he commented in March 2005. 'But instead the British government have treated it as a non-starter'.

Judge Cory was incandescent. He told a House foreign affairs panel in Washington that the government's determination to push the Bill through before complying with its Weston Park commitment to investigate collusion would create an 'Alice in Wonderland situation'. He went further. He advised all Canadian judges asked to play a role to 'decline an appointment in light of the impossible situation they will be facing'.

Geraldine Finucane wrote to all British judges asking them not to participate.

The word was then spread around the establishment that the Finucane inquiry was being thwarted by the Finucane family's intransigence. This not only traduced the family; it showed complete disregard of the scale of criticism. No one connected with the search for the truth about Finucane's murder trusted the British government – not the Irish government, not the US House foreign affairs committee, not a wide range of human rights organisations, and not the Finucane family.

NOTES

1. Cited in Jane Winter's searching critique, *Justice Delayed*, BIRW 2000.
2. Stevens III, Summary and Recommendations.
3. Philip Stevens, *Financial Times*, 7.4.03.
4. Ibid.
5. For more on Nelson, Stobie, Moloney and Ingram, see chapters 14 and 15.
6. Natalie Zemon Davies, Fiction in the Archives: Pardon Tales and their Tellers in Sixteenth Century France, Polity 1987.
7. Nicholas Davies, 2005, op cit, p137.
8. John Kampfner, *Blair's Wars*, Free Press 2003.

18. Collusion chronicle

I have focused on the killing of lawyers because these murders take us to the lengths that the state was prepared to go to in its attack on state citizens, perceived enemies and the rule of law. The story of these lawyers belonged to the handful of collusion chronicles that attracted enough momentum to become part of the politics of the settlement. But they also exposed its limits. The SDLP and Sinn Fein had been inexplicably chaste in their demands that Britain address collusion. Demands do not a movement make, and at critical moments power escaped lightly: in 2001, when Tony Blair agreed to an inquiry about an inquiry, he was making an unavoidable *tactical* concession – though admittedly, by sanctioning a judge of international standing to adjudicate on the evidence, Britain for the first time exposed itself to an external eye and it began to lose control of the story.

Collusion still appeared in political discourse as conspiracy *lite*. This was remarkable: collusion was inscribed in the management of the conflict in this small place that had been the most violent of Europe's conflict zones. Brendan O'Leary and John McGarry remind us that, proportionately, the conflict claimed ten times more lives than those lost by the Americans in their Vietnam war.[1] The codicil *never again* was branded on the post-Vietnam consciousness of the United States. Until the presidency of George W. Bush, the Americans' enthusiasm for war as a way of doing its business was cautioned by the despair of a vanquished super-power. But Britain never seemed to have had its own 'never again' moment, and Northern Ireland was traded as a mature marque of British post-colonial counter-insurgency.

In her critique of those inclined to promote Britain as a template for 'new imperial' wars in the twenty-first century, the historian Caroline Elkins cautions that Britain 'inscribes a legacy of violence' on the governments established in its wake, all too obvious in societies where the 'real outposts of tyranny are the institutions bequeathed by colonial and military strategies'.[2] Northern Ireland was already a post-colonial settlement, and political protest had been translated as incipient insurgency. Indeed, the management of the conflict exemplified the military theorist Frank Kitson's thesis that opposition and resistance are always a potential state of insurgency.[3] According to Kitson, that insurgency must be answered by gangs mobilised from among the people themselves – to intimidate resistance, and destroy the sea in which it swims (again, the people themselves). Elkins reminds us, however, that though Kitson's doctrine 'touched nearly every corner of the world where the British had imperial and strategic interests', and though it became a 'gold standard' of counter-insurgency, it was hardly emancipatory: it depended upon over-arching 'police-state control', with a medley of instruments available, from internment to curfew, to subdue the population.

COLLUSION FOREVER

It is appropriate in this chapter to summarise the shadow that collusion cast over the entire conflict. Fionnuala Ni Aolain, the author of path-breaking research into the use of lethal force in Northern Ireland, suggests that the importance of collusion is that it reveals the state's orientation: 'it positions the state'. She also argues that the repertoire of emergency laws available to 'police-state control' in Northern Ireland were 'entrenched and normalised as a daily part of state procedure'.[4] Thus, from the start of the conflict in 1969, 'it is no exaggeration to argue that Northern Ireland has functioned in a state of legal limbo'. The 'surgical remoulding' of ordinary law both responded to, and defined, the conflict. Ultimately it led to the collapse of the distinction between the ordinary and the extraordinary. In Northern Ireland the taking of life by the state was 'a front-line rejoinder' to political crisis – during the first phase of militarisation after 1969, the military were responsible for 90 per cent of the deaths caused by the use of lethal force.

Elements of the state had imagined its adversaries as insurgents, and counter-insurgency was their answer. And collusion was the logic of counter-insurgency. Despite the perception in the 1960s, shared by the Cabinet, the Home Affairs Ministry, the RUC, and Terence O'Neill himself, that the 'protestant extremism threatens the stability of the state'[5] – rather than the civil rights movement – the protestant militias were to become a ready-made resource to draw on for the Kitson doctrine of counter-insurgency.

Collusion began from the start of the conflict – former combatants have testified that they were trained by the army at the beginning of the 1970s. Former police officers and soldiers have given evidence of wide-spread, known and sanctioned collusion between loyalists, police and soldiers, in ambushes and assassinations, sanctioned by senior officers.[6]

A secret intelligence report in August 1973, *Subversion in the UDR*, described 'widespread' joint membership of the Ulster Defence Regiment (formed in 1970) and the loyalist militia Ulster Defence Association (formed in 1971), and reckoned that any attempt to make the protestant UDR non-partisan 'could very well result in a very small regiment indeed'. The UDR was therefore a proxy loyalist regiment within the British Army.

The UDR was 'the best single source of weapons (and the only significant source of modern weapons) for protestant extremist groups'. Some of these weapons had been used by 'the most violent of the criminal sectarian groups in the protestant community'. But this was not the perceived problem. Control, not collusion, was the concern. If the government's actions were 'perceived to be unfavourable to "loyalist" interests' ... 'these men could act as a source of information, training and weapons for their fellows, and might even work within the UDR to make it unreliable'. Since the UDA was not above contemplating independence, risk was built into the relationship; loyalists might follow the example of white settlers in Rhodesia by making a 'unilateral declaration of independence', in which case 'the loyalty of UDR members to HMG might be sorely tried.'

When Justice for the Forgotten, the Dublin and Monaghan bombing relatives' movement, and the Pat Finucane centre found this report during their annual search of newly-released documents in the National Archive, they gave the story to the *Irish News*; and the paper also published evidence that prime minister Harold Wilson had arranged in 1975 for the leader of the opposition, Margaret Thatcher, to be briefed about the report. 'This is the first time evidence has come to light that shows not only the scale of collusion, but also that the British government was aware of it at such an early stage', commented the nationalist *Daily Ireland*.[7] 'Astonishingly, instead of doing something about it the British government went on to increase the regiment's role and presence in many nationalist areas where tensions were already very high.' This story went largely unnoticed in the London media.

The government's worry about control of loyalists was vindicated in 1974, when collaboration between loyalist militias, unionism and the UDR swiftly brought down Northern Ireland's first power-sharing government. During the period of the strike Ireland's biggest single atrocity since World War II occurred: the bombing of its capital city (and the border town of Monaghan), killing 33 people. The perpetrators are said to have belonged to UVF networks active in Belfast and in South Armagh that collaborated with members of the UDR and the

RUC. In September 1974 the British Prime Minister told the Taoiseach that Britain was holding people responsible for the bombings. They had been involved in the UWC strike. But it would not disclose their identities, due to 'circumstances of grave embarrassment to the Crown'. Dublin did not put London under pressure on this until 1999,[8] when Taoiseach Bertie Ahern met the relatives and survivors (no Taoiseach had done anything like this in nearly a quarter of a century) and launched a commission of inquiry. Britain refused to co-operate.

The Barron Commission that followed quickly spread its net to other, connected killings on both sides of the border. It was the beginning of a process that challenged the historic audit of atrocities by asking how many assassinations claimed by the paramilitaries (on all sides) had been procured or perpetrated (or tolerated) by the security services. In 2002 Judge Henry Barron met the then British Secretary of State John Reid and again asked for co-operation. John Reid declined.

The Barron Commission did, however, hear witnesses from the British security forces, including whistleblowers John Weir (RUC) and Colin Wallace (a British army officer whose career was destroyed by a dirty tricks campaign to criminalise him).[9] Barron found them impressive. Allegations of collusion in the Dublin and Monaghan bombings were 'neither fanciful nor absurd'.[10] He lamented Britain's lack of co-operation.

Ni Aolain characterises the period between 1975 and 1980 as 'normalisation' – a period when there was an attempt to shift control of the conflict onto normal law-enforcement. But after the 1981 hunger strikes the state adopted a strategy of active counter-insurgency. MI5 appeared to be running counter-insurgency through the army and the police and a crowd of agents and informers within the loyalist militias. In 1979 the Force Research Unit, stationed at the Army HQ and staffed by specialists under the eye of MI5, was acting independently and without rules, according to a former officer. In 1981 the Walker Report, written by the head of MI5 in Northern Ireland, structured Special Branch within the RUC and also accorded it autonomy. They ran a multitude of agents and informers. One officer calculated that two thirds of the loyalist organisation he handled were agents.

By the end of the decade there had been crest of political violence. The question routinely asked is: did Downing Street know? That was always the wrong question. Downing Street knew. But at the end of the 1980s the loyalists' revelations ensured that the world knew, too. As Ni Aolain argues, when the state contracts out the killing to 'unaccountable, autonomous agencies' it loses the ability to control it, and therefore 'it puts itself at risk of disclosure'. It also forfeits internal discipline: 'it doesn't have control over those other organisations; it is a high-risk strategy for a democratic state. It is an act of desperation.'

OMAGH BOMBING

Collusion began in the early days of the conflict, and it was to continue after the Agreement had been signed. In 1999 the breakaway Real IRA bombed the town of Omagh. Twenty-nine people lost their lives. Three years later the officer investigating the bombing, Detective Chief Superintendent Eric Anderson, appeared at a press conference and broke down as he begged for help to find the perpetrators. Kevin Fulton watched him on television, amazed. Fulton was a former FRU agent operating in republican milieux and he had warned his RUC handler that an attack on Omagh would take place on 15 August 1998; he had alerted a CID contact to the perpetrators and his strong suspicion that a bomb had been made. The CID contact passed it on immediately to Special Branch. One of the bombers was a British agent.

Fulton contacted Eric Anderson, and realised that the detective knew nothing of those warnings. He then complained to the Ombudsman, who picked up the trail. Her report concluded that the victims, their relatives and the officers of the RUC had all been let down by 'defective leadership, poor judgement and a lack of urgency'.[11] The Ombudsman had identified 360 documents in Special Branch that were potentially relevant to the bombing – and 78 per cent had not been passed on to the investigation. Fulton's information had fallen into a Special Branch pond, where it was 'not assessed or considered'. What happened then provoked one of the most bizarre public rows in recent times, between Chief Constable Ronnie Flanagan and the sedulous Ombudsman Nuala O'Loan. O'Loan hailed from the great and the good, and was an impeccable establishment figure. Flanagan was a Special Branch veteran and an affable public presence. No one like her had ever before taken on someone like him. And no one like her had ever before published such an unrelenting critique of a police operation.

Ronnie Flanagan's retort produced gasps: he would commit public suicide if she was right – and she wasn't – he said. There was no sound of support for the Ombudsman from Downing Street. The then secretary of State Peter Mandelson toured the press. 'Very poor work', he said. 'I'm afraid her credibility has been damaged.'[12] The NIO let it be known that Northern Ireland needed a police force, but it didn't need an Ombudsman. 'It was scary,' said an insider.

Certainly, no one had expected the Ombudsman to act like this: the NIO expected a tame civil servant who would stealthily have words in ears, not one who would go around truth-telling or trying to change things. She wasn't a 'usual suspect'. But she was 'naive', said her critics. She survived, though chastened.

The Omagh bombing, like the bombing of Dublin and Monaghan twenty-five years earlier, and the assassination of Rosemary Nelson (whose suspected perpetrators also boasted about bombing Dublin), all involved collusion; and all were designed to destabilise the political settlement. They were spectacular and conjunctural.

THE MCCORD MURDER

If collusion was part of the logic of counter-insurgency, so were crime and violence. The McCord case was an example of chronic and criminal, rather than conjunctural, collusion; it was a reminder of the army's secret dossier on 'subversion' thirty years earlier, when it had reported that army weapons had been deployed by some of the most violent protestant criminals. If Flanagan was enraged by the Omagh report, there was more to come. The Ombudsman's report on the murder of Raymond McCord Jnr was a devastating challenge to the prevailing orthodoxy.

Raymond McCord had been unable to get justice for his son, Raymond Jnr, and took his grievances about the police, by now the PSNI, to the Ombudsman. Raymond Jnr had apparently been slaughtered by his loyalist comrades in a UVF gang operating in Mount Vernon, a small north Belfast neighbourhood bordering leafy surbubia. The case ignited a larger investigation – by the Ombudsman – into a score of murders. What her investigators discovered was a long-standing paramilitary gang heavily penetrated by Special Branch, killing with impunity, and untouched for many years after the 1994 ceasefires.

The McCord report was published in 2006. But by then Ronnie Flanagan (still the Chief Constable when McCord went to the Ombudsman) was in another job. He had not been asked to stay on as Chief Constable by the Policing Board. Instead he had been crowned chief inspector at Her Majesty's Inspectorate of Constabulary. And he was still working there in December 2007, when Mr Justice Weir delivered a scalding critique of the Omagh investigation and acquitted the sole accused, Sean Hoey.[13]

O'Loan's team had done what no one had expected of them: taken their mission seriously. The resistance they met confirmed that the system was in unstable equilibrium between old habits and new beginnings. 'There's only one way out of this', said a staffer, 'and that is change!'.

SUSPENDED BELIEF – COLLUSION AND THE COUP

The limits of change were further dramatised by two seemingly disconnected events: the audacious raid on the Stevens archive at Castlereagh in March 2002, when thousands of documents on members of the security forces and their agents were stolen; and the raid on an alleged Sinn Fein spy ring at Stormont. One man linked the two events: Denis Donaldson, an MI5 mole in Sinn Fein.

The raid on the apparently impregnable Stevens inquiry archive was instantly described by Ronnie Flanagan as an inside job. But ultimately the only suspect became Larry Zaitschek, an American chef who had recently quit his job in the Castlereagh kitchens. Zaitschek had met republicans – including Donaldson – in the US before he arrived in Northern Ireland. That was enough to put him in the frame, and there he stayed. After the police interviewed him he was allowed to go back to the US, and over the years the police, who had placed his wife and child under secret protective custody, questioned him. But 'Larry the Chef' was never arrested or charged, and nor was anyone else.

When the police raided the Stormont Assembly in 2002, seizing computer disks from the Sinn Fein office, they arrested three Sinn Fein staff. One of them was Denis Donaldson. That had brought to an end Northern Ireland's experiment in power-sharing government.

Donaldson was a middle-ranking apparatchik, regarded by some of his colleagues as a rather sour operator. Monica McWilliams recalled, 'he'd stop by the Women's Coalition office and say, "Hello girls, what's the gossip?"' To which she'd reply, 'We're not girls and we don't gossip'. But gossip mushroomed when suddenly on 8 December 2005 the men were released and the police announced that a prosecution was 'no longer in the public interest'. A week later Sinn Fein disclosed that Donaldson had, in fact, admitted to having been an MI5 agent for twenty-one years, and Donaldson himself announced that the spy ring had been a fiction. This episode became known as Stormontgate – when an elected and sovereign government had been undone by dirty tricks. It was a coup d'etat, said Sinn Fein – a view that attracted somewhat greater currency among political observers than Sinn Fein was used to. BBC journalist Martina Purdy summed up the consensus in December 2005: 'What is clear is that Stormontgate killed the executive and undermined faith in the political process'.

It was widely believed that these events were the work of different anti-Agreement factions within the security forces; after all there was only evidence for one spy at Stormont, and he had been working for MI5. This was the final act of the counter-insurgency. There was no official inquiry. No-one faced any parliamentary hearing or public tribunal. The 'coup' and the collusion reports fell into a becalmed polity.

Truth-telling is a contingent process – it is dependent on social movements beyond the secretive state to hurl the stories into popular consciousness. The evidence was astounding, and yet the archive remained as raw material. Making the story register on the radar was dependent on the work of interpretation and imagination; acting upon its radical revelations was dependent on parliament and the political culture.

CONCLUSION

Scrutiny of violence and collusion could have acted as a prism through which to understand power and its manipulation of the law, the distinction between 'what is legal and what is legitimate'.[14] This is critical. If Northern Ireland is to be permitted to flourish as a society where egalitarianism and human rights – the promise of the Agreement – mark the break with its pitiless past, then, as Ni Aolain put it, 'the past needs and demands definition'. But as a potential detonator, the collusion story has been simultaneously eloquent and muted. Truths cannot speak for themselves, nor can they stand up for themselves. Evidence exists only in the eye of the beholder. It has no power of its own, its transformative potential is contingent on political will.

There was a will to release testimony in South Africa, the model of truth-for-amnesty, because, of course, the black majority had at last escaped from apartheid, and truth telling was a gesture of the greatest cultural importance. The Truth and Reconciliation Commission has been both celebrated and criticised, but at the very least it asserted the end of the era of white domination: even if white power had not relinquished its economic power, it could no longer decide what could be said, who could be heard, what might be made to matter.

Truth tribunals depend upon states as their patrons. The British state kept to itself control over the process of revelation – it would be sequestered and lawyered; and above all it would be thrown into another time, a dimmed future. It would also make up the rules as it went along about how, and how much, and how many truths might be told. John Stevens's ultimate acknowledgement that collusion had been institutionalised induced no shock to the British political or legal system.

Stevens's inquiries began just before Peter Brooke's creative tenure of Hillsborough castle in 1989, and just after the UDA had confirmed collusion by revealing its cache of secret security documents. But Brooke never believed that it was institutional or systemic. The idea was 'ludicrous', he said. And what if he was wrong, I asked. 'Then it is very bad news indeed', he replied. A decade after the Agreement the British government was still simultaneously commissioning – and manipulating – inquiries and keeping its own mouth shut about this 'very bad news indeed'.

Counter-insurgency and collusion remained active in the post-

Agreement formation of the new state. They enabled Britain to dominate the decisive years of the new dispensation through its capricious or strategic suspensions of Stormont's sovereignty. Britain determined when or whether the past would be defined; it re-interpreted the constitution; it decided that the equality and human rights discipline would not apply to the big things – and it would not apply to Britain.

The collusion chronicles could not be staunched, but they could not flourish without the imprimatur of the state; and nor could they become a resource for renovation and a new dispensation. Only state-sponsorship could give it that transformative potential to become the national narrative, the story the society tells about itself. 'The star role in this modern morality play is given to the state', says Ni Aolain. 'The state's first soliloquy should be the acknowledgment that it has not been a neutral nor passive actor in the experience and management of societal conflict'.[15]

NOTES

1. O'Leary and McGarry, 1997, op cit.
2. C. Elkins, 'The wrong lesson', *Atlantic Monthly*, July/August 2005.
3. Kitson, op cit.
4. Ni Aolain, op cit, 2000.
5. O'Callaghan & O'Donnell, 2006, op cit.
6. Former RUC officer John Weir made a full statement on 3 February 1999, which was deemed vital and credible testimony by the Barron Commission. See also M. Dillon, *The Dirty War*, Arrow 1991.
7. P. McKenna, 'There's a Sinister Hush Over Collusion Evidence', *Daily Ireland*, 10.5.06
8. Justice for the Forgotten, *Why the Garda investigation was wound down in 1974*, Justice for the Forgotten, Dublin.
9. See Weir evidence to Barron Commission; on Wallace see P. Foot, *Who Framed Colin Wallace*, Macmillan 1989.
10. Report of the Independent Commission of Inquiry into the Dublin and Monaghan Bombings, Dublin 2003.
11. Police Ombudsman for Northern Ireland, *Investigation of Matters Relating to the Omagh Bombing on August 15, 1998*, Belfast 2001.
12. 'Mandelson says Omagh Report is "Very Poor Work"', *Independent*, 15.12.01.
13. J. Weir, NICC, The Crown v Sean Hoey, ref WE17021, 20.12.07, published January 2008.
14. M. Mamdani, 'Amnesty or Impunity? A Preliminary Critique of the Report of the Truth and Reconciliation Commission of South Africa', *Diacritics*, Vol 32, No 3-4, 2002, pp37-59.
15. Ni Aolain, 2000, op cit.

Conclusion

At the beginning of the conflict, the symmetry of the global civil rights and liberation movements were riveting, the lyrical protests of Parliament's youngest and most irreverent MP Bernadette Devlin were unforgettable, internment was terrifying. Thereafter, the explosion of armed conflict in Northern Ireland obscured everything – the *conflict* became the *armed conflict,* an alienating, dirty business.

This book is the outcome of my own voyages in and out of that dingy mist, among citizens whose lives and whose stories overturn the hegemonic version of events that obscured what was being contested and represented peace as simply the end of war. In that narrative, the peace process was nothing more than a long-unrequited call to the men of the gun to lay down their arms so that normal life could resume. My aim here is to tell a different story.

This book has two themes. The first is the great story of the Agreement and how it became more than a peace treaty, a thing of beauty; its radical novelty the gift of non-violent movements for more than peace, for change. The second is an exploration of the resistance it met, and the struggles to implement it.

There are many reasons for the protracted difficulty of implementation, of course, and two of them are: Pat Finucane and Rosemary Nelson. Their deaths take us to the resistance. The lives of these lawyers were taken by loyalists, the killers included British agents, their deaths were either planned or tolerated by security services who offered them no protection. Their deaths signify a pitiless era of collusion – the high-risk retort of the repressive state apparatus that had always colluded with paramilitary organisations, and which in the 1980s re-armed them and inaugurated an assassination strategy that targeted public figures, including lawyers.

Where these apparently parallel universes meet, then – the movements for change and the forces that resisted them – is in the space of the state. The moment when the movement for equality begins to show critical mass is also the moment when republican and loyalist combatants are contemplating a peaceful, power-sharing settlement. And that is the moment when the security state re-invigorates the war, re-arms, stewards and steers loyalist death squads, and spreads terror. We know, too, that the security state penetrated the IRA's internal security system and apparently participated in a culture of brutality that enabled Britain to dispose of its own unwanted agents. The state that constructed for itself a self-deluding legend as a reluctant and neutral administrator was also a hydra, having its head in all the armies, accusing the society of the incorrigible sectarianism and terrorism which it sponsored.

When a settlement based on equality and power-sharing is at last thinkable, its prospects are simultaneously extinguished by the state; it takes another decade of death, political disappointment, despair and deception before Northern Ireland's protagonists discover together a capacity for creativity and, with the help of good friends in the US, Ireland and the UK, confound pessimistic expectations. During the decisive decade after the Agreement resistance re-grouped, disarmament was delayed, optimism was squandered. In the struggle to understand the reasons for the state's apparent subsequent sabotage of a peace process of which it had been a constituent part, the contradictions and battles within the British state itself become apparent.

One of the novelties of the Agreement was that it made it explicit that the state had a duty to promote equality, and the participation of those with an interest. This was reasonable, and it was respectful of the people whose polity had been so barren and brutalising. Here was a recognition that inequality was the root cause of the conflict, and that the state had to be involved in attempts to address it. Yet the notion that the state's main duty was as an enforcer, and its lingering attachment to the Unionist establishment, was almost always a more dominant driver of policy. The Agreement's equality duties languished for want of implementation, and the security hydra surfaced again and again. New Labour appeared unwilling to re-position the state within the process of reform in Northern Ireland. The effect was to quell renovation and self-discovery on both sides of the Irish Sea – for Northern Ireland's problems were not only its own, and its secrets were the secrets of the British state. Westminster's repudiation of a truth and reconciliation process meant as much to the metropolis as to this little corner of the archipelago.

The point of the Agreement was, precisely, that its values had been constitutionalised: implementation was to be the duty of any and all conceivable governments in Northern Ireland. But the transformative potential of the most egalitarian and expansively democratic constitution of its time was muted by Westminster and then cauterised by political crisis. The Labour government ensured that the constitutional innovations would not be allowed to travel across the Irish Sea to the rest of the United Kingdom, where inequality was growing and party political engagement was declining. Recidivism within the state apparatuses governing Northern Ireland was compounded by the 'unilateral declarations of direct rule' by Westminster that dominated most of the decade after the deal had been done.

The Assembly election of 2007 produced the apparent polarisation that the politicians and commentariat of the centre and of Westminster had dreaded and deemed unmanageable. But the centre was located in 'narrow ground', whilst the election result affirmed the real locus of energy in Northern Ireland's dominant force fields. Within months the voters were presented with spectacles that no one ever expected to see: Ian Paisley bowing to the only opportunity for devolved power, breathing the same air as Gerry Adams, engaging amiably with erstwhile sworn enemies; Ian Paisley sharing power as an equal with Martin McGuinness. They performed as First Ministers with decorum, with normal collegial manners. Before the year was at an end they sat together in the White House, where McGuinness told George Bush that before that election result they'd never spoken to each other, and after they'd never said a bad word to each other.

Northern Ireland's most enduringly successful and destructive politician, Dr No, the anti-Agreement demagogue who had taken no part in its production, embarked on the last lap of his political life sharing responsibility for its implementation. But this was a society that needed to surprise itself – and if the Agreement sought to create a consensus where there had been none, this seemed to be its effect at last. 'Rights' had for three decades connoted an enemy agenda to most loyalists. And yet their experience of a 'rights' culture in relation to their own state was for most of that time impoverished, and when they were encouraged by the equality and human rights movements to assert their own human rights as citizens, the discovery was sometimes ecstatic. 'It is discovering that you're not shite. It is more than wonderful!' said Fiona McCausland, a loyalist community activist whose discovery led her to champion the movement for a Bill of Rights.

Paisley's populist party had to deliver for its constituencies – who included, of course, poor protestants, women, disabled protestants, gay protestants, harassed protestants – something better than No. The best chance of something better was the new beginning and the equality ethic that were inscribed in the Agreement.

At the time I am writing this, the new Northern Ireland is reaching its tenth anniversary. The great and the good were by 2008 talking about a truth commission. But talk was always a way of Britain ... talking, as if talking about something was the same as doing it. The nature of the counter-insurgency – and this could not be more salient for states in the aftermath of 9/11 and in the context of the 'war on terror' – was traduced by Britain's story about itself as a law-abiding democracy. Counter-insurgency compromises the law itself; it creates a crisis for a peace treaty such as the Agreement, precisely because the state is so indifferent to the wounds it inflicted on the rule of law.

After a decade of fitful implementation the Agreement was still Northern Ireland's new heart'. Whether it would be allowed to 'take' depended upon whether or not power would be exercised in the way the Agreement prescribed, and allow the people affected by policy-making to participate in its production; and whether public power would accept the constitutional duty to enlist dialogue with respect rather than dominion; and it depended on how the parties wielding power in the Assembly behaved – as orthodox political parties, or as servicers of that emancipating innovation.

It had never been embraced with enthusiasm by the British establishment. Indeed it attracted not one single word in *Great Hatred Little Room*, the supercilious and weary narrative of the peace process published in 2008 by Tony Blair's main man, Jonathan Powell. His indifference – or was it ignorance? – signalled Downing Street's adhesion to the status quo rather than the radical transition invited by the Agreement.

A decade after the deal Northern Ireland was still living with an unanswered question: would power accept responsibility for the 'huge change' promised by the new beginning? What was not in question, however, was that after a decade the context had been created for the new beginning ... to begin.

Acknowledgements

I am grateful to these people who agreed to be interviewed and consulted over the years, and to others who cannot be named:

Gerry Adams, Catherine Acton, Chris Anderson, Martina Anderson, Peter Archer, Annie Armstrong, Alex Attwood, Jim Auld, Nora Bailey, Adie Baird, Brian Barrington, Ray Bassett, Evan Bates, Sharon Beattie, Maggie Beirne, Christine Bell, Paul Berry, Anne Bill, Louis Blom Cooper, Linda Bowes, Norman Boyd, Brenda Bradley, Peter Brooke, Johnston Brown, Anne Cadwallader, Maureen Cain, Eileen Calder, Mary Clark-Glass, Evelyn Collins, Dan Connolly, Paul Connolly, Pauline Conroy, Pat Conway, Andy Cooper, Colin Crawford, Niall Crowley, Tim Cunningham, Sam Cushnahan, Nicholas Davies, Rosaleen Davison, Bairbre De Brun, Jim Deery, Mary Ellen Campbell, Martina Devlin, Brice Dickson, Nigel Dodds, Pat Doherty, Tom Donahue, Jeffrey Donaldson, Paul Donnelly, Padraign Drinan, Colin Duffy, Joe Duggan, John Dunlop, Frances Dunseath, Mary Enright, Terry Enright, David Ervine, Lisa Ervine, Sean Farren, Brian Ferguson, Michael Ferguson, Josie Ferris, Michael Finucane, Ronnie Flanagan, Vera Fletcher, Philomena Flood, Kevin Fulton, Briege Gadd, Hazel Gambles, Roy Garland, Sharon Gibson, Tom Gillen, Una Gillespie, Joanne Girvan, Harold Good, Tim Gracey, Isabel Grann, Diane Hamill, Laura Hamill, Norman Hamilton, Angela Hegarty, Bronagh Hinds, Colin Holliday, Billy Hutchinson, Martin Ingram, Helen Jackson, Joseph Jamison, Neil Jarman, David Jones, Gerry Kelly, Joe Kelly, Avila Kilmurray, Stephen King, Seanie Lamb, Paul Lashmar, Pauline Leeson, Patricia Lewsley, Michael Liggett, Brendan MacCioneath, Paul Mageean, Harry Maguire, Brendan Maillie, Martin Mansergh, John Marshall, Alex Maskey, Elissa Massimo, Nelson McAusland, Jean McBride, Jim McCabe, Stuart McCartney, Fiona McCausland, Gerry McConville, Inez McCormack, Jim McCory, Christopher McCrudden, Margaret MacCurtain, Darach McDonald, Sally McErlaine, Kieran McEvoy, Brendan McFarlane, Martin McGartland, Fiona McKenna, Sorcha McKenna, Vincent McKenna, Patricia McKeown, David McKittrick, Eithne McLaughlin,

Mitchell McLaughlin, Avila McMurray, Gerlayn McNally, Pat McNamee, John McStea, Philip McTaggart, Robbie McVeigh, Monica McWilliams, Francie Molloy, Chris Moore, John Morison, Bruce Morrison, Marie Mullholland, Danny Murphy, Paddy Murray, Rosemary Nelson, Dermott Nesbit, Fionualla Ni Aolain, Chris Notorantonio, Martin O'Brien, Donncha O'Connell, Paul O'Connor, Martin O'Hagan, Rita O'Hare, Nuala O'Loan, Dennis Paisley, George Patten, Paul Magill, Edna Peden, Stephen Pitten, Joy Poots, Mike Posner, Jim Potts, Dawn Purvis, Karen Quinliven, Ciaran Quinn, Sue Ramsay, Byron Rushing, Clara Reilly, Mike Richie, Tessa Robinson, Brid Rodgers, Eileen Rooney, Bride Rosney, Peter Shirlow, Shirley Simpson, Ailbhe Smyth, Marie Smyth, Gusty Spence, Jonathan Swallow, Mark Thompson, Aidan Troy, Margaret Urwin, Nomfundo Walaza, Debbie Walters, John Ware, Des Wilson, Monica Wilson, Tom Winston, Jane Winter, Patrick Yu.

Special thanks to:
Atlantic Philanthropies and the Joseph Rowntree Charitable Trust for grants that contributed to this work; to CAJ, BIRW, Unison, and many other organisations for critical intelligence;

Judith Jones who has shared the burden of this book and who has worried-over and challenged my ideas – endlessly; Adah Kay for uniquely generous friendship; Sharon Mier for her mindfulness; Richard Barker for critical support; Jess Barker for structural thinking; Adam Dawson and Helen Pringle for their administrations; Daniel Dawson for cottage pies and pasta during his gap year; Sally Davison for good – old fashioned – editing; and the late Professor Ian Taylor who insisted that the story should be a book.

Index